Resourcing Archbishops

Resourcing Archbishops

The second report of the
Archbishops' Review Group on
bishops' needs and resources

 CHURCH HOUSE
PUBLISHING

Church House Publishing
Church House
Great Smith Street
London
SW1P 3NZ

ISBN 0 7151 3864 2

Cover design by Sarah Hopper
Typeset in 10.5 pt Sabon
Printed in England by
Creative Print and Design,
Ebbw Vale, Wales

Published 2002 by Church House
Publishing

Contents

Chairman's preface

The Archbishops of Canterbury and York asked us to carry out our review of the needs and resources of bishops and archbishops in two phases. Our first report, published in 2001, dealt with the needs and resources of bishops. This, our second and final report, deals with the needs and resources of the archbishops. Much of the information which we obtained in the first phase of our work has been directly relevant to the second phase.

As in the case of our first report, we have assumed that readers of this report will include those who have a general interest in the subject, and a concern for the general well-being of the Church of England, but without necessarily having a detailed knowledge of the background. We have, therefore, sought to explain at some length the present position and context, as well as to make our recommendations. This is particularly true of the chapter on the Anglican Communion.

We have written this report as a self-standing volume but, reflecting the fact that we have been engaged on one overall review, we have provided close cross-references to our first report.

We have conducted our review against a background of increasing financial stringency affecting the Church of England. Throughout our work we have felt a tension between on the one hand providing the archbishops with the resources which we would like to see them have and on the other hand the amount which we judge might realistically be expected to be provided by the Church Commissioners in present circumstances.

In formulating our recommendations, we have assumed that throughout the forthcoming decade there will continue to be two provinces of the Church of England and that the provinces will comprise the same dioceses as at present. We have been concerned only with the resourcing needs of the two archbishops, but in many instances it has been necessary to take into account the implications for the wider Church. Throughout we have endeavoured to maintain a proper balance between the Archbishop of Canterbury and the Archbishop of York, and between them together on the one hand and other bishops on the other hand.

We are most grateful to those who have helped us in our work. We have consulted widely, and without exception all whom we have approached have helped us willingly. In dealing with the property aspects of the second phase of our work, we were greatly assisted by Mr Paul Orchard-Lisle who acted as our property consultant and participated in several of our meetings. We are also very grateful to the correspondents whose views are reflected in Appendix C, and to the Archbishop of Canterbury's Lay Assistant and the Joint Provincial Registrars for their permission to reproduce the memorandum which forms Appendix E. We also had the advantage of having before us the report into the see of Canterbury under the chairmanship of The Lord Hurd of Westwell, and of being able to consider the recommendations in that report which related to resourcing.

We should like to record our appreciation of the constructive and courteous help which we have received from many members of the personal staffs of the Archbishop of Canterbury and the Archbishop of York, as well as members of the staffs of the Church Commissioners and the Archbishops' Council. We are particularly indebted to our secretary, Stuart Deacon, who was seconded to us by the Church Commissioners and whose diligent attention to our affairs has greatly facilitated our work. In addition, we should like to record our thanks to my personal secretary, Debbie Bishop, who, since the beginning of the review, has spent hours too numerous to count in labouring on many papers for our work, as well as on drafts and the final versions of our reports.

Each of us has regarded it as a privilege to be engaged in this review. As it has proceeded, we have grown together in prayer and cohesion, while not in any way losing in our deliberations the spark of vigorous debate.

As was our first report, this report is unanimous.

I conclude on a personal note. The work of this review has been demanding. Taking both phases together, we have met in thirty-five plenary sessions, of which two have been residential. In addition, we have been engaged in many other meetings, interviews and endeavours. All of my fellow members of the Review Group are heavily engaged in their own walks of life, but their consistency of attendance and respective contributions at our meetings have been remarkable. I shall for ever be grateful for their unfailing support.

Anthony Mellows

The Review Group and its terms of reference

The following were appointed by the Archbishops:

as Chairman   Professor Anthony Mellows, TD, LLD, Emeritus Professor of Law at King's College in the University of London

as Members   Mr Richard Agutter, senior adviser to KPMG, chartered accountants, and formerly Chairman of KPMG International Corporate Finance. Currently an alderman of the City of London

The Reverend Canon Bob Baker, parish priest, until December 2000 a Church Commissioner elected by the General Synod and a member of the Church Commissioners' Bishoprics and Cathedrals Committee, and since December 2000 Prolocutor of the Province of Canterbury

The Venerable Richard Inwood, Archdeacon of Halifax

Mr Alan King, Chairman of the Bath and Wells Diocesan Board of Finance since 1990 and Chairman of the Consultative Group of Diocesan Board of Finance Chairmen and Secretaries since 1999. Member of the General Synod. Until 1998 Managing Editor of the *Bristol Evening Post*

Mr Luke March, Corporate Governance Director of British Telecommunications until April 2000. Currently Chief Executive of the Mortgage Code Compliance Board

The Right Reverend Peter Nott, Bishop of Norwich until 1999

Mr Peter Parker, TD, Fellow and sometime Vice-President of the Institute of Actuaries. Formerly Chairman of Phillips & Drew International Limited

Mrs Lou Scott-Joynt, wife of the Bishop of Winchester, Associate Member of the Church Commissioners' Bishoprics and Cathedrals Committee as Representative of Bishops' Wives

as Property Consultant Mr Paul Orchard-Lisle, CBE, TD, DL, senior partner of Messrs Healey & Baker from 1987 to 1999. Past President of The Royal Institution of Chartered Surveyors

as Secretary Mr Stuart Deacon, on secondment from the Church Commissioners

Terms of reference

The terms of reference of the Group for the second phase of its work, which is the subject of this report, were:

In relation to the Archbishop of Canterbury:

'To assess the staff and other resources which are needed now and which are likely to be needed in the next decade in order to provide adequate and efficient administrative and other support for the ministry of the Archbishop of Canterbury in his various roles; to assess the cost of providing such support; to assess the resource implications for the Church Commissioners and the wider Church; and to make recommendations to the Archbishops. In so doing, to consider the numbers and roles of staff employed at Lambeth Palace; organizational structures within the Palace, including the Lambeth Palace Library; and the relationship between the Archbishop on the one hand and the Church Commissioners on the other hand (recognizing that the Archbishop is the Chairman of the Governors of the Church Commissioners).'

In relation to the Archbishop of York:

'To assess the staff and other resources which are needed now and which are likely to be needed in the next decade in order to provide adequate and efficient administrative and other support for the ministry of the Archbishop of York in his various roles, more particularly relating to the Northern Province and the North of England generally; to assess the cost of providing such support and to assess the resource implications for the Church Commissioners and the wider Church, and to make recommendations to the Archbishops. In so doing, to consider the numbers and roles of staff employed at Bishopthorpe, as well as the organizational structures within the Palace.'

Expressions and their meanings

The Archbishops

In this report we use the expressions 'Dr Carey' and 'Dr Hope' when referring to Archbishop Carey and Archbishop Hope personally. We use the expressions 'Archbishop of Canterbury' and 'Archbishop of York' to refer to the person who is at the time the Archbishop of Canterbury or York (which expressions may include Dr Carey or Dr Hope, but are not restricted to them); we use 'Archbishop' to mean the Archbishop of Canterbury or the Archbishop of York (and 'Archbishops' to mean both of them); and we use 'archbishop' to mean an archbishop, whether of Canterbury, York, or elsewhere.

The archiepiscopal palaces

Lambeth Palace and the Old Palace at Canterbury are referred to throughout this report as such. Bishopthorpe Palace is frequently spoken of as 'Bishopthorpe', and it is variously referred to in this report as 'Bishopthorpe' or 'Bishopthorpe Palace'.

Other expressions

Unless it appears otherwise from the context, in this report we use the following expressions and abbreviations with the following meanings:

Bishoprics and Cathedrals Committee	The Bishoprics and Cathedrals Committee of the Church Commissioners.
Bishoprics and Cathedrals Department	The Department of the Church Commissioners overseen by The Bishoprics and Cathedrals Committee.
Commissioners	The Church Commissioners for England.
DBF	Diocesan Board of Finance.

ecclesiology	The principles which underlie the structure and organization of the Church of England and the roles of its office holders, both ordained and lay, including their respective rights, duties and obligations.
First Report	*Resourcing Bishops* (the first report of the Review Group) (CHP 2001).
FTE	In relation to posts, full-time equivalent. So two half-time posts would be 1 FTE.
HR Department	The Human Resources Department of the Archbishops' Council.
Hurd Report	*To Lead and to Serve* (The Report of the Review of the See of Canterbury, under the chairmanship of The Lord Hurd of Westwell) (CHP 2001).
IT	Information technology, particularly computers and electronic communications.
National Church Institutions	The following bodies so prescribed by the National Church Institutions Measure 1998:

a. The Archbishop of Canterbury (in his corporate capacity)
b. The Archbishop of York (in his corporate capacity)
c. the Church Commissioners
d. the Archbishops' Council
e. the Trustees of the Lambeth Palace Library Trust
f. the Advisory Board for Redundant Churches
g. the Church of England Pensions Board
h. the National Society for Promoting Religious Education.

operational costs	The costs of an archbishop's personal support staff; of his and their working accommodation; and travelling and official hospitality expenses.
President of the Anglican Communion	All of the offices which the Archbishop of Canterbury holds in the Anglican Communion: see paras 3.9.1. and 16.7.1.
pro bono	Voluntary or free of charge.
province	A group of dioceses which comprise the area of jurisdiction of an archbishop as metropolitan. In the Church of England there are two provinces, those of Canterbury and York. For the meaning of the word generally in relation to the Anglican Communion, see para. 16.5.1.
Provincial Episcopal Visitors	Suffragan bishops who provide alternative episcopal oversight under the provision of the Episcopal Ministry Act of Synod 1993. See First Report, para. 16.34.1.
see	The office held by an archbishop or other bishop. All sees have a territorial title, but the powers, rights, duties and responsibilities may, and in the case of the Archbishops do, extend beyond that territory.
see house	Living and, usually, working accommodation provided for a diocesan bishop and his personal support staff. Although a suffragan bishop has a see, the house in which he resides and, usually, works is provided by the Diocesan Board of Finance and is known as the 'official' rather than the 'see' house.
state rooms	Rooms, usually large, originally set aside for formal or ceremonial occasions, and in archiepiscopal palaces now often used for meetings and official receptions.

working costs	The expression given to operational costs by the Commissioners in their annual reports and accounts.

Inclusive references

Most of the posts mentioned in this report can be held by men or women. For convenience, we refer to 'him' or 'his' in the wide sense of embracing both the masculine and feminine.

Other references

References to paragraphs or chapters, without elaboration, are references to paragraphs or chapters of this report. By contrast, references to paragraphs or chapters of our First Report are throughout described as such.

chapter 1

Overview and summary of recommendations

Overview

1.1 Our general findings are that:

1 It is remarkable what the Archbishops achieve with the limited resources available to them.

2 The demands upon and the expectations of the Archbishops are at the very limit of what is realistic. The jobs are approaching the point at which they will become impossible.

3 Although some of the Archbishops' roles in the leadership of the Church of England nationally are prescribed, in many respects the allocation of those roles is a matter for agreement between them. In general, role priorities are not externally established or validated.

4 There are similarities in the circumstances of the two Archbishops, but for resourcing and some other purposes the dissimilarities are greater. Much caution therefore needs to be exercised before making comparisons between them.

5 The loyalty of the personal staffs of both Archbishops is outstanding.

6 The time is right for a new approach to be made to the staffing support provided for the Archbishop of Canterbury and the management of that staff.

7 The present arrangements for providing resources do not encourage the Archbishops or senior members of their staffs to exercise overall financial control of their activities.

8 The Archbishops live and work in the archiepiscopal palaces.[1] In other contexts the word 'palace' can give the impression of grandeur. That is very far from an accurate description of the style within the archiepiscopal palaces.

9   The private residential accommodation provided for the Archbishops within the palaces ranges from the mediocre to the totally unacceptable.

10   There is the potential for much greater income to be derived from Lambeth Palace and Bishopthorpe consistent with the proper use of those palaces by the Archbishops and their staffs.

11   More generally, there is under-utilization of palace buildings and their grounds.

12   Very broadly, the nature and scale of the resources provided for the Archbishops to enable them to exercise their ministries as presently conceived are about right.

13   There is a tension between the resources which could helpfully be provided for the Archbishops and the amount which, in the present financial circumstances of the Church of England, could reasonably be expected to be applied for those purposes.

14   There is also a tension between on the one hand making changes to the present arrangements in the interest of making better use of resources for the good of the Church generally and on the other hand ensuring that the changes do not make the lives of the Archbishops even more difficult than they are now.

Main recommendations

1.2   We make 21 keynote recommendations:

General

1   Subject to certain specific exceptions, the same arrangements as apply to the resourcing of other diocesan bishops should apply to the Archbishops (para. 4.3.1).

2   The provision of all resources for the Archbishops should be measured against clearly established principles (para. 4.5).

3   In certain respects, the nature and scale of resources provided for the Archbishops can be properly judged only in the light of broader policy considerations. In such instances, the policy considerations should be decided first, and the issues not determined by resourcing implications (see, for example, paras 15.26.2 and 16.84).

Personal staff

4   The Archbishops should continue to have personal staffs at Lambeth Palace and Bishopthorpe (paras 14.19, 19.9.3).

5   There should be created a new post of Chief of Staff to the Archbishop of Canterbury (para. 12.16.2). He should have the closest working relationship not only with the Archbishop of Canterbury, but also with the equivalent officer at Bishopthorpe; and with the Secretary General of the General Synod and the Secretary of the Church Commissioners (para. 12.24.1).

6   A major responsibility of the Chief of Staff should be to ensure that the Archbishop of Canterbury has a stable, harmonious and integrated staff (para. 12.17.1).

7   The principles of the human resources regime which was introduced in 1998 should continue to apply to the staff of the Archbishops, but there should be some modification to its application (para. 12.50.3 and 19.25.3).

Financial

8   Lambeth Palace and Bishopthorpe should each be centres of financial management. The Archbishops, or their staffs, should have a wide measure of financial control over their activities (para. 5.4.2).

9   Most of the funds to be made available by the Commissioners for the provision of resources should be devolved to the Archbishops by way of block-grant (para. 5.4.2).

10   There should be separate block-grants to the Archbishops, one to provide resources for them as diocesan bishops and the other for them as metropolitans, primates and archbishops (paras 5.11.1, 5.12.2). The amount of the block-grant to be devolved to the Archbishops in their capacities as diocesan bishops should generally be calculated according to the same formula as should apply to other diocesan bishops, but with a modification in the case of the Archbishop of Canterbury.

Archbishops' wives

11   The wife of an Archbishop should be properly resourced in respect of those matters with which she deals when acting directly in support of her husband in the exercise of his ministry (para. 10.14.1).

Induction and handover

12 There should be structured induction and hand-over programmes for newly appointed Archbishops and their wives (paras 8.12.1 *et seq*).

The palaces

13 The Commissioners should retain the archiepiscopal palaces, provided that there is a modification to their use and provided also that they become income-generating (para. 6.4.2).

14 New holding and management structures, based on the trust concept, should be established for each of the palaces (paras 6.11, 6.12, 14.26, 15.38.1, 21.41.1).

15 Determined measures should be taken to eliminate under-utilization of the palaces (para. 6.6.3).

16 So far as consistent with the proper use of the palaces as places in which the Archbishops live and as places in which they and their staffs work, there should be conducted in the palaces activities with a view to generating income. In the case of Lambeth Palace the objective should be to cover all of the costs of maintaining the palace in this way, and in the case of Bishopthorpe the objective should be to cover most if not all of such costs (paras 6.7.2, 14.31.3).

17 The Archbishops should be provided for their private residential use with self-contained accommodation which meets acceptable modern standards (paras 10.9, 21.24.1, 14.29.4).

Specific issues

18 The provision of resources for the Archbishops should be sufficiently flexible to meet not only the evolution of their own ministries, but also any reallocation of primatial and archiepiscopal roles between them (para. 4.7). Any such reallocation might include a redeployment, but not an increase in the total, of resources (para. 18.18.2).

19 The Archbishop of Canterbury should continue to be provided with living and working accommodation and other facilities at the Old Palace at Canterbury (para. 15.24.1).

20 The Commissioners should continue to support the Archbishop of Canterbury in his roles within the Anglican Communion, but the amount to be provided for this purpose should be identified and accounted for separately (para. 16.80.3).

21 Very serious consideration should be given to the future location of the Lambeth Palace Library while maintaining intact the Collection (para. 17.35.1).

Other recommendations

1.3   We make further recommendations. Some amplify the keynote recommendations and others are independent of them. These further recommendations are as follows:

1 Funds for the provision of resources for the Archbishops should be calculated by formula but there should be no requirement for the devolved funds to be spent according to the elements of the formula (para. 5.2.2 and 5.17.1).

2 The formula should be seen to be fair and the process of devolution should be transparent (para. 5.7.2.b).

3 Transitional arrangements should apply in determining the amount to be devolved to the Archbishop of Canterbury (paras 5.7.2.a, 5.10.2).

4 The formula to govern the amount to be devolved to the Archbishop of Canterbury should not take account of the Lambeth Palace Library (para. 5.9.1.a).

5 The formula should include provision for overseas travel (para. 5.9.4).

6 The Archbishops should have power to delegate the responsibility for the application of the funds devolved to them as diocesan bishops (paras 5.11.1, 5.12.2).

7 The fees payable to the Vicars-General and the Provincial Registrars should continue to be paid directly by the Commissioners (para. 5.14.1).

8 On future reviews of the formula consideration should be given to including an element for ministry and mission initiatives of the Archbishops (para. 5.16.1).

9 Neither Archbishop should be present for that part of any meeting of the Board of Governors of the Commissioners or of any committee of the Board of Governors at which their own resources are to be considered (para. 5.8.3).

10 Should there be any surplus from the devolved funds after resources have been procured, the relevant Archbishop should have

power to apply it for other purposes for which the Commissioners could properly apply their funds (para. 5.16.2).

11 Any funds so applied should be accounted for as mission costs and not bishops' operational costs (para. 5.16.3).

12 Full advantage should be taken of opportunities for the provision of resources for the Archbishops on a local collaborative basis (para. 5.18.2).

13 Bishops' Resources Groups should be established for the bishops of the Diocese of Canterbury (paras 5.20.2, 13.14) and the Diocese of York (para. 5.20.3).

14 The trustees of The Lambeth Fund should act as the Resources Group for the Archbishop of Canterbury in his metropolitical, primatial, archiepiscopal and Anglican Communion roles (paras 5.20.1, 13.14).

15 The Bishops' Resources Group for the bishops of the Diocese of York should also be concerned with the metropolitical, primatial and archiepiscopal roles of the Archbishop of York (para. 5.20.3).

16 The Archbishops should have power to delegate the responsibilities for appointing the members of the Bishops' Resources Groups (paras 5.20.2, 5.20.3).

17 The Archbishops' staffs should continue to be responsible for the conduct of banking arrangements (para. 5.21.2).

18 Any proposal for new Church legislation which would impose additional duties on either or both of the Archbishops should be accompanied by time and resource analyses (para. 5.24.2).

19 If rooms in an archiepiscopal palace which are set aside as official guest bedrooms or for other purposes are not used on average for 20% of the time, there should be a presumption (which could be rebutted) that those rooms should be put to some other use (paras 6.6.1, 9.14.2).

20 The palaces should be strategically managed together with adjoining or adjacent properties owned by the Commissioners (paras 6.16.2, 14.45.3).

21 There should continue to be disclosed the operational costs incurred by the Archbishops and there should also be disclosed their premises expenses (paras 7.11, 7.2, 7.7, 13.23).

22 The direct operational costs incurred by the Archbishop of

Canterbury in his roles within the Anglican Communion and the direct operational costs incurred by both Archbishops in their roles as metropolitans, primates and archbishops should be separately disclosed (paras 7.3.4, 7.4.1, 7.5).

23   In general, the same resourcing provisions which are requisite for newly appointed diocesan bishops should be made for newly appointed Archbishops (para. 8.1).

24   An Archbishop-designate and his wife should be given full and early exposure to the palace or palaces in which they will live (para. 8.4.2).

25   There should be kept to the shortest the period between when a candidate is approached to see whether, if invited, he would accept an archbishopric and when the public announcement of his appointment is made (para. 8.6.1).

26   Before he takes up his office a newly appointed Archbishop should have both a good holiday (para. 8.7.1) and also time for reflection and personal preparation (para. 8.7.2).

27   There should be clear and early agreement between an Archbishop of Canterbury and the Bishop of Dover as to their respective roles in relation to the Diocese of Canterbury (paras 8.9.1, 15.23.2). That agreement should be recorded (para. 15.23.2).

28   There should be clear and early agreement between the two Archbishops as to the division of primatial and archiepiscopal responsibilities (para. 8.9.2).

29   That agreement should also be recorded (para. 18.13.2).

30   There should be a support team responsible for planning and guiding the arrangements to be made for an Archbishop-designate until he takes up his office (paras 8.11.2, 8.11.3).

31   That team should be constituted at the very earliest opportunity (para. 8.11.4).

32   Induction programmes should be progressively developed, and for that purpose a detailed memorandum should be prepared following the completion of each programme (para. 8.14.2).

33   A retiring Archbishop should participate in the enthronement service of his successor (para. 8.15).

34   The Commissioners should pay the removal expenses which an Archbishop incurs on his retirement (para. 8.16.2).

35   Appropriate resourcing provision should be made for a retired Archbishop while he continues to be active in the service of the Church (para. 8.17.2).

36   There should be at least one press officer on the staff of each Archbishop (para. 9.11.1).

37   Archbishops should be always able to have immediate access to their press officers (para. 9.11.2).

38   The Archbishops' press officers should have the equipment necessary to enable them to prepare and transmit material of broadcastable quality (para. 9.11.2, 18.25).

39   The Archbishops' press officers should work in close liaison with each other, and with corresponding officers in Church House and the Anglican Communion Office (para. 9.12.2).

40   Adequate housekeeping support should be provided for both Archbishops (para. 9.16.2).

41   There should be provided the most appropriate and cost effective facilities for the Archbishops to travel by car (para. 9.18.2).

42   When travelling by air the class of travel should depend on the need, not the standing, of the traveller (para. 9.23).

43   There should be clear guidelines governing the class of air travel by an Archbishop, his wife, members of his staff, and others travelling at his request and on his behalf (paras 9.26 to 9.33).

44   After each overseas visit by an Archbishop there should be a value-appraisal of the visit (para. 9.34.1). It should be initiated by the Archbishop's Chief of Staff (para. 9.34.2).

45   The planning of resources for the Archbishops should be on the basis that their wives might well have their own careers (para. 10.3).

46   An Archbishop's Chief of Staff should be particularly supportive of the wife of a newly appointed Archbishop (para. 10.7.3).

47   Where appropriate, the induction programme for the wife of a newly appointed Archbishop should include advice in relation to the running of a large heritage property (para. 10.8).

48 All questions of policy relating to the nature and style of refurbishment and improvements to a palace should be formulated jointly by the Archbishop and his wife, the Chief of Staff and the Commissioners, and they should have external expert advice where appropriate (para. 10.10.3).

49 That policy should be implemented in accordance with arrangements to be made by the Chief of Staff (para. 10.10.3).

50 The wife of an Archbishop should not be the line manager of any member of staff except, possibly, any secretary who is allocated to her (para. 10.11).

51 The Chief of Staff should have direct access to the Resources Group (para. 12.27).

52 Save in the most exceptional circumstances, the Archbishop of Canterbury's Chief of Staff should be lay (para. 12.28.1).

53 The Archbishop of Canterbury should continue to have an Anglican Communion Officer and a Secretary for Ecumenism (para. 12.31).

54 There should be created the new post of Premises Manager at Lambeth Palace (para. 12.35).

55 For so long as a member of the Commissioners' own staff acts as agent for Lambeth Palace, he should concurrently be a member of the Archbishop of Canterbury's personal staff (para. 12.38.1).

56 The Chief of Staff should review all staff posts at Lambeth Palace and the method by which they are monitored. The staffing requirements should be subject to the same principles of evaluation as apply to staff employed by the other central institutions of the Church of England (paras 12.12.3, 12.42.3).

57 He should have wide scope to reshape the staff in the light of the vision and expectations of the Archbishop (paras 12.20, 12.33.1).

58 So far as possible, the Chief of Staff or a member of his staff and not the Archbishop should be a party to any employment proceedings (para. 12.21).

59 The Archbishop of Canterbury's Chief of Staff should have a close working relationship with the Secretary-General of the General Synod and the Secretary of the Commissioners, as well as with his counterpart at Bishopthorpe (para. 12.24.1).

60 The Chief of Staff should have a contract of employment for a sufficiently long term to afford him a degree of independence (para. 12.26.2).

61 His salary should be commensurate with his responsibilities (para. 12.29.2).

62 If it is required and requested, an initial outfitting allowance should be made to the wife of a newly appointed Archbishop (para. 10.16.3).

63 Proper periods of leisure should be built into the Archbishops' programmes (para. 11.4.2).

64 The post of Bishop at Lambeth should be discontinued (para. 12.15).

65 The Chief of Staff should attend meetings of the Resources Group (para. 13.15.1).

66 The Chief of Staff should be a major contributor to the formulation and implementation of the Archbishop's policy (para. 12.17.2).

67 He should manage all staff employed at the palace (para. 12.18).

68 All appointments of new members of staff should be made by a panel (para. 12.52).

69 The Chief of Staff and not the Archbishop should deal with any issues in staff relations (para. 12.53.2).

70 When the Commissioners appoint a professional firm as agent, the Premises Manager should liaise with that firm and also so far as possible serve the Commissioners' interests (para. 12.38.2).

71 There should be a continuance of the present arrangements under which an Archbishop pays for any personal catering from which he benefits (para. 12.39.4).

72 There should be a Financial Secretary to the Archbishop of Canterbury with responsibility for overall financial control of all activities within Lambeth Palace (paras 12.34.3, 13.8).

73 There should be a costed business plan for all activities within Lambeth Palace (para. 13.8.b).

74 Regular management accounts should be prepared in respect of all operations within Lambeth Palace (para. 13.8.c).

75   Separate overall accounts should be prepared in respect of the Lambeth Palace Library (para. 13.10).

76   There should be close coordination between the Archbishop of Canterbury and the Bishops of Dover and Maidstone about charitable or discretionary grants made for purposes related to the Diocese of Canterbury (para. 13.17).

77   The accounts of the Archbishop's Discretionary Fund should be independently reviewed (para. 13.19).

78   There should be a new strategy for Lambeth Palace (para. 14.23.1).

79   If and when larger-scale development takes place, it should make provision for offices at Lambeth Palace which meet modern criteria (para. 14.30.4).

80   There should be a member of the Archbishop of Canterbury's staff specifically charged with generating income from Lambeth Palace (para. 14.31.1).

81   With minor, specified, exceptions, flats in the buildings at Lambeth Palace and cottages in its grounds should be let on commercial terms (paras 14.34.1 to 14.34.4).

82   There should be available for the Archbishop of York at Lambeth Palace a small flat for his priority, but not exclusive, use (para. 14.35.2).

83   The amounts of all rents and service charges should be reviewed at least annually (para. 14.37.2.a).

84   The amounts of all salary reductions which are made because accommodation is provided free of rent and service charge should be reviewed at least annually (para. 14.37.2.a).

85   The amounts of all such salary reductions should be reflected in the management accounts to be prepared in respect of Lambeth Palace (para. 14.37.2.b).

86   In relation to accommodation which is provided free of rent and service charge to ordained members of the Archbishop's staff who are in receipt of stipend but not salary, the amount of rent and service charge which could be obtained if such accommodation were let on commercial terms should also be included in the management accounts (para. 14.37.2.c).

87   There should be written agreements governing the use and occupation of all residential accommodation (para. 14.37.3).

88   Determined steps should be taken to increase materially the income derived from events held within Lambeth Palace and its grounds (para. 14.38.3).

89   There should be a detailed appraisal of the possible use of part of Lambeth Palace for the holding of conferences or the provision of commercial hospitality (para. 14.40.2.a).

90   If there is to be such use, it should be introduced on a step-by-step basis (para. 14.40.2.b).

91   Pending such an appraisal there should be no change to the existing catering arrangements (para. 14.42.2).

92   Or to the existing gardening arrangements (para. 14.43).

93   There should be considered the possibility of building in the grounds of Lambeth Palace a small number of residential units to provide subsidized housing for clergy or others (para. 14.46.2).

94   Very serious consideration should be given to the future of the post of the Archbishop's (part-time) Canterbury Chaplain (para. 15.15.2).

95   The working offices of the Archbishop and the Bishop of Dover at Canterbury should be combined (para. 15.25.3.a).

96   The Archbishop should continue to have a Private Secretary at Canterbury (para. 15.25.3.b).

97   There should be a detailed feasibility study of a programme for a major conversion of the Old Palace at Canterbury with a view to much greater effective utilization (paras 15.30.1, 15.30.2).

98   The chapel in The Old Palace should be brought into daily use (para. 15.31).

99   The reception and meeting rooms at The Old Palace should be available for greater use (para. 15.32.1).

100   The management of each part of the Canterbury precinct should have regard to the other parts of the precinct (para. 15.33.2).

101   The Commissioners' legal powers in relation to The Old Palace should be extended (para. 15.34.2).

102   The amount spent on the Archbishop's work in relation to the Anglican Communion should be separately identified and disclosed (para. 16.80.3.b).

103   The Commissioners' legal powers to support the Archbishop in relation to the Anglican Communion should be clarified and, if necessary, extended (para. 16.81.2).

104   For so long as the Anglican Communion Office is in premises away from Lambeth Palace, the Archbishop should continue to have his own staff to support him in dealing with Anglican Communion affairs (para. 16.86.4.a).

105   The size of that staff should be considered by the Chief of Staff (para. 16.86.4.b).

106   The issue should be reconsidered if the Anglican Communion Office is relocated to Lambeth Palace (para. 16.86.4).

107   On certain visits made by the Archbishop in relation to the Anglican Communion, he should have both communications and press support (para. 16.94.2).

108   If the Anglican Communion Office is relocated to Lambeth Palace, there should then be considered the possible formation of a joint communications and press office (para. 16.93).

109   Visits made by the Archbishop in relation to the Anglican Communion should be subject to post-visit evaluation (para. 16.90).

110   Much caution should be exercised before a bishop from elsewhere within the Anglican Communion is appointed to serve at Lambeth Palace (para. 16.98.3).

111   The Commissioners' legal powers in relation to the Lambeth Palace Library should be extended (para. 17.37.2).

112   The Lambeth Palace Library should be regarded as a separate cost centre (para. 17.39.1).

113   Overall management accounts in respect of the Lambeth Palace Library should be prepared (para. 17.25.1).

114   The costs incurred by the Commissioners in relation to the Lambeth Palace Library should be identified and disclosed as such (para. 17.40).

115   For so long as the Library is located within Lambeth Palace the Librarian should also be a member of the Archbishop's personal staff (para. 17.43.a).

116 He should fall within the purview of the Chief of Staff (para. 17.43.b).

117 The Archbishop or his Chief of Staff should determine the use of all space within the palace, having regard to the requirements of the Library (para. 17.43.c).

118 If an Archbishop of York is to have an enhanced national role he should have additional staff (paras 18.18.1, 19.14).

119 There should be paid particular regard to the time and direct cost implications of such an enhanced national role (para. 18.18.3).

120 The staff of the Archbishop of York should continue to work at Bishopthorpe (para. 19.2.2).

121 They should continue to do so in their existing offices (para. 19.3).

122 There should be a press officer on the Archbishop of York's staff (para. 19.11.6).

123 The Archbishop of York should be provided with research assistance (para. 19.12.2).

124 There should be greater use of information technology by the staff of the Archbishop of York (para. 19.19.3).

125 There should be considered the appointment of a Chief of Staff to the Archbishop of York (para. 19.16.1).

126 No change should be made at present to the gardening arrangements at Bishopthorpe (para. 19.21).

127 The arrangement whereby the Archbishop of York is the managing employer of his personal staff should continue (para. 19.27.3).

128 The arrangement should, however, be reconsidered upon the happening of certain possible future events (para. 19.28.1).

129 Management accounts should be prepared to show the total financial operations within Bishopthorpe (para. 20.14.2).

130 Details of the Archbishop of York's operational costs, both as diocesan bishop and as metropolitan, primate and archbishop, should continue to be disclosed (para. 20.16.a).

131 Premises expenses in relation to Bishopthorpe should also be disclosed (para. 20.16.b).

132   There should be carried out a detailed feasibility study of a possible programme for conversion works at Bishopthorpe (para. 21.35.2 and 21.35.3). Most of the associated recommendations are dependent on the outcome of that study and of the first quinquennial inspection to be made at Bishopthorpe (para. 21.1.2).

133   The feasibility study should be carried out jointly by the Commissioners and the Archbishop of York (para. 21.35.4).

134   The possibility of relocation of the York Diocesan Office to Bishopthorpe should be taken into account in a feasibility study (para. 21.38.3).

135   A small private garden should be provided for the Archbishop of York on the Bishopthorpe estate (para. 21.24.2).

136   There should be a review as to those who, apart from the Archbishop, need to live on the Bishopthorpe estate (para. 21.28.1).

137   In general, residential accommodation at Bishopthorpe should be available for letting on commercial terms (para. 21.28.2).

138   That principle should not apply to the Ramsey flat or to flats occupied by those who need to live on the site (para. 21.27.5, 21.28.2).

139   Where residential accommodation is provided for a member of staff free of rent and service charge as part of the terms of service, the amount of the rent and service charge which could have been received had that accommodation been commercially let should be reflected in the overall palace accounts (para. 21.28.3).

140   So far as is consistent with maintaining the atmosphere and ethos of Bishopthorpe, and its suitability as a place in which the Archbishop lives, and in which he and his staff work, activities with a view to generating income from the palace should be substantially increased (para. 21.33.2).

141   Consideration should be given to providing facilities for those attending conferences at Bishopthorpe to be able to stay overnight (para. 21.37.2).

The Hurd Report

1.4.1   In March 2000 the Archbishop of Canterbury appointed a group under the chairmanship of the Lord Hurd of Westwell to reflect upon the growth and evolution of the office[2] and role of the Archbishop of Canterbury; to consider possible future developments; and to make recommendations to ensure that that office might continue to be discharged effectively. The report of that group was published in September 2001.

1.4.2   In the course of our work we have considered all of the recommendations in the Hurd Report. Some of the issues covered in it do not affect resourcing. In other instances we ourselves have had to consider the underlying position in order to form our own view on the resourcing implications. In many, but not all instances, we generally support the recommendations contained in the Hurd Report, and in some respects we develop them.

1.4.3   Where appropriate we comment in subsequent chapters on recommendations in the Hurd Report, and in Appendix B we give an index to those observations.

Part I: General

chapter 2

Archbishops, Metropolitans and Primates

Introduction

2.1.1   Throughout the work which led to our First Report we reflected on the theology and historical development of episcopal ministry; we sought to engage in similar reflections on archiepiscopal ministry as the foundation for this report. However, we encountered the immediate difficulty that although there is a substantial amount of material concerning the history and theology of episcopacy, there is comparatively little consensus among scholars concerning archbishops, let alone biblical material which throws light on the subject.

2.1.2   We were, therefore, very grateful to Bishop Peter Nott, one of our members, for writing the essay which is reproduced as Appendix C, and to Lord Habgood, Professor Owen Chadwick and Archbishop Rowan Williams for their permission for correspondence with them to be quoted extensively in that appendix. We very much hope that that appendix will be read in conjunction with this chapter.

2.1.3   There is general agreement that there is no distinctive theology of archbishops, only of bishops. Theologically, what applies to bishops applies to archbishops also.[1]

2.1.4   In this report, therefore, there is no section entitled Theology, but the established theological principles and implications which apply to all bishops are inherent in every chapter.

Ecclesiology

2.2   As well as theology, we were concerned in our First Report with ecclesiology which we defined[2] as 'The principles which underlie the structure and organization of the Church of England and the roles of its office holders, both ordained and lay, including their respective rights, duties and obligations'. It will be apparent in this report that almost every aspect of the work of the Archbishops has ecclesiological significance.

The expressions

2.3   As is shown in Appendix C, the expressions 'archbishop', 'metropolitan' and 'primate' have been used during the last two millennia with various meanings. This chapter examines those expressions, and demonstrates that they now represent separate offices which in the Church of England are held by the same person. In later chapters we consider[3] whether those separate offices should be separately resourced.

Single Order of Bishops

2.4.1   Although the meanings of the expressions 'archbishop', 'metropolitan' and 'primate' have varied, in one respect they have been constant: the expressions have always referred to bishops who are in some sense in a senior position.

2.4.2   None of the expressions has indicated a separate order of ordained ministry. It is clear that:

> a.   archbishops, metropolitans and primates[4] are all bishops; and
>
> b.   together with all other bishops, they belong to the same episcopal order. They are senior bishops who hold a particular office in the Church: they do not comprise a fourth order, in addition to bishops, priests and deacons.

2.4.3   That archbishops belong to the same order as bishops is demonstrated by the fact that although serving archbishops are styled 'The Most Reverend', on ceasing to hold office they normally[5] revert to the general episcopal style of 'The Right Reverend'.[6]

2.4.4   It is also underlined by the fact that in the Church of England there are no distinctions in dress between archbishops and other bishops.[7]

Styles or offices

2.5.1   Canon law[8] states that 'By virtue of their respective offices, the Archbishop of Canterbury is styled Primate of All England and Metropolitan and the Archbishop of York Primate of England and Metropolitan'.

2.5.2   This Canon asserts that:

   a.   the Archbishop of Canterbury and the Archbishop of York hold *offices* as archbishops; and

   b.   their descriptions as primates and metropolitans are *styles*.

While that might have been correct when the canon was first written, it will be seen that what were styles are now offices.

2.6.1   The concept of an 'office' is that of a substantive post which is occupied by different individuals in succession and which has an existence independent of the individual who holds it at any particular time. It carries its own rights, duties and responsibilities and, usually, its own expectations.

2.6.2   An office may be created by an act of a person or body with authority to do so. Alternatively, it may come into existence by being generally recognized as such.

2.6.3   By contrast, a 'style' is a title or description: in general it does not carry responsibilities and does not carry rights or duties.

2.6.4   What is originally a style may with the passage of time attract what are generally regarded as rights, duties and responsibilities, and so develop into an office.

2.6.5   The office of archbishop emerged in this way.[9]

2.7   Similarly, as will be seen, the words 'primate' and 'metropolitan' may previously have been mere styles, but the concepts have been developed so that at the present time the expressions are the titles of *offices*, which, in the case of the Church of England, are held concurrently with that of the office of archbishop.

Archbishops and metropolitans: the historical background
2.8   Statements about the origins and historical meaning of the expressions 'archbishop' and 'metropolitan', as well as 'primate', can only be made with much caution. As is shown in Appendix C, various expressions were often used more or less interchangeably with the same meaning and with little if any awareness of their different derivations. Furthermore, in the absence of comprehensive contemporary evidence, some propositions can be matters only of speculation.

2.9.1 However, two things are clear. The first is that there are no biblical references to archbishops (or metropolitans or primates).

2.9.2 The second is that with the emergence of bishops by the middle of the second century,[10] it was early established that all bishops are equal.[11]

2.10.1 Notwithstanding this essential equality of bishops, it came to be recognized that, in practice, some bishops had a standing which was different from that of others. Various expressions were applied to them, including what in translation is 'archbishop'.[12]

2.10.2 An 'archbishop' is a 'chief bishop' or an 'eminent bishop'.

2.10.3 There may have been a two-way process. On the one hand, someone whose personal qualities stood out might by virtue of those qualities have become bishop of a diocese centred on an important city, a *metropolis*. On the other hand, the bishop of a diocese might have been regarded as being in some way senior by virtue of the importance of the city. Bishops of dioceses centred on important cities sometimes came to be referred to as metropolitans.

2.10.4 With the passage of time, the separate derivations of the expressions 'archbishop' or 'metropolitan' were largely lost, and the words were used interchangeably, with no discernible differences of meaning.[13]

2.11.1 In early centuries, the primary role of archbishops (or metropolitans) appears to have been to convene meetings, or councils, of other bishops in the region, or 'province'.[14]

2.11.2 Archbishops had no special authority expressly conferred on them by any external body, and they certainly could not claim authority over other bishops from any biblical source. However, as the convener of, and presider at, the councils or meetings of bishops, the archbishops were expected to foster unity, and to prevent error, and by custom they came to be recognized as having authority, *inter alia*, to correct any error which did occur.

Archbishops after the Reformation

2.12.1 With the passage of time a difference of nuance emerged in the meanings attributed to 'archbishop' and to 'metropolitan'.

2.12.2 'Archbishop' came to denote chief or principal bishop with emphasis on his spiritual leadership and the moral authority which went with it. The Archbishops of Canterbury and York were the chief ministers or pastors in their provinces, and the Archbishop of Canterbury the chief minister or pastor in the nation.[15] Their positions as such, under the Sovereign,[16] were reaffirmed at the Reformation.

2.13 Just as all bishops are equal but some have a different standing from others, so, within the Church of England, the Archbishops are equal, but in some respects the position of the Archbishop of Canterbury is different from that of the Archbishop of York. The Archbishop of Canterbury is said to have primacy of honour.[17]

2.14.1 In the Church of England, the office of archbishop is primary in the sense that the other styles or offices have been conferred on the Archbishops of Canterbury and York in consequence of their archbishoprics and not independently of them.

2.14.2 Furthermore, the office of 'President' of the Anglican Communion is held by the Archbishop of Canterbury by virtue of his archbishopric. (Formally, there is no office of President of the Anglican Communion and we use the expression to mean all of the offices which the Archbishop holds in the Anglican Communion.[18])

Archbishops as corporations

2.15.1 Before considering the concept of metropolitans, it is convenient to refer to the concept of an archbishop as a corporation. This notion, which has its origins in Roman law, is of the legal fiction of a body which is a legal entity separate from the individual or individuals who comprise it. The overwhelming majority of corporations are trading companies which are entities separate from the shareholders who are the members.

2.15.2 As are other bishops, the Archbishops of Canterbury and York are corporations, known as 'corporations sole'. It is as if the office of archbishop to which we have referred[19] was itself incorporated.[20]

2.15.3 Occasionally, it may not be easy to discern whether an archbishop acts in his personal capacity, or in his corporate capacity, particularly because the corporation can act only through the individual who is the archbishop at the time. However, the Archbishops have seals, and whenever their seal is impressed on a document, they are acting in their corporate capacity.

2.15.4   The fact that an Archbishop is a corporation sole means that:

    a.   that corporation can acquire and hold property;[21]

    b.   acts done by an Archbishop in his corporate capacity bind his successors;[22] and

    c.   rights acquired by an Archbishop in his corporate capacity are exercisable by his successors.

2.16   The issue is particularly pertinent during an interregnum in an archbishopric. Although at that time there is no individual in office, the corporation continues. Thus, when a new archbishop takes up office, he will automatically enjoy the rights which attach to the office and be subject to the liabilities of that office. One result of this is that members of staff who are employed[23] by an Archbishop will continue to be so employed notwithstanding that there is an interregnum.[24]

Metropolitans

2.17.1   We turn now to the significance of the expression 'metropolitan'. By contrast with the spiritual and pastoral connotation of 'archbishop', 'metropolitan' has come to denote canonical authority and jurisdiction. The Canon[25] provides that 'the bishop of each diocese owes due allegiance to the archbishop of the province *as his metropolitan*' (our emphasis). It is as metropolitan that an archbishop confirms the election of a diocesan bishop[26] and, together with fellow bishops, consecrates new bishops.[27]

2.17.2   The use of language is by no means consistent, but a metropolitan, when acting as such, acts not only in his individual capacity, but also as the representative and embodiment of his Church. Thus, in the Book of Common Prayer, the oath of obedience made by a new bishop is:

> 'I ... do profess and promise all due reverence and obedience to the Archbishop and to the Metropolitical Church of N'.[28]

The oath of obedience is not included in the corresponding form in the Alternative Service Book 1980, but is made prior to the consecration in very similar form.[29]

2.18.1 The relationship between a bishop and his metropolitan is direct and personal. Hence, in relation to a bishop, the Canon quoted in paragraph 2.17.1 refers to 'his' metropolitan.

2.18.2 However, the role of the metropolitan is not confined to his relationship with the diocesan bishop. The metropolitan has, throughout his province, at all times metropolitical jurisdiction, as superintendent of all ecclesiastical matters within it, and responsibility and canonical authority to correct and supply the defects of other bishops.[30]

2.18.3 A further example of metropolitical jurisdiction is that it is as metropolitan that an archbishop releases an ordained person from orders.

2.18.4 Furthermore, during the time of a Visitation – that is a formal Visitation, as contrasted with a visit[31] – the metropolitan has jurisdiction as Ordinary.[32] The jurisdiction therefore extends to those within the diocese as well as to the diocesan bishop himself.

2.19 Within the Church of England, a key role of the metropolitan is to be the final determiner of various disciplinary matters, a role which will be redefined if the Clergy Discipline Measure 2000[33] comes into law.

Primates

2.20.1 The word 'primate' appears to have been first used in the Church in Roman Africa to denote a bishop who had a role somewhat less than that of a metropolitan, but wider than that of other bishops. Originally, therefore, a primate was inferior to a metropolitan.

2.20.2 However, that original significance was overtaken, and the word 'primate' came to be used interchangeably with 'archbishop' and 'metropolitan'. Subsequently, the word was used to denote the bishop of the primary see in a region.

2.21.1 From its more modest origins of denoting a senior bishop who was inferior to a metropolitan but superior to other bishops in the region, in modern times the word 'primate' has come to mean a senior bishop with a role which may be *geographically* wider than that of a metropolitan.

2.21.2 The modern idea of the role, which is emerging within the Anglican Communion, has a distinct parallel with that of the archbishops in early times, namely that of a convener of, and presider at, meetings of bishops, including archbishops.[34] So, for the purposes of the Anglican Communion, a primate is the 'principal' archbishop or bishop in a Church which is a member of the Communion.[35]

2.22 A primate, as such, does not have legal or canonical jurisdiction unless it is conferred on him by a provision in the constitution of the Church of which he is a member.

2.23.1 There is an important distinction in the concept of primate as used within the Church of England on the one hand and elsewhere within the Anglican Communion on the other.

2.23.2 As will be seen in the next section, within the Church of England 'primate' denotes a role which extends over an area which is *wider* than that of a province, whereas within the Anglican Communion it generally denotes a representative headship *of* a province.[36]

Primates in the Church of England

2.24.1 The word 'primate' has a special significance within the Church of England, where the Archbishop of Canterbury is styled as Primate of All England and the Archbishop of York as Primate of England. These styles were conferred by the Pope in the middle of the fourteenth century,[37] and were continued after the Reformation.

2.24.2 By using the expressions 'All England' and 'England', the Pope was intentionally not using titles which were restricted to the provinces, but geographically went beyond them.[38]

2.24.3 In the case of the Archbishop of York, until more recent times the title of primate may have been of little[39] practical significance, but in the case of the Archbishop of Canterbury it has had significance for many centuries. Although for most purposes the provinces of Canterbury and York are independent of each other, the Archbishop of Canterbury, as Primate of All England, has in certain very limited respects jurisdiction which extends to the northern province. The best-known example is the power to grant special licences throughout England.[40]

2.25 The concept of primate has developed from that of a convener of, and a presider at, meetings of bishops to that of a presider at meetings, often on a national basis, of bishops and other members of the

Church and, by extension, the leader of the Church and the representative head of the Church to other churches and other bodies.

Patriarchs

2.26.1 Before proceeding, reference should be made to a further expression which is used within parts of the Christian Church, namely 'patriarch'. A patriarch was originally a metropolitan who convened episcopal meetings across a number of smaller provinces, each having their own metropolitan.

2.26.2 The term is not in use in the Church of England and is not considered further here.

Archbishops, metropolitans and primates: summary

2.27.1 There are no clearly defined and universally recognized distinctions in the present use of the expressions archbishop, metropolitan and primate. Different people use the expressions in different ways, and the language is sometimes inconsistent. However, there is now emerging a broad consistency in the meanings which are attributed to these words.

2.27.2 Despite the imprecision of usage, the general connotations at the present time are:

> a. archbishop: the chief or principal minister or bishop, with the emphasis on spiritual leadership and pastoral care;

> b. metropolitan: the holder of canonical authority and the exerciser of canonical jurisdiction within a province; and

> c. primate: a convener of meetings of bishops, and others, the exerciser of broader powers, in the case of both primates in England, throughout the Church of England, and the leader and representative head of the Church.[41]

The offices of the Archbishops of Canterbury and York: a possible classification

2.28.1 The Archbishops of Canterbury and York are diocesan bishops, of the Dioceses of Canterbury and York respectively.

2.28.2 Apart from being diocesan bishops, the Archbishops of Canterbury and York hold the separate offices of primate and metropolitan. They hold those offices by virtue of their archbishoprics.

2.29 There can be much debate as to which duties, responsibilities and expectations attach to each office, and there is often overlap between them, but a possible classification is as follows:

2.29.1 As Archbishops:

a. the chief ministers within the nation;

b. the holders of offices recognized by the law and custom of the State; and

c. the representative heads of the Church of England within the nation;

2.29.2 As Metropolitans:

the holders and conferers of canonical authority and the exercisers of canonical jurisdiction within, in the case of the Archbishop of Canterbury, the southern Province, and, in the case of the Archbishop of York, the northern Province, and the conveners of the convocations of those provinces;

2.29.3 As Primates:

a. the presiders at meetings of national bodies of the Church, such as the General Synod, the Archbishops' Council and the Church Commissioners; and

b. particularly in the case of the Archbishop of Canterbury, but also in certain respects[42] the Archbishop of York, the representative head of the Church of England in dealings with other Churches and bodies.

2.30 The Archbishop of Canterbury alone has the further office of President of the Anglican Communion.[43]

The offices and resources

2.31 We have made this analysis of the offices held by the Archbishops as part of our seeking to understand their work. We have kept in mind these separate offices in considering to what extent, if at all, the Archbishops should be separately resourced in respect of each of the offices.

chapter 3

The Archbishops of Canterbury and York

Introduction

3.1   In some respects there are similarities between the roles of the Archbishops of Canterbury and York, and in other, often major, respects, there are significant differences between them. These differences lead to different resourcing needs, and can make comparisons unhelpful.

3.2   In this chapter, we consider some of the similarities and dissimilarities so far as they are relevant for resourcing purposes. The pattern of the remaining chapters of this report is to deal first with resourcing issues which apply to both Archbishops, and thereafter the separate considerations which apply first to the Archbishop of Canterbury and then the Archbishop of York.

3.3   During almost every archiepiscopate, the ministry of the archbishop will evolve: whatever resourcing arrangements are in place must be sufficiently flexible to meet those changing circumstances.

Similarities

3.4   The starting point is that:

  a.   both Archbishops are priests,[1] and can be expected to have the priestly pastoral instincts; and

  b.   both Archbishops are bishops, and not members of a separate archiepiscopal order.[2]

3.5   We have shown[3] that although the Archbishop of Canterbury has the additional office of President of the Anglican Communion, we regard each Archbishop as holding concurrently four offices, namely those of:

    i.   Archbishop;

    ii.   Diocesan Bishop;

    iii.   Metropolitan, with a role in relation to a group of dioceses which comprise a province; and

    iv.   Primate, with a role in relation to the whole of the Church of England, and, by extension, the nation.[4]

Dissimilarities

3.6.1   Although both Archbishops hold those four offices, there are marked differences in the substance of the offices.

3.6.2   The Archbishop of Canterbury is the diocesan bishop of the Diocese of Canterbury, but at the present time most of his powers and functions as such are delegated to the Bishop of Dover.[5] By contrast, the Archbishop of York has made very limited delegation of his powers and responsibilities as the diocesan bishop of the Diocese of York. In practice, although not in legal responsibility, therefore, the Archbishop of York is much more fully a diocesan bishop than is the Archbishop of Canterbury.

3.7   There are no differences in the fundamental nature of the powers and responsibilities of the two Archbishops as metropolitans, but in practice there are major differences. In the first place, the *scale* is very different. The Northern Province (York) comprises[6] fourteen dioceses with a total population of about 15 million, an area of about 15,500 square miles (about 40,000 square kilometres) and about 2,750 stipendiary diocesan clergy. The Southern Province (Canterbury) comprises thirty dioceses with a total population of about 35 million, an area of about 35,250 square miles (91,000 square kilometres) and about 6,750 stipendiary diocesan clergy. In the second place, the *character and ethos* are different. The smaller size of the Northern Province enables the Archbishop of York to develop a closer relationship with this province and its clergy than is possible for the Archbishop of Canterbury – and this would be so even if the Archbishop of Canterbury did not also have his additional responsibilities within the Anglican Communion. In the third place, as is shown in Appendix E, there are a number of *statutory* obligations imposed on the Archbishop of Canterbury as metropolitan which do not apply to the Archbishop of York.

3.8   There are also substantial differences in the primatial roles. In part this is because by law or custom specific responsibilities are allocated to the Archbishop of Canterbury.[7] In part this is because the Archbishop of Canterbury is generally regarded in the country as the leader or representative of the Church of England as a whole, and so, for example, he is the immediate point of reference for comment on major issues on behalf of the Church of England; and he is the prime national representative of the Church of England in its dealings with the leaders of other churches and of other faiths.

3.9.1   In many respects, it is as the President[8] of the Anglican Communion that at present the position of the Archbishop of Canterbury is most markedly different from that of the Archbishop of York.[9]

3.9.2   The Archbishop of York currently leads the Church of England in its relationship with the other churches within the Porvoo Communion,[10] but the nature of that commitment, as well as of the time which it takes, is very much less than that of the Archbishop of Canterbury in relation to the Anglican Communion.

3.9.3   The result in practice is that whereas the Archbishop of York is one of the leaders *of* the Church of England, the Archbishop of Canterbury is the leader of a much larger agglomeration which *includes* the Church of England.

Self-direction

3.10.1   There are four general observations which apply to both Archbishops. The first is that to an extent the ministries of the Archbishops are self-directing.

3.10.2   There are many constraints. Legal and moral obligations, as well as expectations and external events, dictate how the Archbishops spend much of their time. Apart from that, however, it is for the Archbishops to decide how they divide their time between their various offices, and between the various functions within those offices.

The extent of accountability

3.11.1   Secondly, the scope for self-direction is related to the subject of accountability. Self-direction encourages the use of individual gifts and talents, but unlike most secular models,[11] it is not accompanied by formal operational accountability.

3.11.2   This is not to suggest that the Archbishops are unaccountable. Their dealings with members of the Archbishops' Council, or of the House of Bishops, or of the General Synod, involve in practice some element of (mutual) accountability. But there is no relationship akin to that of a Managing Director of a company to his Board; or of a Headmaster to his Governors; or of the Chairman of a body of trustees to his fellow trustees.

3.11.3   The absence of a formal structure of accountability not only encourages self-direction, but also results in the Archbishops not being subject to the system of ministerial review in the same way as most clergy.[12] On the other hand, Archbishops are subject to continuing, and sometimes unrelenting, public scrutiny.

3.11.4   It is not within our terms of reference to comment on the merits or demerits of a system in which there is no formal accountability or arrangements for review. The system is, however, relevant for our purposes because it predicates the need for flexibility in the provision of resource.

The primatial roles

3.12.1   The third general observation relates to the allocation of primatial roles between the Archbishops. Not only does each Archbishop have the scope for self-direction, but to a material extent the allocation of primatial roles is a matter for agreement between them. There is no governmental or other external body which generally allocates the roles to one Archbishop or the other.[13]

3.12.2   Furthermore, the allocation of primatial roles is itself a continuing process. So, for example, in recent years Dr Hope has in practice chaired many meetings of the Board of Governors of the Church Commissioners; both Archbishops share the chairing of the House of Bishops; both Archbishops share the presidency of General Synod, as well as chairing that body for some items of business; and they share the chairing of the Archbishops' Council.

Evolving ministries and evolving relationships

3.13.1   The fourth, and final, general observation is to note that the ministries of the Archbishops, just as the ministries of other bishops, evolve.

3.13.2   Furthermore, from the two preceding sections it follows that the relationship between the two Archbishops evolves.

3.13.3   Accordingly, many statements about the ministry of any Archbishop, or of the relationship between the Archbishops, can only be valid in the light of the particular circumstances which prevail at the time when those statements are made.

Support for the Archbishops

3.14.1   There is a final observation which applies to both Archbishops: their jobs are lonely. The confidentiality and great sensitivity of some of what they do intensifies this; and the isolation and often hostile public scrutiny serve only to increase the pressures.

3.14.2   This subject falls well outside the provision of resources, save that in our considerations we have been mindful of the absence – subject to the crucial exception of prayer – of many types of support for the Archbishops.[14]

Part II: Principles

chapter 4

Resources and resourcing principles

Resources

4.1.1   In our First Report we defined[1] the resources provided for bishops. Exactly the same categories of resource apply to the Archbishops, namely:

    a.   somewhere to live;

    b.   somewhere to work;

    c.   staff to assist in that work;

    d.   somewhere for the staff to work;

    e.   the means to travel for official purposes;

    f.   the means with which to provide official hospitality;

    g.   the means with which to communicate;

    h.   the means with which to be trained;

    i.   the equipment to do the work; and

    j.   the legal, medical and other professional support necessary to do the work.

4.1.2   Although we consider in this report an Archbishop's personal staff, we do not consider the many others who directly or indirectly assist an Archbishop in his ministry.[2]

4.2   All resources used by the Archbishops are provided by or paid for by the Commissioners. The Commissioners acquired about one quarter of their funds from the former episcopal and archiepiscopal estates.[3]

The general approach

4.3.1   In general, we consider that the approach which we adopted in our first report in relation to bishops should also apply to archbishops.

4.3.2 Thus, we consider that, except in very limited respects, the same principles with regard to resourcing should apply.[4]

4.3.3 We also consider that the same approach should apply in relation to:

   a.   the devolution of Commissioners' funds by block-grant;[5]

   b.   the support given by wives of archbishops;[6] and

   c.   transparency and disclosure.[7]

4.3.4 We do, however, take a different approach with regard to:

   a.   the equivalent of a Bishops' Resources Group in relation to the Archbishop of Canterbury;[8] and

   b.   the ownership of the archiepiscopal palaces.[9]

Principles

4.4 In Chapter 9 of our First Report we set out 15 principles against which we recommended that the provision of resources for bishops should be measured.

4.5 Without repeating the discussion in that chapter, and as adapted to the Archbishops, the principles which we **recommend** should be applied in the case of the Archbishops are (retaining the same numbering as in our First Report) as follows:

4.5.1   No 1: Necessity

An Archbishop should have the resources which are necessary to enable him to carry out his roles and responsibilities.

4.5.2   No 2: Objective determination of necessity

The resources which are necessary should be objectively determined and should be reflected in published national guidelines.

4.5.3   No 3: Individual gifts and skills

So far as practicable, resources should be provided in such a way as will facilitate an Archbishop's exercising of his ministry according to his individual gifts and skills.

4.5.4   No 4: Married Archbishops

The nature and scale of resources provided for an Archbishop should be sufficient to enable him to do his job irrespective of whether or not he is married.

4.5.5   No 5: Need not status

Resources should be provided according to need not status.

4.5.6   No 6: Cost effectiveness

Resources should be provided in a cost-effective manner.

4.5.7   No 7: Simplicity in operation

Resources should be provided in the manner which leads to the greatest simplicity in operation.

4.5.8   No 9: Accountability

An Archbishop should be accountable for the expenditure of funds to the body which provides them.

4.5.9   No 10: Transparency

There should be transparency about the use of funds.

4.5.10   No 11: Involvement in expenditure statements

An Archbishop should be involved in the preparation of any statement to be made to others about the expenditure of funds made available to him, so that to the fullest practical extent he can be satisfied as to its accuracy.

4.5.11   No 12: Subsidiarity

Decisions as to the amount and expenditure of financial resources should be taken at the nearest practical level to that at which the expenditure is incurred.

4.5.12   No 13: Openness

To the fullest practical extent, there should be openness about the nature and scale of resources provided and the principles by which they are determined.

4.5.13   No 15: Discretion

Where there is any discretionary element in the provision of resources, there should be made known:

a. the parameters within which the decision is taken;

b. the method by which the decision is taken; and

c. the person or persons by whom the decision is taken.

4.6.1 Principle No 8 in our First Report related to categorization for budgeting and accounting purposes. As will be seen,[10] we propose a modification to that, to take account of the separate offices held by each Archbishop.

4.6.2 Principle No 14 in our First Report related to equity between one bishop and another. We do not regard the circumstances of either Archbishop as being, for this purpose, comparable to those of another bishop[11] or, as has been seen,[12] comparable to those of each other.

Evolution of ministries

4.7 Almost certainly the ministry of an Archbishop will change during his archiepiscopate, and the balance of the relationship between the two Archbishops will also change. For these reasons, the system for the provision of resources for the Archbishops should be sufficiently flexible to accommodate these changes with the minimum of difficulty. This requirement underlies many of our recommendations.

Devolution of responsibilites

4.8.1 Finally, in this Chapter we make one comment on workload. Both Archbishops work excessively hard, and both would value more time in which to do that work.[13] It is tempting to suggest[14] that some of their work should be devolved to diocesan bishops and others, ordained or lay.

4.8.2 While there may be some, very limited, scope for this, we counsel great caution. Our assessment[15] is that, generally, diocesan bishops are already overloaded. We do not consider that any scope that there might be for devolution of work is sufficiently great in itself to warrant any reduction from the present level of resources which are provided for the Archbishops.

chapter 5

Archbishops and the new regime

Introduction

5.1.1   In our First Report we recommended a new regime for the provision of resources for bishops. Main features of our proposals were that:

> a.   the activities to be conducted by the Church centrally should be clearly defined and restricted;
>
> b.   most of the funds to be provided by the Commissioners in support of episcopal ministry should be made available to the diocesan bishop of each diocese by way of block-grant;
>
> c.   the amount of the block-grant should be determined by formula;
>
> d.   the block-granted funds should be used to procure resources for all bishops in the diocese;
>
> e.   many of those resources should be procured locally; and
>
> f.   in the local provision of resources the diocesan bishop should be advised by a Bishops' Resources Group.

5.1.2   In this chapter we consider the application of these proposals to the Archbishops.

5.2   We deal elsewhere in this report with the application to the Archbishops of other recommendations which we made in our First Report. These include recommendations relating to the measurement of resources against stated principles,[1] the provision of resources on taking up office,[2] transparency and disclosure,[3] the provision of resources for the wives of archbishops[4] and the maintenance and ownership of premises.[5]

Central activities

5.3.1   We recommended[6] that there should only be conducted at the centre (by which we meant by the Commissioners and the Archbishops' Council and their respective staffs):

41

a.   those activities which it is necessary to carry on at the centre in order to prescribe common minimum standards;

b.   those activities which it is necessary to carry on at the centre because they relate to matters which are wider than those affecting one diocese. We cited the setting of nationwide IT protocols as an example; and

c.   those activities for which value is demonstrably added as a result of their being carried on at the centre rather than locally.

5.3.2   We also recommended[7] that, in addition to the major role of generating spendable funds, the Commissioners should:

a.   through a committee constituted for the purpose, set the minimum standards and scales of resources;

b.   operate the block-granting system;

c.   outsource the provision of certain facilities; and

d.   deal with the Inland Revenue in relation to the general principles governing the income taxation of bishops.

5.3.3   The nature of the ministries of the Archbishops differs in a number of respects from that of other bishops,[8] and their specific circumstances need to be considered separately. However, we **recommend** that except to the extent that these circumstances make different treatment essential, the approach which we have proposed should apply to other bishops should also apply in relation to Archbishops.

Devolution of funds

5.4.1   Our recommendation for the devolution of funds by the Commissioners to diocesan bishops was made because:[9]

a.   it would give bishops empowerment over the use of funds made available for their support;

b.   it would encourage local financial control;

c.   it would enable cost-effective advantage to be taken of local opportunities; and

d.   it would save central administrative costs.

5.4.2   All of these considerations apply equally to the Archbishops. We **recommend** that the Archbishops should be given much greater financial control over their affairs.

The calculation of the block-grant

5.5.1   We recommended[10] that the amount to be devolved to diocesan bishops should be calculated from a completely new base, and should be determined by a formula.

5.5.2   We also recommended[11] that although the formula would have various elements, the funds calculated by it should be devolved as one block sum, and that the recipient should not be required to expend it according to those elements. We **recommend** that this approach should also apply to funds devolved to the Archbishops.

5.6   We now consider:

a.   aspects of this approach which should apply to both Archbishops; and

b.   separate considerations which apply to:

i.   the Archbishop of Canterbury;

ii.   the special circumstances of the Diocese of Canterbury; and

iii.   the Archbishop of York.

Considerations applicable to both Archbishops

5.7.1   The Commissioners will need, having regard to advice from the Archbishops' Council, each year to determine the total amount which they apply in the provision of resources by way of support for episcopal (and archiepiscopal) ministry.[12] The Commissioners will also need to determine the manner in which that amount is to be applied in the provision of resources for the archbishops on the one hand and all other bishops on the other hand.

5.7.2   We **recommend** that:

a.   the amount to be applied for archbishops as well as bishops should be determined by formula, but subject in the case of the Archbishop of Canterbury to a transitional arrangement; and

    b.   the elements of the formula and other aspects of the process governing the devolution of funds should:

        i.   be transparent;[13] and

        ii.   be seen to be fair.

5.8.1   The Archbishop of Canterbury is chairman of the Board of Governors of the Church Commissioners, although in recent times meetings have in practice generally been chaired by the Archbishop of York. No one has made to us the slightest suggestion whatever that either Archbishop receives greater support from the Commissioners by virtue of these roles.

5.8.2   The circumstances are such, however, that there may be a *perception* of a conflict of interest between the position of the Archbishops as leaders of the funding body on the one hand and recipients of funds from that body on the other.

5.8.3   Although this would do no more than to state more formally the existing practice, we **recommend** that neither Archbishop (nor, indeed, any other bishop) should be present for any discussion at any meeting of the Board of Governors or of a committee of the Board of Governors[14] at which their own resources are to be considered.

The Archbishop of Canterbury

5.9.1   We **recommend** that there should be separate block-grants:

    a.   to the Archbishop of Canterbury in his metropolitical, primatial, archiepiscopal and Anglican Communion roles which, broadly, comprise his ministry at and from Lambeth Palace; and

    b.   to the Archbishop of Canterbury in his capacity as diocesan bishop for himself and the other bishops of the Diocese of Canterbury.

5.9.2   We further **recommend** that the first of these grants should exclude the Lambeth Palace Library because, in a later chapter,[15] we make separate recommendations to the effect that the Library should be treated as a separate cost centre and funded in a different way.

5.9.3   The formula in respect of the first block-grant would include elements for overseas travel and the Archbishop's roles in relation to the Anglican Communion.

5.10.1   We consider that a satisfactory formula in relation to the Archbishop of Canterbury could not be devised until the Chief of Staff who, in a later chapter, we recommend[16] should be appointed, has, in conjunction with the Archbishop, been able to effect whatever restructuring is necessary. We also consider, however, that when that has been done, a common understanding could be reached between the Archbishop and his staff on the one hand and the Commissioners on the other as to the appropriate staff and other resources which are needed at Lambeth Palace.

5.10.2   During a transitional period, until that stage has been reached, we **recommend** that the amount of the block-grant should be the subject of a budget bid from the Chief of Staff. The bid would be considered on the same bases as are applied[17] to bids from other National Church Institutions.[18]

The Diocese of Canterbury

5.11.1   We **recommend** that the block-grant to be made for the bishops of the Diocese of Canterbury should be made to the Archbishop as diocesan bishop of the diocese. From it there would be provided the resources required by the Archbishop for his ministry as diocesan bishop as well as the resources required for the Bishop of Dover and the Bishop of Maidstone.[19] We further **recommend** that it should be for the Archbishop to decide whether and to what extent responsibility for the application of those funds should be delegated to the Bishop of Dover.

5.11.2   The main resources which we consider should be provided for the Archbishop in relation to his ministry at Canterbury would be one or more members of his staff to be based at Canterbury,[20] together with his official hospitality and travelling costs. We deal separately[21] with the premises at Canterbury.

5.11.3   We **recommend** that in constructing the formula account should be taken of the amount of his time which the Archbishop spends in his ministry in and to the diocese. Solely for the purposes of example, if the Archbishop spends 25% of his time on his diocesan ministry and as there would continue to be the Bishop of Dover and the Bishop of Maidstone, the formula should be on the basis that there were two and a quarter bishops in the diocese. Apart from that, the block-grant would be calculated according to the standard formula.

The Archbishop of York

5.12.1 The resourcing needs of the Archbishop of York can be fairly seen as those of a diocesan bishop, but with additional requirements in respect of his provincial, primatial and archiepiscopal duties.

5.12.2 We **recommend** that:

> a.   there should be a block-grant to the Archbishop of York, as diocesan bishop of the Diocese of York, for the provision of resources for the Archbishop as diocesan bishop and for the other bishops of the diocese;
>
> b.   that grant should be calculated according to the standard formula; and
>
> c.   the Archbishop should be able, if he so wishes, to delegate the responsibility for the application of those funds.

5.12.3 We **recommend** that in addition, the Archbishop should receive a separate, supplementary, block-grant in respect of his resourcing needs as metropolitan, primate and archbishop.

National responsibilities

5.13.1 We discuss elsewhere[22] the possibility of some modification to the sharing of national responsibilities between the Archbishop of Canterbury and the Archbishop of York.

5.13.2 If that resulted in the Archbishop of York having greater responsibilities, and needing an adjustment to his formula amount, we would expect that, in ordinary circumstances, there would be a decrease in the formula amount for the Archbishop of Canterbury.

Provincial responsibilities

5.14.1 The only resources which at present are provided for an Archbishop as metropolitan are the services of the Vicar-General and the Provincial Registrars.[23]

5.14.2 We **recommend** that they should continue to be paid for directly by the Commissioners, and should not be brought within the formula amounts.

Ministry and mission initiative

5.15.1 The Commissioners provide the resources which are necessary to enable the Archbishops to do their work, but they do not, in addition, make any specific allocation to the Archbishops of funds which they can apply in meeting the costs of mission and other initiatives which they wish to take in furthering their ministries. In general, if such initiatives are to be funded by the Church,[24] they should be subject to the ordinary process of evaluation and budgeting allocation.

5.15.2 To a minor extent these initiatives are in fact funded by the Commissioners. For example, the present Archbishop of Canterbury established a chaplaincy at Strasbourg, and the cost is treated as part of the Archbishop's operational costs.

5.15.3 With this minor exception, if an Archbishop wishes to take a personal initiative in mission or in some other way in furtherance of his ministry, he needs to meet the cost either from a charitable fund[25] or by raising new money specifically for the purpose.

5.16.1 In the present financial circumstances of the Church of England, we do not think that it would be right to include in the formula any specific amount for personal initiatives of the Archbishops. We **recommend**, however, that this possibility should be kept in mind on future reviews of the formula.

5.16.2 We do, however, **recommend** that if an Archbishop is able to effect a saving from the block-grant in the provision of resources, then he should be at liberty to apply that surplus for any purpose in the furtherance of his ministry, provided that that purpose is one for which the Commissioners could lawfully apply their funds.

5.16.3 We also **recommend** that any of the Commissioners' funds which are in fact applied in initiatives of this nature should be accounted for as mission costs of the Church and not, as at present, as part of the Archbishops' operational costs.[26]

Non-hypothecation

5.17.1 As in the case of block-grants made to other bishops,[27] although the amount of the grant would be calculated according to a formula with a number of elements, we **recommend** that the devolved funds should not be restricted so that they could only be expended on those purposes, but that the Archbishops should be able to expend them as they think fit.

5.17.2   We do, however, make recommendations[28] for the disclosure of the manner in which the devolved funds are actually applied.

Local procurement of resources

5.18.1   In our First Report, we envisaged[29] that full advantage would be taken of local opportunities for the provision of resources for other bishops, and for collaboration with DBFs and others in making bulk purchases.

5.18.2   We **recommend** the same general approach to the provision of resources for the Archbishops. This is particularly so in the case of the Archbishop of York, with potential opportunities for collaboration with the Diocesan Board of Finance of the Diocese of York and, perhaps, those of adjacent dioceses. In the case of the Archbishop of Canterbury, there may be scope for collaboration with other central Church organizations.

Resources Group

5.19   We recommended[30] that each diocesan bishop should appoint a small Bishops' Resources Group. This group would advise the bishop with regard to the longer-term planning and more immediate procurement of resources from block-granted funds. Furthermore, that Group, or individual members of it, would be available to negotiate the terms on which resources were obtained, and would also be available to solicit supplementary provision or *pro bono* support.

5.20.1   There is already available to the Archbishop of Canterbury a body, namely the trustees of The Lambeth Fund,[31] which could readily perform this function, and we do not think that a separate resources group would be helpful in relation to his roles as metropolitan, primate and archbishop.

5.20.2   We **recommend** that a Bishops' Resources Group should be established for the bishops of the Diocese of Canterbury, and that that Group should have responsibilities in relation to the provision of resources for the bishops of that diocese, including the Archbishop of Canterbury in his capacity as diocesan bishop. We further **recommend** that the Archbishop should be able, if he so wishes, to delegate the responsibility for appointing and chairing that Group.

5.20.3   We also **recommend** that the Archbishop of York should set up a resources group (which would have the additional responsibility of being concerned with the provision of resources for his archiepiscopal, metropolitical and primatial roles) and that he also should have power, if he so wishes, to delegate the responsibility for the appointment and chairing of that Group.

Banking arrangements
5.21.1   We suggested[32] that Diocesan Boards of Finance should act as bankers in respect of funds devolved to other bishops.

5.21.2   The number of financial transactions and money movements relating to the Archbishops, particularly the Archbishop of Canterbury, is much larger than those relating to other bishops, and we **recommend** that the Archbishops' staffs should continue to be responsible for their own banking arrangements.

Partnership with DBFs
5.22   There are, in practice, partnerships between the Commissioners and DBFs in the provision of resources for other bishops.[33] Such arrangements are not applicable to the Archbishop of Canterbury in relation to his activities at Lambeth Palace, but our recommendations with regard to the Old Palace at Canterbury[34] and with regard to Bishopthorpe[35] are designed to strengthen that approach.

Provincial Episcopal Visitors
5.23.1   There are two Provincial Episcopal Visitors who are, formally, suffragan bishops in the Diocese of Canterbury and one who is formally a suffragan bishop in the Diocese of York.[36]

5.23.2   We made recommendations with regard to Provincial Episcopal Visitors in our First Report,[37] and do not need to add to them in this report.

Resource analysis
5.24.1   Finally, in our First Report we recommended[38] that before any new Church legislation which would impose duties on bishops and, indeed, others, the proposed legislation should be accompanied by an assessment of the time and resource implications.

5.24.2   We specifically **recommend** that that should apply to the Archbishops.

chapter 6

The archiepiscopal palaces

Introduction

6.1　　The Archbishop of Canterbury lives in and works in Lambeth Palace and the Old Palace at Canterbury. The Archbishop of York lives in and works in Bishopthorpe Palace, York. Specific observations are made later[1] about these three archiepiscopal palaces: in this chapter we deal with:

    a.　the approach to the use of the palaces;

    b.　their future ownership; and

    c.　certain other general considerations which apply to all three properties.

6.1.2　　We make the preliminary observation that although in general usage the word 'palace' may have the connotation of grandeur, it is more apt to regard the archiepiscopal palaces as being large, and special, rather than as grand.

6.1.3　　We also observe that there is a tension between providing proper living and working accommodation for the Archbishop and making the best use of the buildings.

The use of the palaces

6.2.1　　There are three initial issues. The first is to discern the uses to which the palaces are put. Lambeth Palace and the Old Palace at Canterbury are frequently described as the homes of the Archbishop of Canterbury, and Bishopthorpe as the home of the Archbishop of York.

6.2.2　　These descriptions are true – in part. The Archbishops do, indeed, live in parts of the palaces, and welcome visitors to other parts with warmth and, sometimes, the explanation that they are their homes.

6.2.3　　Yet, although the Archbishops live in these properties, they occupy only very small parts of the total space for their private residential purposes. With the possible exception of the Old Palace at

Canterbury, the *predominant* use of the palaces is that of operational or headquarter buildings for the Church of England. This is so notwithstanding their special characters and ethos.

Retention or disposal

6.3.1   The second initial question is whether the Commissioners should, in contemporary circumstances, retain these properties, and continue to put them to, broadly, their present use, or whether the Commissioners should dispose of them.

6.3.2   We have considered separately each of the properties, having regard to their financial and other values and costs.

6.3.3   With regard to financial values, the Commissioners bring each of the palaces into account at the nominal sum of £1, on the ground that there has been no intention of disposing of them.[2] In our evaluation, we have made certain assumptions about capital values, but we have not commissioned any professional valuation, particularly because the capital values could only be reliably ascertained by actually exposing the properties for sale on the open market.

6.3.4   We have also taken into account other values. We are conscious of the historical and symbolic significance of the properties; the facilities which they represent as places in and from which the Archbishops can exercise their ministries; and, whether or not the personal staffs are to be maintained at their present levels, the need for the members of staff to be provided with working accommodation.

6.4.1   We examine in subsequent chapters the issues in relation to each of the palaces.[3]

6.4.2   For the reasons given in these chapters we **recommend** that the three properties should be retained, but on three inter-related conditions, namely that:

 a.   there is a modification to the way in which the use of the palaces is regarded;

 b.   there is a more efficient use of space within the palaces; and

 c.   in the case of Lambeth Palace and Bishopthorpe, they are put to additional uses which will enable funds to be generated which are sufficient to cover all or most of the recurrent cost of maintenance, repairs, insurance and management.

A home or a place in which to live?

6.5.1   The first condition relates to the way in which the palaces are regarded. The Archbishops regard the palaces as their 'homes', yet, as we have stated,[4] only small parts of the palaces are used by the Archbishops for their private residential purposes. On the other hand, as in the case of other see houses,[5] visitors appreciate the warmth and, as many would regard it, the privilege of being welcomed by an Archbishop into his home.

6.5.2   Some of our major recommendations – not only those relating to income generation – would involve some change of ethos. We describe this change as being from one where the palace as a whole is in some sense regarded as the Archbishop's home to one as a place in which he lives.

6.5.3   We **recommend** that *within* the curtilage of each palace there should be physically self-contained accommodation for the private residential use of the Archbishops. Another way of describing the change of ethos which we recommend is from the position in which the palace itself is regarded as the home to one in which the home is within the palace.

6.5.4   We do not consider that such a change need significantly affect the manner in which visitors are received, nor the enjoyment which they derive from their visits. We do, however, think that it will affect the approach to some of the activities which are carried on within the palaces.

Space utilization

6.6.1   The second condition is that there should be a more efficient use of space. In the case of Bishopthorpe and the Old Palace at Canterbury, there is gross under-utilization of parts of the buildings, particularly those set aside as official guest bedrooms. The availability of such rooms is clearly helpful to the Archbishops, but the use of these rooms needs to be considered as part of the overall use of resources. We **recommend** that if such rooms are not used, taking one year with another, for, say, 20% of the time, then there should be a presumption that they should be put to some other use. The presumption should be capable of being rebutted if the continued setting aside of rooms as official guest bedrooms could be justified.

6.6.2   There is not this type of under-utilization at Lambeth Palace, but, as will be seen,[6] in some respects we consider that parts of the palace buildings could be used more beneficially.

6.6.3   In general, we **recommend** that all the space in the archiepiscopal palaces should be fully and effectively used.

Income generation

6.7.1   All of the palaces are in themselves actually or potentially expensive to keep in a proper state of repair and decoration; and to keep heated, lighted and cleaned. In addition, either members of staff or outside contractors are necessary to keep them in a proper state in which they can be used. Security and the upkeep of the grounds are examples of these activities.

6.7.2   We **recommend** that Lambeth Palace should be put to uses which enable sufficient income to be generated in order at least to cover the costs of maintaining, heating, lighting, cleaning and keeping secure the entire palace and its grounds. We **recommend** that Bishopthorpe should be put to uses which will generate sufficient income to cover a substantial part of these costs.

Reasons for recommendations

6.8   There are two broad reasons for the conditions which we have attached to our recommendation that the palaces should be retained. Those are that:

  a.   in the present financial circumstances of the Church of England, it is difficult to justify the continued level of expenditure on the properties; and

  b.   irrespective of the financial circumstances, it is, in our understanding, one aspect of stewardship that the use of any asset should be kept under review to ensure that, so far as practicable, that use is good and effective.

Ownership of the palaces

6.9.1   In our First Report we made various recommendations in respect of see houses. In outline, these were that:

a.   there should be a review in each diocese of the living and working accommodation provided for all bishops in the diocese;[7]

b.   if a see house were found to be no longer appropriate, it should be replaced at the expense of the Commissioners;[8]

c.   ultimately the Commissioners should transfer without charge the ownership of see houses to DBFs;[9]

d.   the amount to be paid by the Commissioners for the maintenance and repair of see houses should be re-defined and limited;[10] and

e.   the ultimate transfer of the ownership of see houses to DBFs should be accompanied by a transfer to DBFs of the obligation to maintain and repair them.[11]

6.9.2   We made further recommendations in respect of heritage properties which would cease to be used as see houses.[12]

6.10.1   We consider that the three palaces should not fall within this regime, but that they should be subject to separate measures.

6.10.2   In the case of Lambeth Palace and Bishopthorpe, this is because of the substantial income-generating activities which we recommend, and in the case of all three palaces because of the interests which are much wider than those of the diocese.

6.11   We **recommend** that:

a.   the Commissioners should continue to own the palaces; but

b.   separate holding arrangements based on trusts should be established in respect of each of them.

6.12.1   The trust arrangements which we propose are similar to, but are not identical with, those which the Commissioners have established at Auckland Castle.[13] Although the arrangements may conveniently be referred to as being in the nature of a trust, more accurately they depend on the use of charitable companies limited by guarantee.

6.12.2 We **recommend** that in respect of each of the three palaces:
a.   a separate charitable company limited by guarantee should be established;

b.   the Commissioners should grant a lease of the palace to the company, subject to protection of the personal interests of the Archbishop;

c.   the principal objects of the company should be:

i.   to safeguard private residential accommodation within the palace for the Archbishop and working accommodation for the Archbishop and his staff; and

ii.   to maintain and preserve the fabric of the palace and its grounds;

d.   the Archbishop should be a director of the company and should have the right to be the chairman of its Board;

e.   the directors of the company should have the power to form one or more trading companies as wholly owned subsidiaries to conduct income-generating activities;

f.   the net income of the trading company or companies should be paid up to the charitable company; and

g.   the charitable company should, to the extent of its available funds, pay the maintenance and associated costs of the palace.

6.13.1 The main differences between the arrangements for Auckland Castle and those which we propose for the archiepiscopal palaces are that:

a.   the arrangements should apply to the entire archiepiscopal palaces (and not, as in the case of Auckland Castle, only to public and mixed-user rooms);

b.   the provisions for the appointment of directors of the charitable company should be simpler than those for the Auckland Castle company; and

c.   should the charitable company realize a surplus, that surplus should be available, after making provision for future liabilities, for any purpose in furtherance of the Archbishop's ministry.

6.13.2   With regard to the last point, the constitution of the charitable company established for Auckland Castle provides for any surplus to be returned to the Commissioners,[14] although in practice[15] no surplus has arisen. However, the arrangement would be for the benefit of the Commissioners, in their being totally or partially exonerated from meeting maintenance costs[16] and it would encourage endeavours on the part of the Archbishops' staffs for any surplus from the archiepiscopal palaces to be applied as the Archbishop thought proper.

6.14.1   When the system was fully in operation, the roles of the Commissioners would be restricted to:

>   a.   satisfying themselves periodically that their obligations[17] with regard to the maintenance and repair of the properties were being discharged;
>
>   b.   perhaps in the case of Bishopthorpe and the Old Palace at Canterbury, contributing towards the maintenance costs;
>
>   c.   approving any proposals made by the directors which would affect the fabric of the buildings; and
>
>   d.   funding any capital improvements which the Commissioners themselves wished to see effected.

6.14.2   It would follow that the only funds which, in ordinary circumstances, the Commissioners would be required to provide in relation to the properties themselves would be to make any necessary contributions to the maintenance costs of the Old Palace, Canterbury and, perhaps, Bishopthorpe and for any capital improvements which they wished to carry out.

6.15   It would be part of the arrangements that were the income to be generated from the palaces to exceed that required to meet the requisite costs, that surplus would be available for any other purpose for which the trust was established.

Adjacent properties

6.16.1   A further point which is common to all three palaces is whether, together with their grounds, they should each be regarded as discrete entities. In some respects they are. However, the optimum use of the properties is likely to be achieved when there are taken into account adjoining or adjacent properties.

6.16.2   We therefore **recommend** that the palaces should always be strategically managed together with the adjoining or adjacent properties which are owned by the Commissioners, and, accordingly, that there should be the closest cooperation in so doing between the trustees or directors (in respect of the palaces) and the Commissioners (in respect both of the palaces and of the adjacent properties).

Image

6.17.1   In our First Report, we raised questions about the image of see and suffragans' houses.[18] The issues are far wider than matters of resourcing, but our primary concern was that bishops should not be provided with living and working accommodation of a nature or style which made the exercise of their ministry more difficult than would otherwise be the case.

6.17.2   For the same reason, we have reflected on the image presented by the archiepiscopal palaces. It is our perception that the properties are generally seen to be functional, and no representations have been made to us that the Archbishops are criticized for residing in them. More positively, the income-generating opportunities do in part depend on putting this image to appropriate commercial advantage.

6.17.3   Our conclusions on this aspect are that in present circumstances the image of the palaces is not a disadvantage to the Archbishops in the exercise of their ministries; and it is a positive advantage in relation to income generation.

chapter 7

Transparency and disclosure

Introduction

7.1.1   In our First Report we noted that there is at present full disclosure in respect of stipends[1] and we recommended that there should also be full disclosure of bishops' operational costs[2] and premises expenses.

7.1.2   The Commissioners have subsequently disclosed, in respect of the year 2000, operational costs funded by the Commissioners[3] and we understand that the Commissioners intend to repeat the process annually.

7.1.3   Although in several respects disclosure in this form differs from what we recommended,[4] we welcome the significant step which has been taken in what we hope will be a continuing and more comprehensive programme of disclosure.

Disclosure in relation to the Archbishops

7.2   We consider that disclosure is as important in the case of the Archbishops as it is in the case of other bishops. Disclosure brings with it its own form of discipline;[5] it avoids (often ill-informed) speculation; and it enables those who are concerned with the government of the Church of England[6] to make decisions on the basis of established fact.

Categories of disclosure

7.3.1   The present form of disclosure in relation to the Archbishops does not distinguish between the operational costs attributable to their separate offices[7] as diocesan bishop, metropolitan, primate and archbishop and, in the case of the Archbishop of Canterbury, as President[8] of the Anglican Communion.

7.3.2   We have carefully considered whether the Archbishops' staff – not the Archbishops themselves – should supply the Commissioners with information which would enable there to be financial disclosure in relation to each of their offices. We have concluded that, as will be seen, there should be disclosure in some categories, but the effort involved in attributing costs to every one of these categories would not be justified by the result.

7.3.3   We have recommended[9] that the calculation of the block-grants to be made to the Archbishops in their capacities as diocesan bishops should generally be calculated in the same way as those which we have recommended[10] should be made to other diocesan bishops. By this means there can be a proper comparison between the costs of the Archbishops acting as diocesan bishops and those of other diocesan bishops.

7.3.4   We also **recommend** that, in the case of the Archbishop of Canterbury, it would be helpful to identify the costs attributable to him as President of the Anglican Communion. As will be seen,[11] this is part of a wider proposal which we make that there should be full identification of the costs incurred by the Commissioners in supporting the Anglican Communion.

7.3.5   There is a further factor in the case of the Archbishop of Canterbury. At present the costs of the Lambeth Palace Library are accounted for as costs incurred by the Archbishop. For the reasons given in Chapter 17, we regard that as inappropriate and we **recommend** that for accounting purposes the Lambeth Palace Library should be considered as a separate cost centre.[12]

7.4.1   Accordingly, we **recommend** that the operational costs incurred by the Archbishop of Canterbury should be accounted for separately in relation to:

    a.   his role as diocesan bishop;

    b.   his role in relation to the Anglican Communion; and

    c.   his other roles, namely those as metropolitan, primate and archbishop of the Church of England, excluding the Lambeth Palace Library.

7.4.2   Our recommendation applies only to operational costs. We do not regard it as worthwhile, at least at the outset, for there to be an apportionment of premises expenses, which, in any event, we envisage will be totally or mainly met from income generated within the palace.[13]

7.4.3 We further **recommend** with regard to the Archbishop of Canterbury's role in relation to the Anglican Communion that, in order to avoid detailed apportionments, only marginal costs should be disclosed. These would primarily be the stipend or salary costs of the members of the Archbishop's staff who work specifically on Anglican Communion affairs, and the costs of travel by the Archbishop and his staff on the business of the Communion.[14] We regard disclosure of the total cost incurred by the Commissioners in supporting the ministry of the Archbishop in relation to the Anglican Communion as important, but we consider that the time and effort involved in making detailed apportionments of other items would not be justified. We recognize that, by taking only marginal costs, there would not be identification of the full economic cost.

7.5 Correspondingly, we **recommend** that the costs incurred by the Archbishop of York should be accounted for separately in relation to:

a. his role as diocesan bishop; and

b. his roles as metropolitan, primate and archbishop of the Church of England.

7.6 We would like to think that such categorization might be helpful to the Archbishops themselves when they are considering the allocation of time between their various roles.[15]

Method of disclosure

7.7 We **recommend** that disclosure in these categories should be made within succeeding editions of the Commissioners' booklets which disclose figures for other bishops.[16]

chapter 8

Taking up and leaving office

Introduction
8.1   In our First Report we described[1] the process by which a diocesan and a suffragan bishop are appointed, and the resourcing implications of taking up office. In general, we **recommend** that the same considerations which apply to diocesan bishops[2] should apply to Archbishops, although in this chapter we propose certain changes of substance and refer to certain changes of emphasis.

Appointment of an Archbishop
8.2   There are some, comparatively minor, differences in the process of appointing a new Archbishop from that of appointing a diocesan bishop.[3] However, these differences are not material for resourcing purposes, and we do not, therefore, comment on them.

Features of the process
8.3   For present purposes, the following are the salient features of the appointment process:

8.3.1   There will usually be three phases:

a.   from when an Archbishop announces his retirement[4] until (usually while the serving archbishop is still in office) there is an announcement of the appointment of his successor;

b.   from the announcement of the appointment of the successor to the actual retirement of the serving archbishop; and

c.   the interregnum, namely from the retirement of the serving archbishop until his successor takes up his office.[5]

These three phases will together occupy at the very least six months and it may be a good deal longer:

8.3.2   The whole process will be marked by a tension between on the one hand the wish to see it completed quickly and on the other hand the wish for it to be done properly.

8.3.3 During the first phase there is likely to be intense speculation[6] as to the identity of the serving archbishop's successor.

8.3.4 This speculation, and the secrecy which accompanies the process, is likely to put particular pressure on his prospective successor in the period between when he is asked whether, if invited, he would accept the appointment[7] and when the appointment is announced.[8]

8.3.5 It is highly likely that his successor will be a diocesan bishop or an archbishop of another province, and therefore carrying a heavy workload in his existing post. He will, therefore, have to deal with that as well as preparing himself for his new role.

8.3.6 As soon as the announcement is made, the successor is likely to be deluged with letters and requests for comment.[9]

8.3.7 It may be presumed that the successor will have no experience in a role which is so wide-ranging or of such a high profile, or, particularly in the case of the Archbishop of Canterbury, in working with a staff which is anywhere near the size and specialization of that at Lambeth Palace.

8.3.8 The successor will be only too well aware of the enormity of the tasks which he will be called upon to perform and of the expectations of him.

8.4.1 A diocesan bishop-designate may not have seen the see house in which he will live.[10] An Archbishop-designate[11] is likely to have visited the palace in which he will reside, and therefore to know *something* of it, and of its atmosphere – but probably only a small part.

8.4.2 We **recommend** that at the earliest possible stage in the process, an Archbishop-designate and, if he is married, his wife should be given the fullest exposure to the palace or palaces[12] in which they will live. They are large buildings and take some time to get to know.

8.5 The appointment process can be at least as daunting for the wife of an Archbishop-designate. Even if she has lived in a fairly large see house,[13] she will step into a world which in many ways may be totally different from that to which she has been accustomed. We refer to this in a later chapter.[14]

Timing

8.6.1   As in the case of the appointment of diocesan bishops,[15] we recommend strongly that the period between when a candidate is approached to see whether, if invited, he would accept appointment and when the announcement is made should be kept to the shortest, although we recognize that the timing is by no means solely within the control of the Church.

8.6.2   By contrast, the period between when the announcement is made and when the successor takes up official residence needs to be long enough comfortably to enable, among other things, there to be the induction[16] and hand-over[17] programmes which we recommend later.

8.7.1   Suffragan bishops are busy, but if and when a suffragan becomes a diocesan the nature, scope and intensity of his work is often in a different league. When a diocesan bishop becomes an archbishop, his commitments move into yet another league. In no small part this is due to the increased pressures on him which result from greatly heightened national public scrutiny and (often) criticism. It may be pre-supposed that any Archbishop-designate will be robust, but to prepare for this we strongly **recommend** that the programme should permit the Archbishop-designate and his wife to have a good holiday,[18] even if the result is that there is insufficient time for other highly desirable things.

8.7.2   We further strongly **recommend** that the programme should permit the Archbishop-designate to have time for reflection and personal preparation.

Expectations

8.8.1   We recommended in our First Report[19] that when a candidate is approached to see whether, if invited, he would be willing to accept appointment as a diocesan bishop, he should be given as clear as possible an understanding of what would be expected of him and of the means by which he could measure himself against those expectations.

8.8.2   In relation to his office as diocesan bishop, the same applies to an Archbishop-designate of York. The position is more complicated in the case of an Archbishop-designate of Canterbury, who will need to involve very fully the Bishop of Dover in seeking this understanding. For both Archbishops, it may not be realistic for them to be given a clear understanding of the expectations of them in their other[20] roles.

8.9.1 There are two matters affecting the roles of the Archbishops which need to be addressed early in an archiepiscopate. First, in relation to the Archbishop of Canterbury, we **recommend** that the Archbishop should clearly agree with the Bishop of Dover their respective roles in relation to the Diocese of Canterbury.[21]

8.9.2 Secondly, there will be varying expectations with regard to primatial roles, and the division of primatial responsibilities.[22] We **recommend** that the division of these responsibilities should be reviewed and, if necessary, clarified early in the archiepiscopate of either an Archbishop of Canterbury or an Archbishop of York, as well as being kept under periodic review thereafter.

Support team

8.10.1 The Hurd Report recommended[23] that there should be a carefully constructed and authoritative planning team (probably run by the new style Lambeth Chief of Staff[24] when in post) set up immediately when a serving Archbishop of Canterbury decides to retire in order to prepare for announcing that decision and to assist at all of the following stages. These will include in particular the induction of his successor with the object of preparing him for the work which he will undertake and to enable him to make informed choices about how he will address his ministry.

8.10.2 We fully support the general thrust of that recommendation and consider that it should also apply in relation to an Archbishop of York.

8.11.1 We envisage that the support team will be in operation from some time before the time when the announcement is made to the conclusion of the enthronement service.

8.11.2 We **recommend** that the support team should be concerned with:

> a. ensuring that adequate resources are provided for the Archbishop-designate in his existing post when the announcement is made;

> b. arranging for an induction programme[25] and a comprehensive handover programme,[26] including the handover of personal accommodation;

c.   ensuring that proper arrangements are made for the enthronement service and intermediate steps;[27] and

d.   so far as possible, assist in making any advance re-disposition of staff which the Archbishop-designate requests.

8.11.3   We **recommend** that the core members of the support team should be the Chief of Staff, the Secretary General of the General Synod, the Secretary of the Church Commissioners, the Archbishops' and the Prime Minister's Appointments Secretaries and in the case of the Archbishop of Canterbury the Archbishop's Secretary for Public Affairs. Other senior members of the Archbishop-designate's staff and others will also need to be involved. Part of the induction programme would probably be conducted by outside specialists.

8.11.4   The members of the support team will be heavily involved in the other aspects of their work. In order to give them time to prepare – preparation of an individually tailored induction programme will itself be time-consuming – we **recommend** that an Archbishop in office should give to the team on a basis of the strictest confidence an advance indication of his intention to announce his retirement.

Induction programme

8.12.1   As we have just stated, we **recommend** that one of the functions of the support team should be to arrange an induction programme for the Archbishop-designate.[28]

8.12.2   In part, the context of that programme must be informed by the Archbishop-designate's own wishes. However, we **recommend** that it should include:

a.   specific instruction or advice on:

   i.   the nature and scope of the new Archbishop's responsibility;

   ii.   the setting in which the new Archbishop will work; and

   iii.   the responsibilities of the members of staff, particularly the more senior ones, so that when the new Archbishop takes up office he will have a clear understanding of what he can expect from the members of staff and they will have a clear understanding of what they can expect from him; and

b. specific training in:

i. working with a staff of the size and calibre of that which he will find on arrival at Lambeth Palace or to some extent at Bishopthorpe;

ii. programme and commitment management; and

iii. the higher sensitivity which will be required in relations with the media.

8.12.3 We also **recommend** that, if the Archbishop-designate is married and if his wife so wishes, there should be an integral part of that programme for his wife.

Handover procedure
8.13 The process of assuming office can be daunting to the Archbishop-designate and, if he is married, his wife. To ease this, we **recommend** that the support team should arrange a structured handover procedure, in which the retiring Archbishop and, where appropriate, his wife would fully participate.[29]

Monitoring the induction and handover programmes
8.14.1 If the pattern of recent times is followed, it may be expected that in ordinary circumstances an Archbishop will remain in post for, very broadly, ten years.[30] It is, therefore, to be anticipated that at least some members of the support team for one Archbishop will not be members of the team for his successor. Yet experience gained in one set of induction and handover programmes should inform subsequent programmes.

8.14.2 To encourage this process, we **recommend** that when an Archbishop has taken up office, the leader of the support team should arrange for a detailed memorandum to be prepared as a reference point in planning further programmes.

Symbolic transfer
8.15 In our First Report, we referred[31] to the significance of a retiring diocesan bishop participating in the service of enthronement of his successor and in so doing symbolically to transfer the care of the diocese to the successor. Although it is strictly outside our terms of reference, we nevertheless **recommend** similar involvement on the part of a retiring Archbishop in the enthronement service of his successor.

Removal expenses on retirement

8.16.1 Finally, in this chapter we deal with two points relating to the retirement of an Archbishop. First, we recommended[32] that on retirement a bishop's removal expenses should be reimbursed to him.

8.16.2 We recommend that the same provision should apply on the retirement of an Archbishop.

Resources in retirement

8.17.1 Secondly, unless, perhaps, an Archbishop retires on the ground of ill-health, it can be expected that in retirement he will continue to be in demand. He will receive many invitations to write, to preach, to lecture, usually[33] to sit in the House of Lords, and to serve the Church in other ways. Yet, there is at present no official arrangement for him to be provided in retirement with any resources, not even part-time secretarial assistance.

8.17.2 We recommend that:

a. for so long as the retired Archbishop is active in the service of the Church, there should be a power for him to be appropriately resourced;[34]

b. the Resources Group or its equivalent[35] of his last archiepiscopal see should be charged with making that provision;

c. this need should be taken into account in the calculation of the formula;[36] and

d. there should be a change in the legislation to permit this support to be provided.

chapter 9

Specific resources

Introduction

9.1   In this chapter we consider general considerations with regard to the Archbishops' personal staffs and specific resources which should be provided for the Archbishops. We deal in later chapters with particular staff issues and with living and working accommodation.

Employment arrangements

9.2.1   As a background to the specific staffing issues which we discuss later, we note at this stage the employment arrangements which apply to members of the Archbishops' staffs.

9.2.2   Each Archbishop, in his corporate capacity,[1] is one of the National Church Institutions. Some of the others are the Church Commissioners, the Archbishops' Council and the Trustees of the Lambeth Palace Library Trust.[2]

9.2.3   All employed members of staff working within any of these Institutions are:

   a.   jointly *employed* by all of them; but

   b.   at any point of time *managed* by one of them.

9.2.4   There has been a general move towards the Institutions adopting common terms and conditions of employment. However, so that existing rights of individual members of staff were not prejudiced, some differences between those whose circumstances are otherwise comparable continue to exist.[3]

9.4.1   The present employment regime, which came into force at the beginning of 1998, is intended to ensure that the central institutions of the Church of England act as good employers; encourage all members of staff to be treated with fairness and consistency; enshrine principles of equal opportunity; and encourage the relevant institution – for the purposes of this report, the Archbishops – and the member of staff to understand what each can realistically and properly expect from the other.

9.4.2   The regime is also intended to facilitate the movement of staff between one Institution and another.

9.5.1   As part of the arrangements, the Archbishops' Council established the Human Resources Department.

9.5.2   The HR Department:

a.   operates certain aspects of the regime, particularly in relation to the appointment of new members of staff and the transfer of members from one Institution to another; and

b.   provides advice to managers, including Archbishops, on: employment law and practice; management issues which arise during the course of an employment; and the termination of employment.

9.6.1   The HR Department provides its services to the Institutions under Service Level Agreements.

9.6.2   The time spent by the HR Department on its dealings with each of the Institutions is logged; and the cost of the Department is attributed to each of the Institutions according to the respective amounts of time spent.

9.7.1   The HR Department operates the system for making new appointments. Both Archbishops agreed to adhere to it.

9.7.2   The HR Department also provides advice. It is for the Archbishops to decide whether to seek that advice and, if they do, whether to follow it.

9.8.1   Three general points can be made at this stage. First, it is clear to us that there is still some way to go before all the Institutions and the members of staff managed by them are persuaded of the merits of the regime. This results in some resistance.

9.8.2   Secondly, there have been some staffing difficulties within the HR Department itself, and these have resulted in the service provided by that Department in some instances falling short of what it would have wished.

9.8.3 Thirdly, employment law is becoming increasingly complicated and concepts of employment practice are developing. All the Institutions including, but in no way confined to, the Archbishops, need to observe the law and to follow best practice in their relationship with members of staff. It would be bad for the Church as a whole if there were justifiable complaints made to the courts or employment tribunals about the treatment of staff.

9.9 We refer to the application of this regime and other specific staffing issues separately in relation to each of the Archbishops.[4]

Communications: press officers

9.10.1 Archbishops need[5] to be forewarned of issues, both from within the Church and also from outside it, which might affect them or upon which they are likely to be asked to express a view, so that they or someone on their behalf can, if necessary, give an almost immediate, but measured, comment. Archbishops also need to be able to be pro-active in conveying their message when they wish to do so.

9.10.2 The need to be able to give an immediate but informed response predicates a working pattern where the response time is much swifter than that required in most other parts of the Church.

9.11.1 We therefore **recommend** that, in general,[6] there should be at least one press officer on the staff of each Archbishop. The press officer or officers should work in close proximity with the Archbishop and should to the fullest practicable extent know his mind.

9.11.2 We also **recommend** that:

a. the Archbishops should be able always to have immediate access to their press officer, even if they are on a visit or otherwise away from their working base; and

b. initially the press officers of the Archbishop of Canterbury and, prospectively, the press officer of the Archbishop of York, should have equipment which would enable them, from Lambeth Palace or Bishopthorpe, to be able to prepare and send to broadcasters audio, visual and other material of broadcastable quality.[7] We recognize that mutual confidence would need to have built up before national broadcasters would accept such material for direct transmission.

9.12.1   In relation to communications generally, it is important that the Church of England should convey a coherent and consistent message. Policy for the Church of England is determined by General Synod, although in exercising their leadership of the Church, the Archbishops may need to make statements on matters where that policy has not been fully formulated. In other instances, although the policy may have been formulated, its detailed implementation may remain open.

9.12.2   So that there can be consistency of approach, we regard it as important that the Archbishops' press officers liaise closely with each other and with the corresponding members of staff at Church House. On occasions of great urgency, it can require considerable effort and sensitivity for the Archbishop and his staff to make an almost immediate response, but we **recommend** constant vigilance to ensure that this liaison is maintained.

9.12.3   In a later chapter,[8] we comment further on liaison between the Archbishop of Canterbury's press officer and the Anglican Communion Office.

Hospitality: catering
9.13.1   The Archbishops provide hospitality for the official visitors who come to their respective palaces. Particularly in the case of the Archbishop of Canterbury, these numbers can be large.

9.13.2   In general, it can be said that the present physical facilities for limited catering are adequate, but, as will be seen,[9] the catering staff is not large enough to permit full use of the other facilities of the palaces. We make detailed recommendations later.[10]

Overnight accommodation for official guests
9.14.1   Archbishops need to be able to provide overnight accommodation for official guests. In at least two cases,[11] there is a noticeable under-use of the accommodation which is provided.

9.14.2 We are not satisfied that there is at present a proper balance between the use of the accommodation for overnight official guests and the opportunity cost[12] of maintaining it. We **recommend** that there should be adopted as a principle that if there is a year-long average occupancy rate of less than, say, 20%, there should be a presumption, which could be rebutted, that the rooms set aside for that purpose should be put to some other use. As the presumption would be rebuttable, it would be open to Archbishops or members of their staff to demonstrate that, notwithstanding low usage, the rooms should continue to be held available for overnight official guests.

Housekeeping

9.15.1 There is a requirement for a housekeeper in each of the archiepiscopal palaces, although the post should by no means necessarily be full-time. The provision of official hospitality is an inherent part of an Archbishop's ministry.[13]

9.15.2 We see the housekeeping role as including:

a. ensuring that either the whole building or at least the parts of it which are used for official visitors, whether or not accommodated overnight, are kept clean and tidy, and, accordingly, supervising cleaners;

b. ensuring that beds for visitors are made up; necessities are provided for them; sheets are changed and laundered after each visit; and generally meeting their reasonable needs;

c. organizing catering; and liaising with cooks and outside catering contractors; and

d. liaising with gardeners, particularly so that flowers and plants grown in the garden are made available when required for the official reception rooms in the palace.

9.15.3 We do not see the housekeeper as having any other than entirely incidental responsibility for the private residential accommodation of the Archbishop and members of his immediate family living with him.

9.16.1 We assert in the next chapter[14] that it should not be assumed that the Archbishop will be married, or, if he is, that he has a wife who is able and willing to perform the housekeeping role.

9.16.2 Accordingly, we **recommend** that it should be clearly accepted that housekeeping support should be provided for both Archbishops.

9.16.3 We envisage that the provision of funds by way of block-grant to the Archbishops which we propose[15] will be sufficiently flexible to enable this to be done.

Travel
9.17 We consider next travel, by road and by air. The recommendations in our First Report[16] about travel by train apply to the Archbishops as they do to other bishops.

Travel by road
9.18.1 Each of the Archbishops is provided with a car and a driver. The drivers are full time members of staff, but when not acting as drivers they are employed on other duties within the palaces. The Archbishops may on some occasions drive themselves.

9.18.2 As in the case of travel by car by other bishops,[17] we **recommend** that the Chief of Staff[18] or the Resources Group[19] or its equivalent[20] should explore the most appropriate and cost-effective provision of travel by car.

Travel by air
9.19.1 We have considered separately flights between continents, which we describe as 'long-haul', and flights within Europe (and within the United Kingdom), which we describe as 'short-haul'.

9.19.2 The present Archbishop of Canterbury travels by air, particularly in making long-haul journeys, more extensively and more frequently than the Archbishop of York. This is due primarily to the visits which the Archbishop of Canterbury makes as President[21] of the Anglican Communion.

9.19.3 In the case of some of the journeys made by the Archbishops in response to specific invitations, the cost of travel is met by the host.[22] These journeys are not preceded by preparatory visits by staff, and although they involve the Archbishop's time, they do not involve additional cost[23] to the Commissioners. We do not consider these journeys further, although we observe that in these circumstances, by paying the travelling expenses, the host is providing a subvention towards the cost of the Archbishop's ministry.

9.19.4   Other major visits, primarily by the Archbishop of Canterbury, usually do require preparatory visits by one or more members of his staff. The visits may be made by the Archbishop primarily in his capacity as a leader of the Church of England or in the case of the Archbishop of Canterbury in his capacity as President of the Anglican Communion, but may well involve both capacities.[24] The Hurd Report recommended [25] that save in exceptional circumstances, the aim should be for there to be no more than two formal tours a year for the purposes of the Anglican Communion.

9.19.5   Throughout his archiepiscopate, Dr Carey has not built rest or recovery days into his visiting programmes. He is, therefore, available to his hosts on arrival, and is almost invariably expected immediately to assume a high profile and highly demanding role.

9.19.6   When making major visits, the Archbishop will need to be supported in them by one or more members of his staff.[26]

9.20   Official air travel by the Archbishop of York is at present much less. It is usually within Europe, sometimes in his capacity as representative head of the Church of England in its dealings with other Churches within the Porvoo Communion.[27]

9.21   From time to time other bishops travel to different countries on behalf of one or other of the Archbishops.

9.22.1   Overseas travelling and any subsistence costs incurred by the Archbishop of Canterbury, by his wife and by members of staff and by other bishops travelling in the exercise of his ministry, are charged by the Commissioners to an overseas travel account in their books.[28] In the year ended on 31 December 2001 the total charged was £99,000 (2000: £174,000).

9.22.2   The cost of official overseas travel undertaken by the Archbishop of York is chargeable to the overseas travel account. However, it has been the practice of Dr Hope to treat these travelling expenses as part of his operational [29] costs.

Class of travel

9.23   Customarily, Archbishops of Canterbury, when making long-haul journeys, have travelled first class. However, in accordance with one of our general principles,[30] we **recommend** that the class of travel should depend on the need, not the standing, of the traveller.

9.24   We have considered the practice with regard to the class of travel which is followed by some Government departments, commercial bodies, non-governmental organizations and other organizations in the voluntary sector. Some of the recommendations which we make in the following paragraphs are more stringent than those adopted by certain other bodies,[31] but they are made in the context of the present economic circumstances of the Church.

9.25.1   Two particular considerations apply to long-haul travel. First, an Archbishop or, indeed, any other person in a highly visible and responsible position, needs to be alert on arrival. Were there to be an ill-chosen remark by the Archbishop or a member of his staff, the repercussions would be out of proportion to any saving of fare differential. The type of travel should be determined so far as practicable to avoid that risk.

9.25.2   Secondly, in some secular organizations members of staff are entitled to the same class of travel, irrespective of their grade within the organization. We have not followed that approach, for reasons both of cost and need, in the recommendations which we make separately in relation to the Archbishop on the one hand and members of his staff on the other.

9.26   The practices followed by most other organizations which we have considered allow for some discretion. That approach seems to us to be right. Accordingly, although in the following paragraphs we make proposals, we **recommend** that they should be treated as guidelines, and that they should be subject to discretion on the part of the Chief of Staff (at Lambeth Palace) or his equivalent (at Bishopthorpe).

9.27   In the case of the long-haul journeys, we **recommend** that the emphasis should not be on the class of travel, but on the ability within a class (whatever its category) to be able to work with reasonable privacy and, on overnight flights, to be able to sleep in reasonable comfort.

The general rule

9.28   We **recommend** that all official air travel, by whomsoever it is undertaken, should be at the cheapest rate available to meet the traveller's needs.[32] One of these needs will usually be certainty of timetable planning, and in some cases it may be flexibility.[33]

An Archbishop: long-haul

9.29   Because of the need for an Archbishop to be fully alert and presentable on arrival and to be able (not too literally) to hit the ground running, we **recommend** that:

a.   in general, the Archbishop should travel first class; but

b.   if (i) his flight is solely within a day and (ii) the configuration of the seats provides reasonable comfort and privacy of working space, then he should travel business class.

An Archbishop: short-haul

9.30   We **recommend** that, likewise because of the need to be alert on arrival and to be able to spend the journey time usefully, an Archbishop when on official business should also make short-haul overseas journeys in business class.

An Archbishop's wife

9.31   We **recommend** that an Archbishop's wife should travel in the same class as the Archbishop when she is accompanying him and will be undertaking official engagements during the visit.

An Archbishop's staff

9.32.1   In general, we **recommend** that members of an Archbishop's staff should travel economy class, whether they are making reconnaissance visits or accompanying the Archbishop.

9.32.2   However, we **recommend** that they should travel business class if:

a.   they are accompanying the Archbishop and *he* requires recurrent access to them during the journey; or

b.   they are making a long-haul journey and are required to undertake work of significant responsibility immediately on arrival.

Other bishops

9.33 We recommend that the principles which we have just stated in relation to members of an Archbishop's staff should apply to bishops, or, indeed, others, who are travelling on an Archbishop's behalf.

Post-visit reviews

9.34.1 There is a final point about visits made by Archbishops. Every visit will involve not only the Archbishop's time but also cost. If the host pays the travelling expenses, there will nevertheless be incurred staff time in making arrangements for it, and where applicable, in accompanying the Archbishop. If the Commissioners pay, the financial cost to the Church is clearly greater. In our view, there should be a review after each visit so that, by making a value appraisal, a code of best practice can be evolved.

9.34.2 Accordingly, we recommend that after each overseas official visit it should be the responsibility of the Chief of Staff (at Lambeth Palace) or his equivalent (at Bishopthorpe) to initiate a structural review of the visit. Such a review should include (but need not be restricted to):

    a.   the working of the practical arrangements;[34]

    b.   in that context, whether rest days should have been included in the programme;

    c.   whether the objectives of the visit were achieved; and

    d.   an overall consideration of the value of the visit.

9.35 Finally, we observe that even if the host pays the travelling expenses of a visit, that visit will involve a cost to the Archbishop in his time. Accordingly, while offers by a host to pay travelling expenses are to be warmly welcomed, the fact that the host is paying the expenses should not be the determining factor in deciding whether the Archbishop should make the visit.

chapter 10

Archbishops' wives

Introduction

10.1   In this chapter we consider:

a.   the support which is given *by* the wife of an Archbishop to her husband in the exercise of his ministry; and

b.   the support, in the form of resources, which should be given *to* the wife of an Archbishop when she is acting in furtherance of his ministry.

Support of Archbishops

10.2   In our First Report, we recorded[1] as clearly as we could the incalculable debt of gratitude which the Church of England owes to wives of bishops for the support which they give to their husbands in a great variety of ways – some of which may not be obvious. That applies to the wives of archbishops as it does to the wives of other bishops, and we welcome the opportunity of re-stating it here.

Careers

10.3   In our First Report, we predicted[2] that it would become the norm for many bishops' wives to have their own careers. By extension, we **recommend** that the Church of England should now plan on the basis that the wives of Archbishops might well have their own careers.

The basic principles

10.4.1   Our work has involved considering the resourcing needs of the Archbishops generally and not by reference to any particular Archbishop or any particular wife of an Archbishop. However, as our work has proceeded we have very helpfully had two contrasting examples. At one extreme has been Dr Hope, who is unmarried. At the other extreme (for this purpose) has been Dr Carey, who has notably exercised a joint ministry with his wife. It is difficult to conceive of a wife who has been more publicly and privately integrated with the work of her husband as Archbishop than Mrs Carey; this has been greatly appreciated in England and throughout the wider Anglican Communion.

10.4.2 These examples clearly demonstrate two of our basic principles, namely that:

> a. the resources provided for an Archbishop should be sufficient to enable him to do the job, without it being *assumed* that he will have a wife who is willing and able to support him[3] in his ministry; and

> b. where a wife is able and willing to support her husband in the exercise of his ministry, that should be warmly welcomed, appreciated and properly resourced.[4]

10.4.3 Our third basic principle is that no wife of an Archbishop should be prevented from pursuing her career or from following other activities by the demands made on her by her husband's ministry or the place or places in which they are required to live.[5]

Induction and handover programmes

10.5.1 If the wife of an Archbishop considers that, in order to give her husband the support which she wishes, she needs to understand (subject to proper observance of confidentiality) the numerous aspects of his work and the context in which he will perform it, she should be assisted to do so.

10.5.2 Accordingly, we recommended[6] that when an induction programme is being planned for an Archbishop-designate, then if his wife so wishes, it should also be planned for her. The programme for the Archbishop-designate's wife should be an integral part of the whole, and not a mere appendix to it. It follows that we **recommend** that where the wife wishes to participate in the programme, her own view as to its content should be taken fully into account when it is being planned.

10.6 We also recommended[7] that wherever possible there should be a structured handover from a retiring Archbishop to his successor. We **recommend** here that where both a retiring Archbishop and his successor are married, and both wives are willing to participate, then so far as is appropriate there should likewise be a structured handover programme for them.

Accommodation

10.7.1 We make four points about accommodation. The first is that the archiepiscopal palaces are large buildings, and have large grounds.[8]

Moving into them can be daunting – quite apart from the time which it takes to learn one's way around.

10.7.2   Furthermore, although we consider that a newly appointed Archbishop should inherit an efficient, well-running machine,[9] paradoxically that can make the experience of the wife of a newly appointed Archbishop in the first months, or even years, even more daunting. The more efficient the machine running a large building, the easier it is for a wife to feel overwhelmed by it.

10.7.3   This is one of the reasons why we have recommended[10] that an induction programme should be available if requested. We also **recommend** that the Chief of Staff, although not accountable to the Archbishop's wife, should nevertheless be sensitive to these circumstances.

10.8   The second point is related to the first. A newly appointed Archbishop and his wife may these days have had no previous experience of living in a large house, or of living in a house which is a heritage property,[11] or of living in a house with a large garden. Every case will depend on its own facts, but we **recommend** both that the induction programme should take account of these factors, and that the Resources Group or its equivalent[12] should be available to provide advice, if sought, on the particular aspects of living in the new environment.

10.9   Thirdly, we have recommended earlier,[13] but we repeat here, that the private residential accommodation to be provided for an Archbishop and his wife should be physically separate and self-contained, and that it should have its own access. At present, that is not satisfied in any of the archiepiscopal palaces. It should be. We refer to this in greater detail in the chapters which deal separately with the three archiepiscopal palaces.[14] We **recommend** that the provision of satisfactory private residential accommodation for the Archbishops should be a matter for urgent review.

10.10.1   Fourthly, although the private residential accommodation, which in a narrow sense is the 'home' of the Archbishop and his wife, occupies only a small part of the palace, more loosely they may think of, and refer to, other parts of the palace, or the palace as a whole, as being their 'home'. This may be particularly so in the case of state rooms[15] and associated reception areas.

10.10.2 An Archbishop and his wife may both feel that they want to enhance parts of the property, not so much for their own benefit, but for that of their successors and of the Church more widely.[16] Thus, for example, the present Archbishop of Canterbury and his wife, and their predecessors have done a great deal for the lasting improvement of Lambeth Palace. Yet there is always a balance to be struck between issues of personal taste on the one hand and broader suitability, including heritage considerations, on the other. The issue is not unique: the same point can arise with other clergy houses, albeit that the scale of the palaces is usually larger.

10.10.3 The matter should be considered as an integral part of the management of the palace as a whole. We **recommend** that all questions of policy relating to the nature and style of refurbishment and improvements should be formulated by the Archbishop and his wife, the Chief of Staff, and the Commissioners, together with, where appropriate, external expert guidance.[17] We further **recommend** that in general the implementation of that policy should be in accordance with arrangements to be made by the Chief of Staff.

Management of staff

10.11 We **recommend** that, with one possible exception, the wife of an Archbishop should never be the line manager of any member of staff who works in the palace. The possible exception is where the Archbishop's wife is provided with her own (part-time) secretary.[18] With that possible exception, the Chief of Staff should be responsible for all staff in the palace.[19]

Domestic and outdoor staff

10.12 In the ordinary course, the Archbishop's wife is likely to have almost daily contact with domestic staff, and to have influence on decisions taken about the house and garden. However, in our view, the principle should be that the Chief of Staff should be the manager of those members of staff, as well as of all others who are employed in the palace. This requires mutual sensitivity on the part of the Archbishop's wife, the Chief of Staff, and the members of staff.

Housekeeping

10.13 In practice, it is likely that the wife of an Archbishop will be involved in some of the housekeeping functions, particularly in looking after official guests.[20] Where she does so, that should be welcomed and appreciated.[21] However, we re-state here our previous recommendations that in considering the resources to be made available *to the Archbishop* housekeeping services should be provided,[22] and that in making such provision it should not be assumed that the Archbishop's wife will be available and willing to attend to these matters.[23]

Resources for an Archbishop's wife

10.14.1 Following the recommendations which we made in our First Report[24] about the provision of resources for the wives of other bishops, we **recommend** that:

> a.   subject to the one exception which we note in the following section, resources should not be provided for an Archbishop's wife merely because she is an Archbishop's wife; but

> b.   when an Archbishop's wife is acting directly in support of her husband in the exercise of his ministry, then she should be provided with the resources which are necessary for that purpose; and

> c.   it should be for the Resources Group[25] or its equivalent to arrange the provision of these resources.[26]

10.14.2 The resources which are most likely to be appropriate are secretarial (almost invariably part-time), IT and travelling.

10.15.1 We regard these principles as generally applying to the involvement of an Archbishop's wife in relation to the Lambeth Conference.[27] The nature and extent of an Archbishop's wife, for example, in planning and perhaps leading a spouses' programme is a matter to be agreed between those planning the conference and the Archbishop's wife. Where in accordance with that agreement the Archbishop's wife participates, she would be doing so in furtherance of the Archbishop's ministry. She should, therefore, be properly resourced for so doing.

10.15.2 We consider, however, that the cost of providing the resources in these circumstances should be treated as part of the costs of the particular Conference (and not as part of the Archbishop's operational costs).

10.16.1 There is a final point. An Archbishop's wife will be invited to accompany her husband to State and similar occasions and there will be an expectation that she will do so.

10.16.2 We regard the Archbishop's wife in these circumstances as officially participating in such events and in doing so as supporting her husband and furthering the exercise of his ministry. In our view, it would be wrong in principle to expect the Archbishop's wife to be financially disadvantaged for doing so,[28] and it would also be wrong in principle to assume that the Archbishop will meet such cost.

10.16.3 Accordingly, we **recommend** that, if it is required and if it is requested, an initial allowance should be made to an Archbishop's wife upon her husband taking up office, which she could apply for outfitting. The maximum amount of such an allowance might be the same as the grant made by the Commissioners to a newly appointed bishop for robes.[29] We cannot predict to what extent that allowance would in fact be taken up.

10.16.4 In order to implement this recommendation it would be necessary for the Commissioners to take additional legal powers.

Part III:
The Archbishop of
Canterbury

chapter 11

The needs and resources of the Archbishop of Canterbury

The roles of the Archbishop of Canterbury

11.1.1 We have stated[1] previously that we regard[2] the offices held by the Archbishop of Canterbury as being those of:

>   a. diocesan bishop of the Diocese of Canterbury;
>
>   b. archbishop, a spiritual leader of the Church and nation and a member of the House of Lords;
>
>   c. metropolitan, having canonical jurisdiction over the thirty dioceses which comprise the Southern Province;
>
>   d. primate, having the prime leadership role of the Church of England; and
>
>   e. President[3] of the Anglican Communion.

11.1.2 We describe in later chapters:

>   a. the substantial commitment of the Archbishop to and within the Anglican Communion;[4] and
>
>   b. his role as the diocesan bishop of the Diocese of Canterbury.[5]

11.1.3 In this chapter we deal with the other three roles.

11.2.1 Although the Archbishop's metropolitical role is primarily in relation to the Southern Province of the Church of England, the Archbishop also has metropolitical jurisdiction in relation to some churches overseas, by virtue of provisions in their own constitutions.[6]

11.2.2 Further details of some aspects of the Archbishop's metropolitical role are given in Appendix E.

11.3 A material part of the Archbishop's time is occupied by his dealings with other Christian churches and bodies of other faiths. The latter aspect has been particularly important during the currency of our work.[7] We regard the Archbishop as performing these ecumenical and inter-faith roles in either or both of his capacities as Archbishop and President of the Anglican Communion.

Workload

11.4 Each Archbishop structures his work in his own way. Dr Carey has followed a pattern of working for forty days and taking two days off. Apart from a holiday for most of August and a few days off during the Easter and Christmas periods, Dr Carey has planned to take off one weekend in six. Throughout the intervening time, he has expected to work, or to be officially engaged, from 7am until late in the evening, without any distinction between weekdays and weekends and without any planned evening or day off.

11.4.2 No one should be appointed as Archbishop unless he is robust, and the capacity for effective work will vary from one individual to another. We do not comment on the specific instance of Dr Carey, but in general excessive hours of work can damage not only the health of the Archbishop, but impair the well-being of those who work with him. We **recommend** that proper periods of leisure should be built into every Archbishop's programme.

Degrees of independence

11.5.1 The Archbishop of Canterbury has to maintain a delicate balance between on the one hand his relationship with the Church of England and on the other hand his relationship with the Anglican Communion generally.

11.5.2 In relation to the Church of England the Archbishop, together with the Archbishop of York, is the spiritual leader of the Church of England and quintessentially part of it, yet he has some, but not a large, degree of detachment from its structure. The Archbishop is clearly bound by decisions of the General Synod which have the force of law. He is also under the strongest obligation to follow decisions of the House of Bishops when acting as a college of bishops of which he is a member. The Archbishop also will wish to take very careful note of decisions of the General Synod even if they do not have the force of law. But the Church of England is episcopally led albeit synodically governed,[8] and in leading the Church he sometimes has to speak on issues on which there is not, at the time, any clearly established policy.

11.5.3 Perhaps more significantly, the Archbishop is both the President of the Anglican Communion and the representative of the Church of England at meetings of the principal organs of the Communion.[9] Yet on particular issues the views of the Church of England may differ from those of some of the other churches within the Anglican Communion. The Archbishop must, therefore, have some measure of independence from both.

11.5.4 The balance in these relationships is fluid, but we regard the Archbishop at the present time as having a semi-detached relationship with the structures of the Anglican Communion and some, but a lesser, degree of independence from the other structures of the Church of England.

Places of work

11.6.1 The Archbishop's main place of work and residence is at Lambeth Palace. All of his senior personal staff work within the palace, and his principal place of residence provided by the Church is within the palace.

11.6.2 The Archbishop also has living and working accommodation at the Old Palace at Canterbury, where he has a small staff.[10]

11.7 In addition, the Archbishop has a room in Church House which he uses primarily for meetings.

Relationship with the Commissioners

11.8.1 In previous times, it would have been inappropriate to refer to resources being *provided* for the Archbishop. Lambeth Palace and the Old Palace at Canterbury both formed part of the archiepiscopal estates, and the Archbishop would have occupied the palaces as of right. Similarly, he would have met the costs of his ministry (both episcopal and archiepiscopal) from the income of those estates.

11.8.2 However, in the same way as happened with the former episcopal estates, the archiepiscopal estates progressively came to be vested in the Church Commissioners,[11] so that it is now the case that the Commissioners own the palaces and make them available to the Archbishop.

11.9 The Commissioners pay all of the Archbishop's operational costs, as well as the costs of maintaining and repairing the fabric of the palaces.

11.10.1 In broad principle, the relationship between the Archbishop and the Commissioners is the same as that between diocesan bishops and the Commissioners.[12]

11.10.2 However, the standing of the Archbishop is such that the Commissioners endeavour to meet most of the resourcing requests which he makes.[13] This is not because the Archbishop is also the Chairman of the Board of Governors of the Church Commissioners – we have referred previously[14] to the avoidance of a conflict of interest – but because the respect for his office is such that any request will carry weight.

Present resources

11.11 The main resources which are provided for the Archbishop can be summarized as:

    a.   private residential accommodation at Lambeth Palace and at the Old Palace, Canterbury;

    b.   working accommodation in both palaces;[15]

    c.   a total staff of about 50 (including domestic staff and gardeners) of whom about a quarter are part-time;

    d.   working accommodation for the staff;

    e.   reception and meeting rooms;

    f.   two chapels;

    g.   IT and other equipment for the Archbishop and his staff;

    h.   accommodation for overnight official guests;

    i.   a car (and a driver who is included in the numbers given in paragraph c.);

    j.   funds to enable the Archbishop and his staff to travel by land and by air; and

    k.   funds to enable the Archbishop and his staff to provide official hospitality.

Composite provision of resources

11.12.1 As metropolitan, the Archbishop is provided with the specific resources of the services of the Vicar-General and the Provincial Registrar.[16]

11.12.2 Subject to these instances, the resources are provided to the Archbishop without distinction as to the capacity in which he utilizes them.

Observations

11.13.1 For reasons which we give in a subsequent chapter,[17] we are satisfied that it is right for the Archbishop to continue to have his principal residence and main working base at Lambeth Palace, provided that measures are taken to increase the income generated from the property.

11.13.2 We make[18] a number of recommendations with regard to the Archbishop's staff at Lambeth Palace.

11.13.3 Subject to these points, we consider that, looking at the position very broadly, both the nature and quantum of the resources provided for the Archbishop at Lambeth Palace are about right.

11.13.4 Irrespective of the manner in which the role of the Archbishop in relation to the Diocese of Canterbury develops,[19] we have no doubt that he should continue to be provided with accommodation at Canterbury; but

11.13.5 Significant changes should be made in that respect.[20]

Prospective changes

11.14.1 The workload and roles of the Archbishop of Canterbury have been transformed during the last century. Archbishop Frederick Temple was Archbishop between 1896 and 1902, having previously been Bishop of London. He became Archbishop when he was in his mid-seventies and nearly blind. His doctors ordered him to reduce his working time to two hours a day. He did that by becoming Archbishop.[21]

11.14.2 The major change during the twentieth century came with the archiepiscopate of Archbishop Geoffrey Fisher (1945–1961), who developed what has become the very demanding role in relation to the Anglican Communion.

11.14.3 The roles of the Archbishop will no doubt continue to evolve. We anticipate that the Archbishop will be required to spend more time in his metropolitical role, particularly in dealing with appeals if the Clergy Discipline Measure 2000[22] is enacted.

11.14.4 However, except as may arise from implementation of the recommendations made by Lord Hurd's Group,[23] we are not aware of any other events which are likely to occur during the forthcoming decade which would materially alter the Archbishop's proper resourcing requirements.

11.15 As we write this report, it remains to be determined which of the recommendations made in the Hurd Report will be implemented. We have, however, considered all of these recommendations, and we summarize in Appendix B references to those of them which fall within our terms of reference.

Concluding observation

11.16 It is important that the provision of resources provided for the Archbishop is sufficiently flexible to adjust easily to the changing demands of an evolving ministry. We hope that our recommendation for the provision of funds by way of block-grant will facilitate that.

chapter 12

The Archbishop of Canterbury's staff

Introduction

12.1.1   An Archbishop of Canterbury can only exercise his ministry to anything approaching its full potential if he has a well-functioning, trained and stable staff of appropriate size.

12.1.2   This chapter is concerned with the Archbishop's staff at Lambeth Palace. We consider separately the staff employed at the Old Palace, Canterbury,[1] and the staff employed within the Lambeth Palace Library.[2]

The staff

12.2   The Hurd Report observed[3] that at Lambeth Palace there 'is a talented senior staff backed up by industrious and cheerful assistance at all levels'. Those are also our findings. There is high calibre among the principal officers and we comment later on the loyalty and hard work which is evident throughout the staff.

The issues

12.3.1   The staffing issues are:

a.   the size and composition of the staff;

b.   the context in which they work;

c.   where the staff should work;

d.   some specific posts;

e.   management of staff;

f.   turnover;

g.   the application of the Church of England's human resources regime to the Archbishop's staff; and

h.   appointments to posts.

12.3.2   We consider in a later chapter[4] where the staff should work and the remaining issues in this chapter. We deal with the size and composition of the staff after referring to the context in which they work.

A personal staff at Lambeth Palace

12.4.1   The initial question is whether the Archbishop should continue to be based at Lambeth Palace and to have his personal staff with him at the palace. For the reasons given in a later chapter,[5] we conclude that he should, and the remainder of this chapter proceeds on the basis that he will do so.

12.4.2   However, as will also be seen, we propose significant changes to the staffing arrangements.

The context: Lambeth Palace as a place in which to work

12.5.1   If it is accepted that the Archbishop will continue to have a personal staff at Lambeth Palace, it is then necessary to consider the context and ethos within which the members of staff work. It has, not in any order of priority, at least four elements.

12.5.2   First, Lambeth Palace is the primary place of residence of the Archbishop. The private residential accommodation is his home in a narrow sense, and the Archbishop may think of the palace as a whole in a much more general sense as his home. Those who are employed at the palace will always need to be sensitive to this.[6]

12.5.3   Secondly, the palace has an intimate atmosphere which some say is like that of a court.[7] This feeling is encouraged by the fact that the palace is physically enclosed and that main access[8] is by means of a gatehouse, with a door that has to be opened for each visitor. It is said that this atmosphere encourages the idiosyncratic. It also encourages members of staff to act like protective courtiers.

12.5.4   Thirdly, the palace is one part of the central headquarters of the Church of England. Yet it is not fully integrated with the remainder of the headquarters[9] and remains partly independent of them. Its ethos, but not its scale, is similar to that of many see houses.

12.5.5   Fourthly, the palace takes on many different guises. They vary from a palace at which the Archbishop receives Heads of State, Heads of Government or other official overseas visitors, often by arrangement with the Foreign and Commonwealth Office. On other occasions, it can be a setting for seminars, of late particularly in the exercise of the present Archbishop's inter-faith ministry. Or it can be a centre for members of the Church, as when meetings of the Archbishop's Council take place in it. And on yet other occasions it can be a more routine headquarters. This combination of factors makes the atmosphere in the palace unique.

12.6   The ethos of the palace engenders great loyalty on the part of the staff. This is a complex mix of loyalty to the Archbishop as an individual and loyalty to the office of Archbishop. We pay tribute to it.

12.7   Our recommendations with regard to staff are designed:

   a.   to eliminate the aspect of the court – without impairing the sense of loyalty; and

   b.   to establish the palace as a smooth-running, efficient operational centre which is also a place in which the Archbishop and his family live.

The size and composition of the staff

12.8.1   Excluding the staff [10] who work in the Lambeth Palace Library, there are at present 36 full-time and 13 part-time posts at Lambeth Palace. This gives 42½ full-time equivalent posts.

12.8.2   Our classification of these posts (both full-time and part-time) is:

   10 principals or other senior members of staff
   16 administrative and support staff (other than secretarial and
      clerical staff)
   12 secretarial and clerical staff
   11 infrastructure staff

12.9.1   At Lambeth Palace the expression 'principal' is used to denote principal officers appointed by the Archbishop (in his corporate capacity) and not necessarily those of principal grade. The following is a simplified structure diagram showing the key members of the Archbishop's personal staff: [11]

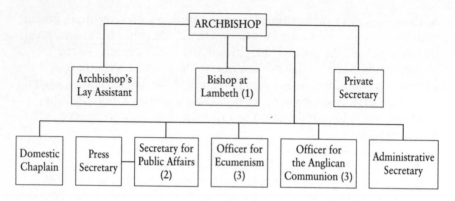

Notes:
(1) The Bishop of Lambeth is also Head of Staff.
(2) The Secretary for Public Affairs is also Deputy Head of Staff.
(3) The Officer for Ecumenism and the Officer for the Anglican Communion are supported by one officer who acts as deputy to both.

12.9.2 The administrative and support staff are generally deputies of or assistants to the principals.

12.9.3 Each principal and some of the members of the administrative and support staff have discrete full-time or part-time personal secretaries.

12.9.4 By 'infrastructure' staff, we mean those members of the staff who maintain the palace and its services as a place in which the Archbishop can live and work and in which the members of his staff can work. Included in this category are the steward, the cook, (part-time) housekeepers, (part-time) cleaners, the maintenance officer, gatekeepers and gardeners (full-time and part-time).

12.10.1 The Commissioners have supplied us with figures for the staff at Lambeth Palace. These figures:

> a. are not in all respects definitive, particularly in respect of the earlier years;
>
> b. do not distinguish principals from other administrative and support staff because the definition of 'principals' has changed over the years;
>
> c. do not include temporary staff;

d. do not distinguish between full-time and part-time staff;

e. treat a person who has two roles as dividing his time equally between them; and

f. have been calculated by taking the actual figures at the end of June and the end of December, and then averaging them. The process of averaging has resulted in halves in some instances.

12.10.2 The figures on these bases for the last decade are as follows:

Year	Principals, Chaplains, Secretaries and Administrative Staff	Drivers	Gardeners	Domestic Staff
1990	20.5	1	1.5	10
1991	26.5	1	2	11
1992	27	1	2	9.5
1993	28.5	1	2	9
1994	28.5	1	3	9
1995	28.5	1	3	9
1996	30.5	1	3	9
1997	27.5	1	3	9
1998	27.5	1	3	9
1999	25.5	1	3	9
2000	27	0.5	3	8.5
2001	29.5	0.5	3	9.5

12.10.3 The corresponding figures for the previous decades are as follows:

Year	Principals, Chaplains, Secretaries and Administrative Staff	Drivers	Gardeners	Domestic Staff
1950	7	1	3	2
1960	9	1	2	3
1970	20	1	1.5	6
1980	20	1	1	8

12.11   It has been suggested to us that during the last decade or so there has been some grade inflation, that is, either that a post has been upgraded while an occupant is in post, or on the retirement of one person the post is upgraded in order to make it more attractive to a prospective successor. On the limited evidence adduced to us it is likely that this has occurred.

Comment

12.12.1   The picture is one of contrasts. On the one hand the size of the staff needs to be large enough to support the Archbishop not only in – if there are such things – ordinary circumstances but also in extraordinary circumstances, perhaps when matters of great urgency arise. It is a demonstration of the loyalty on the part of members of staff to which we have referred that they are prepared to work late, sometimes very late, in order to complete a specific task.

12.12.2   On the other hand, we were surprised at the ratio of the total number of members of staff to the principals.

12.12.3   Later in this chapter we propose the appointment of a Chief of Staff. We **recommend** that one of his early tasks should be to make a complete review of all staff posts within the palace and of working practices, and that, consistent with contractual rights, he should restructure the staff in order best to meet the Archbishop's requirements.

12.12.4   We have not ourselves carried out a staff audit, but our expectation is that the size of the staff would be reduced by that process.

The Bishop at Lambeth

12.13.1   We consider next some of the existing senior staff posts and propose new posts. The first of the existing posts is that of Bishop at Lambeth. During recent archiepiscopates it has been the practice for an experienced bishop to serve at Lambeth Palace. The present post-holder is now designated Bishop at Lambeth and Head of Staff.

12.13.2   Despite the endeavours both of the Archbishops and of the holders of this post, and the benefit of having, in addition to the Archbishop, someone in episcopal orders at Lambeth Palace, the practice has not worked satisfactorily. At the risk of over-simplification and, therefore, of material error: the role of the occupants has not been clearly and consistently defined; they have not themselves usually had managerial or, indeed, any other comparable experience of an organization as large as that at Lambeth Palace; while in the post of Bishop at Lambeth they have not had episcopal oversight of anything; and generally their own episcopal skills and experience have been under-utilized. In short, the Bishop at Lambeth is a bishop, but a bishop who does not exercise an episcopal ministry.

12.14.1 The present Bishop at Lambeth, although carrying the title of Head of Staff, has an unusual relationship with other members of the Archbishop's staff. The job descriptions of the principals[12] provide that they are accountable to the Archbishop, but that the 'Bishop at Lambeth is the Head of Staff and as such has a management role'.[13] The Bishop at Lambeth is not the direct line manager of anyone except his personal secretary, but has general oversight of the work undertaken by the other senior members of staff. Those members of staff normally report directly to the Archbishop, but report to the Bishop at Lambeth on specific issues which the Archbishop has delegated to him.

12.14.2 For present purposes, the essential points are that:

a.   the Bishop at Lambeth is 'Head' of Staff, not 'Chief' of Staff; and

b.   he does not actually manage the staff.

12.15   As did, in effect, the Hurd Report,[14] we **recommend** that this post, in its present form, should be abolished.

Chief of Staff: role

12.16.1 In place of a Bishop at Lambeth the Hurd Report recommended[15] that 'the work of the Lambeth Palace staff should in future be coordinated by a Chief of Staff with authority to ensure that policy preparation is fully coordinated within the Palace and between the Palace and the National Church Institutions, the Anglican Communion Office and Bishopthorpe'.

12.16.2 We wholeheartedly support that recommendation.

12.17.1 We **recommend** that the Chief of Staff should have five main roles. The first should be to provide the Archbishop with a smooth, well-running organization. An Archbishop should not have any anxiety about the capability, effectiveness or method of working of any member of his staff. On appointment, an Archbishop should inherit a smooth-running machine.

12.17.2 Secondly, although an Archbishop will always be the final determiner of the policy which he wishes to adopt, we **recommend** that the Chief of Staff should be a major contributor to its formulation and implementation; and, when it has been fixed, the Chief of Staff should be responsible for the management of the Archbishop's programme, so that the commitments which the Archbishop makes accord with that policy.

12.17.3 Thirdly, by virtue of his experience, which is very likely to have been gained outside the Church, and, progressively, by virtue of the ease and openness of his relations within the Church, he should alert the Archbishop to potential pitfalls or other areas of danger.

12.17.4 Fourthly, he should be responsible for establishing and maintaining good and harmonious relations with his counterpart[16] at Bishopthorpe, and with the Archbishops' Council and the Church Commissioners. In this way, he should ensure the coordination on matters of concern between the Archbishop and these other bodies; and ensure the maximum exchange of information and know-how both to and from Lambeth Palace.

12.17.5 Fifthly, he should have overall responsibility for the income-generating measures which we recommend in a later chapter.[17]

12.18 In order to carry out the first of these roles, we **recommend**, as did the Hurd Report,[18] that the Chief of Staff should directly or indirectly manage all staff employed at Lambeth Palace, as well as being responsible for the management of other resources.

12.19 The Hurd Report recommended[19] that a bishop from elsewhere within the Anglican Communion might be appointed to serve at Lambeth Palace. We comment on that later,[20] but observe at this stage that were that recommendation to be implemented the greatest care would need to be taken in defining the respective areas of responsibility of such a bishop and the Chief of Staff.

12.20   As stated above, we **recommend** that the Chief of Staff should be given wide scope to re-shape the staff in the palace in the light of the vision and expectations of the Archbishop, while paying full regard to the rights and expectations of those working there at the time when the new arrangements come into force. He should also formulate a programme of succession–planning so that so far as possible not more than one member of the senior staff would retire or come to the end of his contract at about the same time.

12.21   We hope that there will not be employment tribunal or court proceedings affecting staff at Lambeth Palace, but, in case there should be, we **recommend** that so far as possible the Chief of Staff (or, perhaps, a member of his staff) should be the effective party to these proceedings rather than the Archbishop personally.

12.22.1 It would be for the Chief of Staff to agree with the principals their working mode. Broadly we see both direct contact between the principals with the Archbishop – which is good in itself – and contact with the Archbishop through the Chief of Staff.

12.22.2 In our view the guiding principles should be that:

a.   any matters which would involve the Archbishop entering into time or resource commitments should pass through the Chief of Staff; and

b.   if, exceptionally, the Archbishop proposed to enter into such commitments as a result of direct access, it should be for him to ensure that the Chief of Staff is fully involved before those commitments are actually made. This should be included in the Archbishop's induction programme.[21]

12.22.3 The Chief of Staff will only be able to perform his coordinating role if he has an overview of the total ministry of the Archbishop.

12.23.1 The Archbishop's ministry is multi-faceted – but it is one ministry. To maximize its effectiveness, his personal staff need to support him as a team. Some of the evidence adduced to us indicates a tendency for members of staff to work directly to the Archbishop as almost independent individuals, rather than as members of a team. In such circumstances, it is easy for individuals (from good intention) to urge the Archbishop to give priority to activities within their own fields rather than seeing his ministry in the round.

12.23.2 We look to the Chief of Staff to reinforce the team building and thereby to assist both the Archbishop and the principals in determining priorities between them.

The Chief of Staff, the Secretary General and the Secretary of the Commissioners

12.24.1 We recommend that the Chief of Staff should have a close working relationship with the Secretary General of the General Synod and the Secretary of the Commissioners, and also with his counterpart at Bishopthorpe.

12.24.2 One of the responsibilities of this group should be to monitor the use and deployment of specialist staff in order to ensure full cooperation between them.

Chief of Staff: further aspects

12.25.1 If, as we have recommended, the Chief of Staff is to contribute to the formulation of the Archbishop's policy, he must have the experience and be of a calibre which commands the Archbishop's respect. There must be a balance between the Archbishop and the Chief of Staff.

12.25.2 The Chief of Staff should be appointed by a panel of which the Archbishop might, but would not necessarily, be the Chairman. It is axiomatic that the Archbishop personally should play the fullest part in the selection of a Chief of Staff. The arrangement will not work without, among many other things, good personal chemistry between the two. Ultimately, however, the appointment is to the Archbishop in his corporate, not personal, capacity.

12.25.3 When the arrangements are in force, we envisage that the term of appointment of a Chief of Staff might come to an end either in the middle of an archiepiscopate (so that there is good opportunity to appoint his successor) or after a few months into the archiepiscopate of a successor-Archbishop (so that he could either be reappointed or a new appointment made).

12.26.1 The Chief of Staff must have an inherently good relationship with the Archbishop. He must have both the degree of independence of office which enables him to advance his views even if they do not accord with those of the Archbishop and the maturity to accept the Archbishop's decision even if it is contrary to his advice.

12.26.2 In case the relationship should break down, there should be a mechanism by which the Chief of Staff's contract could be terminated. However, to give him the required degree of independence and sense of financial security, we **recommend** that the Chief of Staff should have, say, a five-year contract (to expire at either of the times which we have mentioned in paragraph 12.25.3). Any compensation for loss of office would need to be paid from the block-grant.

12.27 We also **recommend** that the Chief of Staff should have direct and open access to the independent group which is recommended elsewhere[22] to assist in the provision of resources for the Archbishop.

12.28.1 The Hurd Report recommended[23] that the Chief of Staff should *probably* be lay. We go further and **recommend** that save in the most exceptional circumstances he *should* be lay.

12.28.2 It seems to us that any ordained person (even if in episcopal orders) is likely to be so influenced, even subconsciously, by considerations of obedience to someone who is an ecclesiastical superior that his independence of stance might be compromised.

12.29.1 The Hurd Report recommended[24] that the Chief of Staff should be paid at a level commensurate with the qualities which are being sought in the individual. It did not mention a figure.

12.29.2 There is a fundamental conflict between the requirement for calibre and the reluctance or inability of the Church of England to pay market rates for staff of that calibre. However desirable it might be from the viewpoint of the Archbishop, we think that it would be unacceptable to the Church as a whole for the Chief of Staff to be remunerated more highly than, say, the Secretary General of the General Synod. We do not consider it necessary for the Chief of Staff to be provided with residential accommodation, either within the palace or elsewhere, and on that basis we consider that he should be remunerated on Senior Civil Service pay bands 6 or 7.[25]

The Archbishop's Anglican Communion Officer and Officer for Ecumenism

12.30.1 The Archbishop has an Anglican Communion Officer, as well as a part-time Deputy Officer. Yet within 15 minutes or so walking distance from Lambeth Palace is the Anglican Communion Office[26] with a staff of about 15. Is there an unnecessary duplication?

12.30.2 The Archbishop has an Officer for Ecumenism and a part-time Deputy. But within both Church House and the Anglican Communion Office, there are specialist officers in this field. Is there unnecessary duplication here too?

12.31 As will be seen from our discussion of the Archbishop's roles in relation to the Anglican Communion,[27] we consider that he should continue to have an Anglican Communion Officer; and for similar reasons we consider that he should also continue to have an Officer for Ecumenism.

Inter-faith

12.32.1 In the latter stages of our work we have noted the considerable time and effort which the Archbishop has spent on inter-faith issues in the aftermath of terrorist action in the United States on 11 September 2001, and it has been suggested to us that he should also have a Secretary for Inter-faith Affairs.[28]

12.32.2 We think the preferable course is for such matters to be dealt with by a change in the composition of the Archbishop's staff rather than increasing it. We do not underestimate the practical difficulties, but the flexibility which we urge should enable a two-way movement between Lambeth Palace and Church House so that the Archbishop has the specialist staff which he needs at any particular point of time.

Senior staff generally

12.33.1 We recommend that the Chief of Staff should have the responsibility, in discussion with the Archbishop, to structure the senior staff, as well as all other members of staff, in a way which will best meet the needs and expectations of the Archbishop. Furthermore, the results of any restructuring would need to be kept under review, and be subject to modification as the Archbishop's own ministry developed.

12.33.2 It would be inconsistent with this view for us to make detailed comments on the existing staff posts – such matters are appropriately left to the Chief of Staff – but we have three specific recommendations.

Financial Secretary

12.34.1 First, we have recommended [29] that the Commissioners should devolve funds by way of block-grant to the Archbishop.

12.34.2 We recommend in a subsequent chapter [30] that there should be a positive policy to maximize so far as proper income generation from the property.

12.34.3 In order to deal with these and the other financial matters, we **recommend** the establishment of a new post, that of Archbishop's Financial Secretary. It would be for the Chief of Staff to consider whether the existing post of Bursar should be merged with this post, but in any event we are satisfied that the Financial Secretary's salary and associated costs would be covered by the additional income generated.

Premises Manager

12.35 Our proposals with regard to income generation will involve a much intensified use of the palace. In order to deal with this we **recommend** that there should be a premises manager for the palace. We do not necessarily regard this as a new post, but one which will be established as part of the income generation programme and which may involve redeployment by the Chief of Staff of existing posts, such as that of the Steward.

The Commissioners' agent

12.36.1 In the case of most see houses, the Commissioners engage a professional firm practising in the area to look after their interests in the properties. At present, in the case of Lambeth Palace and the Old Palace at Canterbury a member of the Commissioners' staff, who is a qualified architect, acts as the agent. His responsibilities are to ensure that the Commissioners' obligations for the upkeep of the fabric of the properties are discharged; to advise with regard to other aspects affecting the structure of the buildings; and to deal with their internal repair and decoration.

12.36.2 The agent is also asked to deal with various incidental matters affecting the running of the buildings, albeit that such matters do not involve the exercise of professional skills.

12.36.3 We understand that it is the Commissioners' intention in the fairly near future to appoint a professional firm to act in relation to Lambeth Palace and the Old Palace at Canterbury so that the arrangements will be similar to those for see houses generally.

12.37 It is a feature of the present arrangements that the Commissioners' agent is *formally* responsible only to the Commissioners, by whom he is in effect employed. However, he naturally also endeavours to give effect to the wishes of the Archbishop, and so in practice also owes loyalty to the Archbishop and his wife.

12.38.1 We **recommend** that for so long as the Commissioners directly employ an agent for the palace then, while continuing to be employed by the Commissioners, he should also be a member of the Archbishop's personal staff and should, therefore, so far as is consistent with his primary obligations to the Commissioners, be within the operational direction of the Chief of Staff.

12.38.2 When the Commissioners have appointed a professional firm to act as agents for the palace, no doubt the Premises Manager would be responsible for liaison with that firm and in that event, we **recommend** that the Premises Manager should also be required to serve the interests of the Commissioners in his dealings with that firm.

Catering

12.39.1 At present there is a cook employed at Lambeth Palace. The cook is able to cater for small-scale official hospitality provided by the Archbishop or senior members of his staff, but outside caterers are engaged when the Archbishop wishes to provide hospitality on a larger scale.

12.39.2 The very restricted in-house catering equipment and facilities prevent more widespread use of rooms at Lambeth Palace for meetings.

12.39.3 The extent of catering equipment and facilities at Lambeth Palace will need to be reconsidered as part of our income-generation proposals;[31] and they will probably be enhanced.

12.39.4 We **recommend** continuance of the existing arrangement whereby the Archbishop and members of his family should, where they so wish, have meals cooked for them on payment of the cost of provision.

Housekeeping

12.40   We have referred previously to the principles which we consider should apply to housekeeping.[32]

Gardeners

12.41   We refer in a later chapter[33] to gardeners.

Staff management

12.42.1 It stands out that there is no overall management of staff at Lambeth Palace. The Archbishop (in his corporate capacity) is the managing employer,[34] but it should not be for him to be cast in the role of manager. The Bishop at Lambeth has an ill-defined role as Head of Staff,[35] but he does not actively manage the staff. The Archbishop's Administrative Secretary and his deputy act as old-style personnel officers. But the absence of comprehensive management is manifest.

12.42.2 To remedy this, we have recommended[36] that the Chief of Staff should have overall management responsibility for staff.

12.42.3 We **recommend** that:

a.   he should conduct a total review of all staff posts, without any assumption that existing posts would continue, or that new posts would or would not be created;

b.   he should institute a system of monitoring the continuing need for the posts which are established following the review; and

c.   there should be applied to such posts the same principles of evaluation as apply to staff posts in the other National Church Institutions.

Turnover

12.43.1 The absence of overall staff management is illustrated by the degree of change in senior staff posts.

12.43.2 This history of the senior posts for the years 1999, 2000 and 2001 has been as follows:

Bishop at Lambeth	One change
Secretary for Public Affairs	No change

Press Secretary	Two changes
Press Officer	One change
Private Secretary	One change
Archbishop's Lay Assistant	No change
Domestic Chaplain	One change
Officer for Ecumenism	One change
Officer for the Anglican Communion	Two changes
Administrative Secretary	One change

12.44   At a more junior level, the history of secretarial[37] and clerical assistant posts during the years 1999, 2000 and 2001 has been as follows:

Personal Secretary or Personal Assistant to:

1. The Archbishop	One change
2. Mrs Carey	Four changes
3. The Bishop at Lambeth	Two changes
4. The Archbishop's Lay Assistant	Two changes
5. The Chaplain	Two changes
6. The Secretary for Public Affairs	One change
7. The Officer for Ecumenism	One change
8. The Officer for the Anglican Communion	Two changes
9. The Assistant Officer for Ecumenism and the Anglican Communion	Two changes
10. Clerical assistant to the Officers for Ecumenism and the Anglican Communion	Two changes
11. The Administrative Secretary	One change
12. The Deputy Administrative and Awards Secretary	One change
13. Clerical Assistant to the Deputy Administrative and Awards Secretary	Two changes

12.45   The Archbishop's ministry will be hampered until he has a staff which has a more stable composition.

The National Church Institutions and the Human Resources regime

12.46   We have outlined in a previous chapter[38] the Human Resources regime which was introduced following the coming into effect of the National Church Institutions Measure 1998. The Archbishop, in his corporate capacity, is one of those Institutions and has, therefore, subscribed to the regime.

12.47.1 It has not been for us to conduct an overall review of that regime, but we support at least some of its objectives, from the viewpoints both of the Archbishop and members of his staff.

12.47.2 In an era of increasing complexity of employment law, the Archbishop, in the same way as any other employer, needs the availability of professional advice and there need to be proper procedures for the appointment and the termination of the appointment of members of staff. The Archbishop needs protection.

12.47.3 From the viewpoint of the members of the staff, we recognize that the values of openness, fairness and consistency of dealing are those which a good employer – and the Church of England should certainly be that – should espouse.

12.48.1 We can also understand that because of the physical proximity of Lambeth Palace to the other London National Church Institutions and because of some contact between the staffs of the Institutions, a move towards the adoption of common terms and conditions of service has merit.

12.48.2 Nevertheless, the overwhelming balance of the evidence which has been adduced to us indicates that the system is not working at Lambeth Palace as well as it should do. This is particularly so with regard to the making of appointments.

Appointments

12.49.1 It is an aspect of the Human Resources regime that when a staff vacancy occurs in any of the National Church Institutions, then the post is to be advertised internally within all of the Institutions, and if no suitable internal candidate is forthcoming then the post is to be advertised externally.

12.49.2 It is a further aspect of the regime that both job and person specifications, to a standard format, are to be prepared for all posts. The decision whether to make an appointment is a matter for the appointing officer (or panel), but, when the decision has been taken, the contract is prepared by the HR Department.

12.50.1 The delays in the appointment process, at least so far as Lambeth Palace is concerned, cause frustration and inefficiency of working.

12.50.2 We **recommend** that, when appointed, the Chief of Staff should discuss with the HR Department a modification of the arrangement, at least to permit concurrent internal and external advertisements.

12.50.3 We also expect that the Chief of Staff will act to ensure that there are no delays in the operation of whatever arrangements are for the time being in force.

The appointment process

12.51.1 We have referred[39] to the need so far as possible to avoid any risk of the Archbishop being required to give evidence in any court or tribunal proceedings relating to staff.

12.51.2 A further factor is that when an appointment is being made, although there will be very much in mind the particular Archbishop who is in office at the time, the appointment is to the Archbishop in his corporate capacity, so that, in principle, the appointment would subsist notwithstanding the death or retirement of an Archbishop and continue into the archiepiscopate of his successor.

12.52 Accordingly, we **recommend** that:

a. senior appointments should always be made by a panel;

b. so far as possible the Archbishop should not himself be the appointing officer;

c. if the Archbishop is not a member of the panel which makes senior appointments, short-listed candidates should meet the Archbishop and, perhaps, make a brief presentation to him; and

d. in that event the appointing panel should take into account observations made to it by the Archbishop.

Employment problems

12.53.1 It is to be anticipated that from time to time problems will emerge in the relationship between an Archbishop and a member of his staff. In such circumstances, the pastoral instincts of an Archbishop will be to attempt to solve them himself.

12.53.2 We strongly **recommend**, however, that he should not do so, but should rely on the Chief of Staff to deal with such matters. To do otherwise will risk greater complications – for both Archbishop and member of staff.

chapter 13

Financial management and control

Introduction

13.1.1   In this chapter we consider the arrangements for financial management and control at Lambeth Palace and make recommendations with regard to them. In doing so, we also refer to recommendations of a financial nature which are made in other chapters of this report.

13.1.2   At the end of the chapter we summarize the amounts which the Commissioners have expended in the years 2000 and 2001 in support of the Archbishop of Canterbury.

Present position: operational costs

13.2.1   In outline, the present arrangements with regard to the payment of operational costs and premises expenses which apply to the Archbishop are similar to those which apply to diocesan bishops,[1] but with some variations.

13.2.2   A budget for operational costs[2] is drawn up by staff of the Bishoprics and Cathedrals Department following discussions with members of the Archbishop's staff.

13.2.3   On occasions, adjustments to budgeted amounts are made during a year. This might be, for example, because a staff post is regraded. The need for such adjustments is agreed between the Archbishop's Administrative Secretary on behalf of the Archbishop and the Bishoprics and Cathedrals Department, together with, in the case of staff matters, the Human Resources Department of the Archbishops' Council.[3]

13.2.4   The salary and office equipment costs are paid directly by the Commissioners and debited to a central account in their books.

13.2.5   The Commissioners remit amounts quarterly to a local bank account, which is administered by the Bursar,[4] and from which smaller operational costs are paid.

13.2.6   The operational costs which are paid in these ways cover not only those incurred by the Archbishop in his capacity as diocesan bishop, but also those incurred by him in his capacities as metropolitan, primate and archbishop.

13.2.7   The Archbishop's staff prepares and sends to the Bishoprics and Cathedrals Department quarterly details of the expenditure made from the local account.

13.2.8   On the basis of that information and details in their own records, the Bishoprics and Cathedrals Department prepares quarterly reports which are sent to the Archbishop's staff.

13.2.9   The Bishoprics and Cathedrals Department monitors during the course of a year actual financial performance against budget.

13.2.10   The Archbishop's staff monitor local expenditure against budget, but they are not able to monitor satisfactorily central expenditure against budget.[5]

Premises expenses
13.3.1   A separate budget for premises expenses is drawn up by the Bishoprics and Cathedrals Department, following discussions with their agent[6] and the Archbishop's staff. Included in this budget are the salary and associated costs of most of the infrastructure staff,[7] such as gatekeepers and gardeners.

13.3.2   The Commissioners themselves pay the major items and debit the housing account in their books.

13.3.3   The Commissioners remit quarterly accounts to a separate local bank account, from which smaller payments are made by the Archbishop's staff.

13.3.4   Financial performance against budget is reviewed by the Bishoprics and Cathedrals Department on an *ad hoc* basis, but not by the Archbishop's staff.

Overseas travel

13.4.1   The Bishoprics and Cathedrals Department draws up in discussion with the Archbishop's staff a separate budget for overseas travel.

13.4.2   The Commissioners remit amounts quarterly to a separate local bank account from which these expenses are paid.

13.4.3   The Commissioners maintain in their books an overseas travel account, to which are debited the costs of such travel incurred by the Archbishop, members of his staff, and others travelling on his behalf and at his request.[8]

Metropolitical resources

13.5   The only separate resources which the Archbishop has in his capacity as metropolitan[9] are the services of the Provincial Registrar and the Vicar-General.[10] Their fees are externally prescribed,[11] and are paid directly by the Commissioners.

Aspects of the present arrangements

13.6.1   There is no single person charged with the financial control of the activities at Lambeth Palace. To a major extent this control is exercised remotely by the Bishoprics and Cathedrals Department, but that Department is dependent in part on information supplied by the Archbishop's staff.

13.6.2   The Archbishop's staff have difficulty in monitoring.[12]

13.7.1   Dr Carey has been sensitively aware of the financial circumstances of the Church of England as a whole and in view of that he has not incurred some expenditure which for all other purposes would be desirable.

13.7.2   Nevertheless, the system is not one which encourages coordinated financial control. In our First Report, we recommended[13] the introduction of a system for other bishops which would give them a substantial amount of financial responsibility and decision-taking authority. We consider that a similar system should be established for Lambeth Palace.

Recommendations

13.8   We recommend that:

a.   there should be an officer on the Archbishop's staff with responsibility for overall financial control of all activities [14] within the palace;

b.   there should be a costed business plan for all activities within the palace, and this plan should be within the purview of the Chief of Staff;[15] and

c.   monthly or quarterly management accounts should be prepared in respect of the total operations within the palace.

13.9   The devolution of funds by way of block-grant and the financial empowerment of the Archbishop which we thereby recommend should result in all necessary financial information being held in the palace.

13.10   Elsewhere [16] we **recommend** that separate overall accounts should be prepared in respect of the Lambeth Palace Library.

Financial Secretary

13.11.1 At present financial procedures within Lambeth Palace are dealt with by the Archbishop's Administrative Secretary, and by the Bursar who works to him. The Archbishop's Administrative Secretary will, when he thinks it appropriate, refer to the Archbishop for decision whether major discretionary expenditure should be incurred, but in practice this rarely arises.

13.11.2 We have proposed [17] that the Commissioners' funds for operational costs should be block-granted to the Archbishop. We propose in a subsequent chapter [18] various measures to increase substantially the income to be derived from the palace. In view of these considerations we have recommended [19] that there should be a Financial Secretary as a member of the Archbishop's personal staff, although this would not necessarily involve increasing the size of the staff.[20] The Financial Secretary would report directly to the Chief of Staff.

Third party support

13.12   Certain third party funds have been used to defray premises expenses which would otherwise have been paid by the Commissioners, or not incurred at all. In this context, we consider:

a.   The Lambeth Fund;

b.   the Archbishop's Charitable Trusts; and

c.   the Archbishop's Discretionary Fund.

The Lambeth Fund

13.13.1 The Lambeth Fund was created in 1983 by well-wishers of
Archbishop Runcie. It was established to raise funds to support
initiatives or objectives of the Archbishop where either Commissioners'
funds were not available or the use of Commissioners' funds was not
considered appropriate.

13.13.2 The Lambeth Fund is constituted and registered as a charitable
trust. The trustees[21] are appointed by the Archbishop. The Archbishop
himself is not a trustee but (by his choice) in practice Dr Carey attends
at least part of almost all ordinary meetings of the trustees.

13.13.3 The trustees of The Lambeth Fund have three broad functions:

a.   to raise funds and apply them in support of initiatives of
the Archbishop;

b.   to act as the direct or ultimate governing body of various
enterprises, such as The Lambeth Partnership[22] and
Springboard;[23] and

c.   either individually or as a body to be available to explore
from an independent concerned stance with the Archbishop
particular issues which he wishes to raise.

13.13.4 Most of the funds raised by The Lambeth Fund have been
applied broadly in the field of mission and so are outside our concern.
However, the trustees have themselves either actively raised, or have
received, funds, almost exclusively from sources in the United Kingdom
or the United States, which have at various times been applied in
effecting improvements to the palace or contributing to the cost of such
improvements. These have included improvements to the garden and to
the main chapel; significantly to the crypt chapel; and some
refurbishment work to the state rooms.

13.13.5 In raising funds, the trustees have consistently followed the
principle of seeking to attract only money which is new to the Church;
and of doing so in a manner which does not impact on any fund-raising
activities of the local Church.

13.14   In the case of bishops in each diocese, we recommended[24] the formation of a Bishops' Resources Group. We do not recommend the equivalent in respect of the Archbishop, but we **recommend** that some or all of the trustees should also act as the Archbishop's Resources Group in relation to his activities at Lambeth Palace. We further **recommend** that the Diocese of Canterbury should have its own Resources Group constituted by the Archbishop or, if the Archbishop so chooses, by the Bishop of Dover.[25]

13.15.1   The trustees of The Lambeth Fund determine their own rules of procedure, and it is not for us to prescribe them. We **recommend**, however, that they should consider inviting the Chief of Staff to be in attendance for at least part of their meetings: this would assist in ensuring coordination with activities conducted by members of the Archbishop's staff.[26]

13.15.2   The concern of the trustees of The Lambeth Fund will no doubt always be, consistent with their legal obligations as charity trustees, to support the Archbishop. However, without diluting their general loyalty to the Archbishop, we have recommended[27] that the Chief of Staff should be afforded access to the trustees for consultation.

The Archbishop's charitable trusts

13.16.1   The Archbishop is a trustee of various charitable trusts[28] and he appoints the other trustees of those trusts. These trusts are administered from Lambeth Palace by members of his staff.

13.16.2   Apart from one grant which was made from one of these trusts towards the improvement of the crypt chapel, no payments are made from these trusts towards the Archbishop's operational costs or premises expenses.

13.17   Payments are made from the Archbishop's charitable trusts to the Bishop of Dover and a rather lesser sum to the Bishop of Maidstone so that they can have their own discretionary sub-funds. Consistent with one of our recommendations about the Diocese of Canterbury,[29] we **recommend**, so that there is no overlap or inconsistency, that there should be close coordination between the Archbishop and the Bishops of Dover and Maidstone about grants which are made either by the Archbishop from the main fund or by the Bishops of Dover and Maidstone from the sub-funds for purposes related to the Diocese of Canterbury.

The Archbishop's discretionary fund

13.18.1 The Archbishop has a discretionary fund which, in common with those of some other diocesan bishops, receives an annual grant[30] from the Central Church Fund and certain other donations. The Archbishop makes various grants and donations from it of a total amount broadly corresponding to the income, so that the balance remaining at the end of each year is small.[31] This fund is not legally charitable.

13.18.2 We have been assured that no payments are made from this fund which are applied for the Archbishop's operational costs or premises expenses, and accordingly this fund falls outside our terms of reference.

13.19 We note that although accounts of the Discretionary Fund are prepared, they are not audited or professionally examined. There is not the slightest indication of any irregularity, but we **recommend** that they should be independently reviewed, and that this should be dealt with in conjunction with the audit of the accounts of the charitable trusts.

Commissioners' financial support

13.20.1 The table in paragraph 13.21.2 summarizes the information about the financial support provided by the Commissioners for the Archbishop of Canterbury during the year which ended on 31 December 2000. It separates expenditure in relation to:

> a. the Archbishop, in all of his roles, at Lambeth Palace, but excluding the Lambeth Palace Library (column (2));
>
> b. the Lambeth Palace Library (column (3)); and
>
> c. the Archbishop at the Old Palace, Canterbury (column (4)).

13.20.2 The figures in columns (2) and (4) of the table include the costs incurred in relation to the Archbishop's ministry in the Anglican Communion. In a later chapter we have separately identified the marginal costs of that aspect of his ministry.

13.20.3 The table uses the expense categories which we recommended in our First Report.[32]

13.20.4 As in the case of see houses, no notional charge for the use and occupation of premises is included.

13.21.1 The figures have been supplied to us by the Commissioners. We do not doubt the broad picture which is presented by them, but as always when considering financial information of this nature, it is necessary to keep in mind that specific figures in relation to one year may be exceptional, and give a distorted impression.

13.21.2 The figures are as follows:

Commissioners' financial support for the Archbishop in 2000

Description (1)	The Archbishop and Lambeth Palace (2) £	Library (3) £	The Archbishop and the Old Palace, Canterbury (4) £	Notes and References (5)
A. Office and Support Staff Costs				
Stipends, pension contributions and employers' National Insurance contributions in respect of the Bishop at Lambeth, the Archbishop's Chaplain and the principals who are clergy	124,000		10,000	(a)
Salaries, pension contributions and employers' National Insurance contributions of lay principals, other administrators and secretaries	690,000	263,000	20,000	
Removal and resettlement expenses of clergy members of staff	6,000			
Other staff costs	19,000			
Staff sub-total	839,000	263,000	30,000	
Office expenses	116,000		2,000	
Office equipment	28,000			
Office furniture	nil			
Miscellaneous	30,000			
Total A	1,013,000	263,000	32,000	

Description (1)	The Archbishop and Lambeth Palace (2) £	Library (3) £	The Archbishop and the Old Palace, Canterbury (4) £	Notes and References (5)
B. Administrative and Operational Costs				
Ordination expenses	nil		nil	
Patronage expenses	nil		nil	
Training expenses	nil		nil	
Legal fees	nil		16,000	(b)
Removal and re-settlement expenses	nil		nil	
Strasbourg Chaplaincy and Apocrisorioi	18,000		Not applicable	(c)
Library operational expenses: see Chapter 17		142,000		
Common Services:				
a. Legal				
b. IT				
c. Office services	56,000	23,000		
d. HR				
e. Communications				
Total B	74,000	165,000	16,000	
C. Individual Working Costs				
Cars	7,000			
Driver's pay and pension contributions	12,000			
Other travel within the United Kingdom and subsistence	30,000		1,000	
Overseas travel	174,000			
Hospitality	30,000		8,000	
Total C	253,000	nil	9,000	

Description (1)	The Archbishop and Lambeth Palace (2) £	Library (3) £	The Archbishop and the Old Palace, Canterbury (4) £	Notes and References (5)
D. Premises Expenditure: Recurrent				
Heating and lighting	45,000		2,000	
Maintenance and repairs (including maintenance contracts) of premises and equipment	203,000	25,000	15,000	
Council tax and water charges	19,000		1,000	
Insurance	18,000	17,000	nil	(d)
Gardeners' pay, domestic staff pay and pension contributions	222,000		27,000	
Garden costs	10,000			
Minor household and garden items	nil		1,000	
Depreciation	3,000			
Furnishings, equipment and restoration of portraits	4,000		1,000	
Sub-total	524,000	42,000	47,000	
Miscellaneous credits	(16,000)			
Total D	508,000	42,000	47,000	
E. Premises: Income: Recurrent				
Rents and service charges receivable	(16,000)		(9,000)	
Total E	(16,000)	nil	(9,000)	
F. Premises: Expenditure: Capital				
General improvement works	55,000	14,000	nil	
Net cost of replacement of house for a clergy member of staff	151,000			(e)

Description (1)	The Archbishop and Lambeth Palace (2) £	Library (3) £	The Archbishop and the Old Palace, Canterbury (4) £	Notes and References (5)
Improvement works to Crypt	107,000			
Total F	313,000	14,000	nil	
G. Summary				
A. Office and Support Staff Costs	1,013,000	263,000	32,000	
B. Administrative and Operational Costs	74,000	165,000	16,000	
C. Individual Working Costs	253,000	nil	9,000	
D. Premises: Expenditure: Recurrent	508,000	42,000	47,000	
E. Premises: Income: Recurrent	(16,000)	nil	(9,000)	
F. Premises: Expenditure: Capital	313,000	14,000	nil	
TOTAL	£2,145,000	£484,000	£95,000	

Notes:
(a) The appointment of the Canterbury Chaplain is part-time.
(b) This excludes the fees paid to the Provincial Registrar and Vicar-General.
(c) These items may not be by their nature operational expenses, but part of the Archbishop's mission. They are included here to accord with the Commissioners' accounting treatment.
(d) This excludes the cost of insuring the Old Palace at Canterbury which is included in the Commissioners' block insurance policy.
(e) Some ordained members of staff are provided with rent-free living accommodation in addition to stipend. This item relates to the net cost of a replacement house for a clerical member of staff who works at Lambeth Palace. The house remains in the ownership of the Commissioners.

13.22 The corresponding figures in respect of 2001 are as follows:

Description (1)	The Archbishop and Lambeth Palace (2) £	Library (3) £	The Archbishop and the Old Palace, Canterbury (4) £	Notes and References (5)
A. Office and Support Staff Costs				
Stipends, pension contributions and employers' National Insurance contributions in respect of the Bishop at Lambeth, the Archbishop's Chaplain and the principals who are clergy	139,000		11,000	
Salaries, pension contributions and employers' National Insurance contributions of lay principals, other administrators and secretaries	756,000	299,000	21,000	
Removal and resettlement expenses of clergy members of staff	8,000			
Exceptional staff costs	11,000			
Staff sub-total	914,000	299,000	32,000	
Office expenses	125,000		2,000	
Office equipment	27,000			
Office furniture				
Miscellaneous	12,000			
Total A	1,078,000	299,000	34,000	

Description (1)	The Archbishop and Lambeth Palace (2) £	Library (3) £	The Archbishop and the Old Palace, Canterbury (4) £	Notes and References (5)
B. Administrative and Operational Costs				
Ordination expenses			1,000	
Patronage expenses				
Training expenses	1,000			
Legal fees			17,000	
Removal and re-settlement expenses				
Strasbourg Chaplaincy and Apocrisorioi	13,000			
Library operational expenses: see Chapter 17		134,000		
Common Services:				
a. Legal				
b. IT				
c. Office services	155,000	25,000		
d. HR				
e. Communications				
Total B	169,000	159,000	18,000	
C. Individual Working Costs				
Cars	4,000			
Driver's pay and pension contributions	11,000			
Other travel within the United Kingdom and subsistence	13,000		1,000	
Overseas travel	99,000			
Hospitality	48,000		11,000	
Total C	175,000	nil	12,000	

Description (1)	The Archbishop and Lambeth Palace (2) £	Library (3) £	The Archbishop and the Old Palace, Canterbury (4) £	Notes and References (5)
D. Premises Expenditure: Recurrent				
Heating and lighting	41,000		3,000	
Maintenance and repairs (including maintenance contracts) of premises and equipment	232,000	23,000	7,000	
Council tax and water charges	23,000		1,000	
Insurance	11,000	17,000		
Gardeners' pay, domestic staff pay and pension contributions	242,000		29,000	
Garden costs	13,000			
Minor household and garden items			1,000	
Depreciation	4,000			
Furnishings, equipment and restoration of portraits	21,000			
Sub-total	587,000	40,000	41,000	
Miscellaneous	7,000			
Total D	594,000	40,000	41,000	
E. Premises: Income: Recurrent				
Rents and service charges receivable	(8,000)		(9,000)	
Total E	(8,000)	nil	(9,000)	

Description (1)	The Archbishop and Lambeth Palace (2) £	Library (3) £	The Archbishop and the Old Palace, Canterbury (4) £	Notes and References (5)
F. Premises: Expenditure: Capital				
General improvement works	104,000	14,000		
Donation towards improvement works to crypt effected in previous year	(50,000)			
Total F	54,000	14,000	nil	
G. Summary				
A. Office and Support Staff Costs	1,078,000	299,000	34,000	
B. Administrative and Operational Costs	169,000	159,000	18,000	
C. Individual Working Costs	175,000	nil	12,000	
D. Premises: Expenditure: Recurrent	594,000	40,000	41,000	
E. Premises: Income: Recurrent	(8,000)	nil	(9,000)	
F. Premises: Expenditure: Capital	54,000	14,000	nil	
TOTAL	£2,062,000	£512,000	£96,000	

Publication and disclosure

13.23 In accordance with our principles of transparency and disclosure,[33] we **recommend** that:

> a. the details of the Archbishop's operational costs should continue to be disclosed together with other bishops' costs;[34] and

> b. unless and until there is also disclosure with them of premises expenses, these should also be disclosed, if necessary, by note to the Commissioners' statutory accounts.

chapter 14

Lambeth Palace and its grounds

Introduction

14.1   In this chapter, we consider Lambeth Palace as a place for the Archbishop and his immediate family to live in, and as a place for the Archbishop and his personal staff to work in; whether it should be retained by the Commissioners; and, if so, how it should be managed and used.

History

14.2   Lambeth Palace became the property of the Archbishop (in his corporate capacity[1]) in 1197, but was probably first used as a residence by St Anselm in the last decade of the previous century.[2] With the exception of the Commonwealth period (1649–60) Lambeth Palace has been continuously in use as a residence for successive Archbishops for over 900 years.[3]

Description

14.3   The palace, its associated buildings and its grounds occupy a site of about 10 acres (4.05 hectares).

14.4.1   The buildings comprise:

a.   the main palace building;

b.   Morton's Tower, within which is the gatehouse to the palace;

c.   Lollard's Tower, which is attached to the main palace building and in which there are a number of flats;

d.   eight cottages around a courtyard; and

e.   the head gardener's house.

14.4.2   Within the main palace building there are:

a.   four flats, which are at present occupied by the Archbishop,[4] the Bishop at Lambeth, the steward and a research assistant, together with three suites for official guests;

b. spacious studies for the Archbishop, and the Bishop at Lambeth, and offices on the lower ground and upper ground floors (which together occupy approximately 7,000 sq ft (650 sq m));

c. three main state rooms[5] and meeting rooms (which occupy approximately 12,420 sq ft (225 sq m));

d. two chapels;

e. the Great Hall, which is primarily used by the Lambeth Palace Library;[6] and

f. other areas used by the Library, which, together with the Great Hall, occupy approximately 19,000 sq ft (1,765 sq m).

14.4.3 Morton's Tower is the gatehouse to the palace. It incorporates the gatekeeper's lodge, but the rooms above are primarily used by the Lambeth Palace Library.[7]

14.4.4 Lollard's Tower is divided into five flats.

14.4.5 The head gardener's house, which occupies a site of about one-fifth of an acre (0.08 of a hectare) is separated from the palace and its grounds by a hostel.

14.5 The gardens, which have an area of about 6.3 acres (2.55 hectares), are a well-maintained mix of formal and informal open space. They are shared informally between the occupiers of the palace, and are used occasionally by third parties. For comparison the formal gardens of Buckingham Palace comprise about 20 acres (8.1 hectares).

Adjacent properties
14.6 The Commissioners also own:

a. a recreational ground known as Archbishop's Park, which comprises about 8 acres (3.25 hectares), and which is separate from the palace. It lies to the east of the palace gardens. This recreation ground is let to the London Borough of Lambeth under a lease which can be terminated on three months' notice. The land is used as a public open space;

b.   an area of about 0.69 acres (0.28 hectares) to the north of Archbishop's Park. This is let to the Special Trustees of Guy's and St Thomas' Hospital for a term which will expire in 2166; and

c.   the land between the eastern boundary of the palace grounds and the head gardener's house on which the hostel stands. This is also let to Guy's and St Thomas' Hospital for a term which will expire in 2106.[8]

Status

14.7.1   Lambeth Palace is not a see house, but is provided by the Commissioners as a London home and office for the Archbishop and his staff.

14.7.2   Prior to the vesting of the palace in the Ecclesiastical Commissioners in 1946[9] there was an agreement between the Commissioners, the Archbishop and other interested parties to the effect, broadly, that the Commissioners would hold the property as an investment and would let it to the Archbishop at a rent. It seems to have been the intention that the Commissioners would have provided the Archbishop with funds with which to pay the rent, and that they would have received that rent as investment income.[10] However, the process of providing an amount and receiving back the same amount as rent subsequently lapsed.

14.8   Although Lambeth Palace is not a see house (but the Old Palace, Canterbury is[11]), Lambeth Palace contains the principal residence of the Archbishop.

Public access

14.9.1   The palace and its grounds are enclosed, and the main[12] access is by means of the gate within Morton's Tower.[13] The palace is not open to the public as of right, but as part of the millennial celebrations in 2000 special arrangements were very successfully made whereby about 85,000 visitors were, in conducted groups, shown part of the property.

14.9.2   Members of the public may now see part of the property when attending charitable events held within the palace,[14] or when participating in tours of the main palace building and the grounds. At present, these tours take place twice a week.

Maintenance costs

14.10   As stated in the previous chapter,[15] the Commissioners'
expenditure in respect of the buildings and the grounds in the years
which ended on 31 December 2000 and 31 December 2001 was as
follows:

	2000 £	2001 £
Heating and lighting	45,000	41,000
Maintenance and repairs	203,000	232,000
Council tax and water charges	19,000	23,000
Insurance (excluding items covered under the Commissioners' block policy)	18,000	11,000
Gardeners' and domestic staff pay and pension contributions	222,000	242,000
Garden costs	10,000	13,000
Other costs	4,000	21,000
Depreciation	3,000	4,000
Miscellaneous costs/(credits)	(16,000)	7,000
	£508,000	£594,000
Rents and service charges receivable	£(16,000)	£(8,000)
Capital expenditure	313,000 [16]	104,000
Capital receipt		(50,000)
Net capital expenditure	£313,000	£54,000

Maintenance and repairs

14.11.1 The maintenance and repairs of the fabric, as well as any
structural alterations or additions, are superintended by the
Commissioners' agent.[17]

14.11.2 The Commissioners discharge all the maintenance and
repairing obligations to which they are subject by virtue of the heritage
nature of the property.[18] All essential work is carried out at the expense
of the Commissioners.

14.11.3 There is a small[19] maintenance staff employed within the
palace, and we make no recommendation for that arrangement to be
changed.

14.11.4 The first quinquennial inspection has not yet been carried out.

14.12 From time to time, certain capital improvements are effected at the expense of the Commissioners.[20] In addition, further improvements have been carried out with the aid of funds donated by third parties.[21] These have either been of a decorative nature, or of a nature which is very beneficial to succeeding users of the property albeit not essential. In both categories, expenditure of Commissioners' funds was not thought appropriate in current financial circumstances.

Capital and rental values

14.13.1 Lambeth Palace is carried in the books of the Commissioners at £1.[22]

14.13.2 We have not commissioned a valuation of the property,[23] but we have proceeded on the assumption that it has a value of not less than £10 million.

14.14 If the value is taken as being £10 million, the rental equivalent value of the property would approach £1 million p.a. The parts of the building used as conference rooms, state rooms and offices have a rental value of about £372,500, but this is only about one-third of the annual cost which would be incurred in providing alternative accommodation in a purpose-built modern building in the area.

Retention or disposal?

14.15 In difficult (financial) circumstances, hard questions have to be asked. The fundamental one is whether the Commissioners should:

> a. retain Lambeth Palace and continue to put it to, broadly, its existing use; or
>
> b. retain the property as an investment, providing alternative accommodation for the Archbishop and his staff; or
>
> c. dispose of the property, likewise providing alternative accommodation for the Archbishop and his staff.

14.16.1 We have approached this question by considering first whether the Archbishop would be given more effective support if his staff were to be relocated to other premises such as Church House[24] and, to put the matter at the extreme, for the Archbishop himself to have his own working accommodation in the same building.

14.16.2 There would, no doubt, be some economies of scale, such as the ability to use common reception and communications facilities.

14.16.3 There would also be greater opportunity for interchange between members of the Archbishop's staff and those employed[25] by the Archbishops' Council. Even if there is not in fact any overlap in staff posts,[26] co-location of staff would help to remove the *perception* of overlap.

14.17.1 Such a move would draw the Archbishop closer to the central structure of the remainder of the Church of England, and it would alter the balance to which we have referred earlier[27] which the Archbishop needs to maintain between his roles in relation to the Church of England on the one hand and those in relation to the Anglican Communion generally on the other hand.

14.17.2 Furthermore, wherever his main working base, the Archbishop will need to be able to provide official hospitality on various scales. The diversity of the Archbishop's ministry is illustrated by the different activities which take place within the palace.[28] For so long as the Commissioners continue to own the property, we consider that the Archbishop should continue to provide hospitality in it.

14.18.1 There could be an intermediate position, in which the Archbishop and a small personal staff continued to work at Lambeth Palace, and the remainder of his staff elsewhere.

14.18.2 We reject that approach. We have no doubt that the Chief of Staff[29] should work in close proximity with the Archbishop; and that the Chief of Staff should work in the same place as those whom he is to manage.

14.19 On balance, we have concluded that the Archbishop is likely to be better served and supported if he and his staff continue to be based at Lambeth Palace. We could not, therefore, recommend a change from the present position on *non-financial* grounds.

14.20.1 We have, however, considered the position from a financial viewpoint.

14.20.2 We have shown[30] that partly because of the nature and size of the property, it has a significant infrastructure staff, although by no means all of the cost of those posts would be saved if the Archbishop lived and worked elsewhere.[31]

14.20.3 We have also shown[32] that, even without taking into account premises expenses attributable to the Lambeth Palace Library, and without taking into account capital expenditure, the recurrent premises expenses are in the region of £500,000 p.a. However, likewise, by no means all of those expenses would be saved if the Archbishop lived and worked elsewhere.[33]

14.21.1 The major unknown factor is the size of the Archbishop's staff (excluding infrastructure staff) after (a) the Chief of Staff has carried out his review[34] and (b) value audits have been carried out as part of the process of bidding for funds.[35]

14.21.2 We understand that the rental value of office accommodation in the area of Lambeth Palace is only about a quarter of the rental value of accommodation in, say, Church House. Accordingly, if, *solely for the purpose of comparison and without making any prediction as to the future size of the Archbishop's staff*, it is assumed that the non-infrastructure staff remains at its present level, it is far cheaper for the Church as a whole to continue to use Lambeth Palace for the Archbishop's staff and let the equivalent space in Church House.

14.22 Our views with regard to the retention or otherwise of Lambeth Palace are influenced by our assessment that if the palace is retained then there are realistic prospects of generating from it sufficient income to meet its running costs. By these we mean the costs of infrastructure staff and premises expenses, other than those which are personal to the Archbishop.[36]

14.23.1 We conclude that the Commissioners should retain the property. We **recommend** a strategy by which the property would continue to contain the London home and office of the Archbishop and the offices for his personal staff, but which would also involve:

    a.   providing improved residential accommodation for the Archbishop;

    b.   providing improved working accommodation for some members of staff;

c. increasing significantly the net income generated from the property, so that, at the minimum, that income would cover all recurrent outgoings; and

d. as part of income generation measures, realizing some of the development value inherent in the property.

14.23.2 This strategy would accord with our general approach[37] that the palace as a whole should not be regarded as the home of the Archbishop, but the place *in which* he has his home.

Ownership structure

14.24 Before examining the elements of this strategy, we consider the future ownership and tenure of the palace. We consider that the arrangements:

a. should involve the Commissioners only to the minimum extent requisite;

b. should fully protect the Archbishop and support his ministry; and

c. consistently with those considerations, should encourage income generation from the property.

14.25 We propose arrangements similar to, but not in all respects identical with, those adopted by the Commissioners in relation to Auckland Castle, the heritage property which is the see house of the Bishop of Durham.

14.26 We **recommend** that arrangements which we have described in Chapter 6 should be brought into effect at Lambeth Palace.[38]

14.27. We envisage that when these arrangements were fully in force:

14.27.1 The Commissioners' main roles in relation to the property would be:

a. from time to time to satisfy themselves that the property was being kept in good repair and condition;

b. to consider any requests which were made by the charitable company for permission to make alterations to the fabric of the building or to effect improvements; and

c.   to pursue any capital improvement projects which they themselves wished to initiate and fund;

14.27.2 All repairing and maintenance costs would be met by the charitable company; and

14.27.3 Any surplus would be available for the other objects of the company.

14.28 The lease would also provide that in the event of any substantial failure on the part of the company to meet its obligations the arrangements would be brought to an end.

The Archbishop's residence

14.29.1 In the light of these proposals with regard to the property, we turn now to specific aspects of the strategy which we have recommended.[39] The first relates to the private residential accommodation provided for the Archbishop.

14.29.2 The Archbishop's flat[40] is in the main palace building. Its area is sufficient, but the flat is by no means grand, and the internal configuration is poor. The demarcation between the flat and the remainder of the building is insufficiently distinct. Many of the fittings fall far short of modern standards. Access to the flat is by means of the central entrance to the main building and through the principal hall and reception area of the main building. In this respect it lacks privacy, a factor which would become more acute in the event of a substantial increase in the use of that part of the palace.[41]

14.29.3 Dr and Mrs Carey – whose aspirations for themselves have been, if we may say so, modest – regard the arrangements as satisfactory. They have found neither this lack of privacy nor the fact that they live directly 'over the shop' disturbing. But we have serious doubts about its suitability. In any event, it is clear that the arrangements would not be suitable for an Archbishop with children of school age.

14.29.4 We are convinced that the Archbishop should live within the palace complex, and we are also convinced that the chapels should, as they are at present, be in constant use. We are not convinced that the Archbishop's flat should necessarily be in the main palace building, and it might be preferable for a self-contained house to be provided for him within the curtilage. We **recommend** that the private residential accommodation which is provided for the Archbishop should be self-contained and have its own private access. Issues relating to obtaining planning permission are considered later in this chapter.[42]

14.29.5 In the shorter term we **recommend** urgent works to improve the quality of the present flat (or the formation of a flat for the Archbishop on the top floor of the main building).

Lambeth Palace as a place in which to work

14.30.1 The Archbishop and the Bishop at Lambeth have good studies, well suited both as rooms in which to work and rooms in which to receive visitors. One or two other senior members of staff also have comfortable offices.

14.30.2 In general, however, the working accommodation within the palace is less than ideal, although none of the members of the Archbishop's staff to whom we spoke complained about it. It is easy for those on the lower ground floor to feel second class; it is unfortunate that until recently some have had to work away from the main building in the cottages; and generally the configuration of the rooms and the inflexibility does not encourage the face to face communication which is now the norm in many other working environments.

14.30.3 These disadvantages in the rooms for working purposes will become more pronounced as working conditions in other places generally continue to improve.

14.30.4 Much of the working accommodation is inefficient. We would like to see the offices brought up to modern standards, but that might only be possible in the event of a major redevelopment. We **recommend** that if any larger-scale development does in fact take place,[43] then it should make provision for offices which meet modern criteria.

Income generation

14.31.1 On the Archbishop's staff is an Events Administrator who deals with events which are held in the palace or its grounds, but there is no member of the Archbishop's staff who is specifically charged with generating income from the palace (while doing so in ways which are consistent with its use by the Archbishop and his staff). We **recommend** that there should be.

14.31.2 We have also recommended[44] that the Commissioners' agent (while remaining a member of the Commissioners' staff) should also become a member of the Archbishop's staff and should thereby be more readily able to contribute to such a policy.

14.31.3 More generally we **recommend** that there should be adopted the clear policy that activities should be conducted at Lambeth Palace which would maximize the income to be derived from the property, consistent with its use as a place of residence for the Archbishop and his immediate family, and as a place of work for the Archbishop and his staff.

14.31.4 By contrast with the other archiepiscopal palaces, there is no issue at Lambeth Palace of under-utilization of space. However, there are issues about the most effective (and cost-effective) use of space, particularly that used by the Lambeth Palace Library. These issues would need to be examined in the context of the income generation policy.

14.31.5 In relation to income generation, there are to be considered:

    a.   residential lettings;

    b.   *ad hoc* other hourly or daily lettings; and

    c.   more widespread, but sympathetic, commercial use.

14.31.6 We consider the realization of development value separately.[45]

Residential lettings

14.32 Some of the cottages and the flats in the Lollard Tower are let. In several respects the position is unsatisfactory. The first respect is the letting policy.

14.33 The following is a summary of these parts of the property and of their occupancies:

Property	Occupier	Use and Basis of Occupation	Remarks
Cottages			
No 1	Gatekeeper	Free of rent or service charge	
No 2	Archbishop's Assistant Officer for Ecumenism and the Anglican Communion	Free of rent or service charge	
No 3	Archbishop's Officer for the Anglican Communion	Free of rent or service charge	
No 4	Various	Offices (and so free of rent or service charge)	These offices are likely to be vacated in the near future
No 5	The Sisters of Religion[46]	Free of rent or service charge	
No 6	A Church Estates Commissioner	Let at a rent	Informal letting by exchange of letters
No 7	Archbishop's Chaplain	Free of rent or service charge	
No 8	Archbishop's Driver	Free of rent or service charge	
Gardener's House	Resident Gardener	Free of rent or service charge	A deduction is made from the Gardener's salary in lieu of the payment of rent or service charge
Lollard's Tower			
Caretaker's Lodge	Staff luncheon room		
Langton Flat	The Steward	Free of rent and service charge	
Chichele Flat	St Thomas' Hospital	Let at a rent and service charge	Yearly tenancy
Laud Flat	Gatekeeper	Free of rent or service charge	Commences October 2002
Matthew Parker Flat	The Archbishop of York	Free of rent or service charge	Used by the Archbishop when at Lambeth Palace
Juxon Flat	Librarian	Free of rent or service charge	A deduction is made from the Librarian's salary in lieu of payment of rent and service charge

14.34.1 We **recommend** that, in general, the cottages and the flats in the Lollard Tower should be let on commercial terms. We would prefer to see these lettings on at least medium (rather than short[47]) leases so that there is some continuity of community within the palace.

14.34.2 To this general approach, there are three exceptions. First, one or two members of the staff may need to reside on the premises for the proper performance of their duties. Examples are the steward and (unless all security arrangements were to be outsourced) the principal gatekeeper.

14.34.3 Secondly, it has been the practice for two sisters of religion to serve at the palace. They are not remunerated, but are accommodated in one of the cottages. We **recommend** that that should continue.

14.34.4 Thirdly, and more generally, we have in mind that the palace is a large building, and that from time to time the Archbishop may be away leaving his wife in the property. We would wish to see that there is at least a small number of persons living on the property – they could be tenants of flats paying a market rent – for the Archbishop's wife not to feel uncomfortably isolated.

14.35.1 We are also concerned with effective use of space. A small flat in the Lollard Tower is kept available for the use of the Archbishop of York when in London. The present Archbishop of York stays in that flat for about 20 nights a year.

14.35.2 We favour the provision of accommodation for use by the Archbishop of York when in London, partly for his own convenience and partly to encourage contact with the Archbishop of Canterbury. We **recommend**, however, that a small flat (one bedroom, sitting room and kitchen(ette)) or official guest suite should be kept available for priority use by the Archbishop of York, but, when not used by him, should be available for use by other bishops or visitors when in London.

14.36 The general observations which we made in a previous chapter[48] about the use of official guest bedrooms apply to those at Lambeth Palace.

14.37.1 Apart from those issues relating to the use of the flats, cottages and official guest bedrooms, there are other aspects of the present letting arrangements which we regard as unsatisfactory.

14.37.2 In the first place, we are not satisfied that where there are lettings, the amounts of the rent (or salary reductions) and service charge arrangements are on full commercial terms. We **recommend** that:

> a.   whether or not this is done at the present time, the amounts of all rents or salary reductions, and service charge contributions, should be reviewed at least annually;
>
> b.   in the case of salary reduction arrangements, the amount of the reduction should be reflected in management accounts, so that the true economic cost of the activity can be determined; and
>
> c.   likewise, the notional rent which could be obtained from flats which are occupied by members of staff who are clergy should also be reflected in management accounts for the same reason.

14.37.3 The other unsatisfactory aspect of the letting arrangements is that, so far as we have been able to ascertain, with few exceptions there are no written agreements governing the use and occupation of the flats or cottages. We **recommend** that there should be written agreements in all cases.[49]

Day and evening events

14.38.1 The Archbishop welcomes Church bodies and other charities, usually those with which he has some connection, to hold events within the palace, or its grounds. During 2001 35 such events were held.

14.38.2 For charities which hold events within the palace, the maximum fee is £450 when the event takes place within the palace building and £500 when it is in the grounds. However, in many instances the Archbishop waives the fee. Enquiries which we have made in respect of professionally managed venues of similar standing show that hirings on commercial terms would attract fees of several multiples of these figures.

14.38.3 We **recommend** that determined steps should be taken to increase materially the income from such hirings, while at the same time giving preferential rates to charities or other similar bodies with which the Archbishop has a connection.

A conference centre?

14.39.1 It would, in principle, be possible to extend further the concurrent use of the palace for other purposes, such as that of a conference centre or as a place for the provision of commercial hospitality.

14.39.2 Various consents would be required, but in outline it seems possible for the palace to be used for such purposes while:

> a. enabling the Archbishop and others who need to do so to live in the palace;[50]
>
> b. for all those who currently work within the palace to continue to do so;
>
> c. for the state rooms to be available for the Archbishop and others within the Church for about 40% of the year; and
>
> d. for the necessary upgrading of the catering facilities to be carried out at the cost of a commercial partner.

14.39.3 There can be no certainty with almost any commercial enterprise, but the initial indications which we have had suggest that within a period of less than five years, and without significant capital outlay, the income from such an activity could be built up so that it was sufficient to meet all recurrent premises expenses and infrastructure staff costs.

14.40.1 Such an activity would be bound to have some effect on the ethos of the palace, and it seems to us that the success or otherwise of such a move would depend largely on the extent to which that change is controlled and restrained. We think that it is possible to achieve a proper balance.

14.40.2 We **recommend** that:

> a. a detailed appraisal of such a project should be carried out; and
>
> b. subject to the results of that appraisal, increased use of this nature should take place on a step-by-step basis.

Catering facilities

14.42.1 At present, some of the meeting rooms are not used to their maximum potential because of the very limited catering facilities.[51] Increased use of the palace (whether or not as a conference centre) would require enhanced catering facilities and an increase in the catering staff.

14.42.2 We **recommend** that that should be considered as part of the appraisal which we have recommended[52] and that in the meantime there should be no changes to the existing arrangements.

Garden

14.43 Materially increased use of the palace would affect the garden. It is common for gardening services to be outsourced, but we **recommend** that gardening should also be included within the appraisal[53] and that in the meantime there should be no changes to the existing arrangements.

The Lambeth Palace Library

14.44 We consider in a later chapter[54] the part of the property which is used by the Lambeth Palace Library.

Development value

14.45.1 Lambeth Palace and its grounds are not covered by any specific land use zoning, so that it is presumed for the purposes of town and country planning that the existing uses will continue. The main palace building is Grade I listed and some of the boundary walls are Grade II listed. The whole site lies within a conservation area, and is within an archaeological priority area. The palace grounds are an important ecological site. Furthermore, there is a planning policy[55] to protect local views around buildings of metropolitan importance, of which the palace is identified as one.

14.45.2 These facts mean that it would be very difficult to obtain the required consents for material alterations or additions to the existing buildings, or for the construction of new buildings within the grounds. Nevertheless, it is not totally impossible to envisage that consents might be forthcoming if a careful strategy is formulated and followed to obtain them.

14.45.3 Planning permission and other consents are far more likely to be obtained if they are sought as part of a wider agreement made with the local planning authority. For this reason we **recommend** that whatever arrangements are made to deal with the property aspects of Lambeth Palace should also deal with adjoining or adjacent land in the

Commissioners' ownership, although such land does not form part of the palace.

14.46.1 We have referred to the possibility of providing a house for the Archbishop in the grounds;[56] to the possibility of providing improved working accommodation;[57] and to the possible concurrent use as a conference centre.[58] There is a further possible type of development which we **recommend** should be considered.

14.46.2 Physically there could be some development within the grounds, away from the main palace building, without impairing the amenity. Although in a narrow sense this would not affect Lambeth Palace as a resource for the Archbishop, we would find it attractive for a small number of residential units to be built in the grounds which could be used to provide subsidized housing for clergy and others whose work requires them to be resident in Central London, but for whom the cost of private sector accommodation is prohibitive.

Concluding observations

14.47　In some respects Lambeth Palace is an under-utilized resource for the Church of England as a whole. In considering its future use, we are sensitive to the need to give the very greatest weight indeed to the proper needs of the Archbishop, his family and his personal staff. We are also sensitive to the economic circumstances in which the Church of England is placed. We believe that, in the ways which we have described in this chapter, it is possible to reconcile the two – and that it would be a dereliction not to try to do so.

chapter 15

The Diocese of Canterbury and the Old Palace, Canterbury

Introduction

15.1.1   The Archbishop of Canterbury is the diocesan bishop of the Diocese of Canterbury, although most of the duties of that office are performed by the Bishop of Dover. The see house with which the Archbishop is provided in this capacity is the Old Palace at Canterbury.

15.1.2   In this chapter we consider the present position with regard to the Old Palace; present and prospective use; and, so far as it is relevant for resourcing purposes, the relationship between the Archbishop and the Bishop of Dover.

The Old Palace: the property

15.2   The original building which was on the present site of the Old Palace was used by Archbishops of Canterbury from about 1070 until it was ruined in the 1650s. The present building, which incorporates comparatively small parts of the original building, was completed in 1902 and has been the house for Archbishops of Canterbury and so the see house for the diocesan bishop of Canterbury since then.

15.3.1   What may loosely be described as the Church of England precinct at Canterbury comprises the Cathedral; various houses in the close, including the Deanery and the International Study Centre[1]; King's School, Canterbury; and the Old Palace.

15.3.2   The Old Palace is situated on the western side of the precinct. It has a gateway to Palace Street, but access is generally through the grounds of the Cathedral.

15.4.1   The Old Palace site has a surface area of approximately three quarters of an acre (0.3 of a hectare).

15.4.2   The building comprises:

a.   various rooms for the private use of the Archbishop;

b.   a study for the Archbishop;

c.   accommodation at the top of the building currently used by the steward;

d.   a 'state' or large room which, together with a spacious hall, is suitable for receptions, dinners and meetings. There is an appropriately sized kitchen to serve these rooms;

e.   a chapel, together with a vestry, which is also used by the Archbishop's Chaplain for interviews;

f.   five bedrooms which are available for official guests (in addition to the bedrooms in the Archbishop's private accommodation);

g.   an office which is shared by the Archbishop's Canterbury Chaplain and his Canterbury Private Secretary;

h.   in a wing of the building which has its own entrance, three ground floor rooms which are used by the Bishop of Dover as the working accommodation for himself and his staff;

i.   two flats above the Bishop of Dover's offices, which are let;

j.   an area, known as 'Theodore', comprising a large room, a smaller room, a kitchen and a lavatory, which is let to the Dean and Chapter at a nominal rent and which had been sub-let by the Dean and Chapter to the King's School, also at a nominal rent; and

k.   a minute flat which accommodates the Archbishop's driver when he needs to be at the property overnight.

15.4.3   The rooms provided for the private use of the Archbishop do not comprise a flat. They are disjointed and have no integral kitchen. The rooms do not in any way form a unit which is physically self-contained.

15.4.4   Within the site there is a small garden which is available for use by the Archbishop, the steward, and their guests. It is maintained by a part-time gardener.

15.4.5   The building is listed Grade I. It is a Scheduled Ancient Monument in both a world heritage site and a conservation area.

Ownership

15.5.1 The Commissioners own the property.

15.5.2 The Old Palace was originally owned by the Dean and Chapter and was sold by them in 1900 to the Archbishop (in his corporate capacity). At the time of the sale it was envisaged that, should at any time the property not be required by the Archbishop for use as a residence, the Dean and Chapter would be able to repurchase it. We regard the arrangement as imposing an obligation[2] on the Commissioners to offer to re-sell the property should it no longer be required for its intended purpose.

15.6 The Bishop of Dover lives elsewhere in a house owned and provided for him by the Canterbury Diocesan Board of Finance.

15.7 The internal configuration of the Old Palace is awkward. Apart from the offices used by the Bishop of Dover and the flats above them, the various parts of the building are intertwined. As noted, the rooms used by the Archbishop do not include a kitchen and afford no real privacy. The steward's accommodation has almost no privacy at all.

The Old Palace: its use

15.8.1 It has been the practice of the Archbishop to be in the Old Palace for Christmas and Easter in each year, and at various other times, particularly at weekends,[3] during the year.

15.8.2 During 2001 Dr Carey was in the Old Palace for all or part of 55 days. We understand that he spent rather more time at Canterbury at the beginning of his archiepiscopate than towards the end, and that this pattern was mirrored by Archbishop Runcie.

15.9.1 Except for senior staff meetings, the state rooms are normally used only when the Archbishop is in residence. During 2001 the state rooms were used on:

> a.   10 occasions for the provision by the Archbishop of official hospitality;
>
> b.   19 occasions for diocesan and senior staff meetings; and
>
> c.   a small number of occasions for other purposes, particularly Ordination retreats.

15.9.2   Usually, the state rooms are not used by the Bishop of Dover.[4]

15.10.1   We understand that, although there are exceptions, in an average year the guest bedrooms are only fully occupied during Ordination Retreats. In 2000 and 2001 these have taken place twice a year and involve the occupation of the bedrooms for three nights on each occasion.

15.10.2   We also understand that as a result of a recent increase in the number of ordination candidates, not all of the candidates can now be accommodated within the Old Palace for these retreats. The candidates are unenthusiastic about sharing rooms whilst on retreat.

15.10.3   When the rooms are being fully used, the hot water system is barely adequate.

15.11   The chapel is well-appointed, but is in general used only when the Archbishop is in residence. It is not normally used by the Bishop of Dover or by members of his staff.

The Old Palace: status

15.12   The Old Palace is provided by the Commissioners for the Archbishop as the see house of the Diocese of Canterbury. We understand that at present the Commissioners do not have power to provide residential accommodation in Canterbury for the Archbishop in any other capacity.

The Old Palace: value

15.13.1   The Old Palace is reflected by the Commissioners in their statutory accounts at a value of £1.[5]

15.13.2   We have not commissioned a valuation.[6] However, we have assumed that if it were offered for sale on the open market and were not subject to the option to which we have referred,[7] then having regard to the constraints of the site and the cost of repair and maintenance it would fetch somewhat in excess of £2 million.

15.13.3   We refer to maintenance costs later.[8]

The Archbishop's staff at Canterbury

15.14.1   The Archbishop's staff at the Old Palace comprises:

    a.   his Canterbury Chaplain;

b.   his Canterbury Private Secretary; and

c.   the steward.

15.14.2 At the present time, the Commissioners' agent for Lambeth Palace[9] also acts as the agent for the Old Palace.

15.15.1 The Canterbury Chaplain works part-time for the Archbishop. He is the line manager of the Archbishop's Private Secretary, and when required provides her with immediate guidance.

15.15.2 There is no doubt that the Archbishop has found it very helpful to have the assistance of his Canterbury Chaplain, particularly in relation to often heavy programmes for visits to the diocese. We have concluded, however, that it might well be possible to provide chaplaincy support for the Archbishop in other ways, by, for example, arranging for the functions to be performed by other clergy in the diocese, including the Bishop of Dover's chaplain. We **recommend**, therefore, that very serious consideration should be given to making the post of the Archbishop's Canterbury Chaplain redundant.

15.16.1 Within the Old Palace, there are two separate working offices, namely those of the Archbishop and those of the Bishop of Dover.

15.16.2 The business conducted in the Archbishop's office includes matters relating to the diocese, but is much wider. Some of the business is confidential. Much of the incoming post and electronic traffic[10] which relates to the diocese is referred to the Bishop of Dover's office.

15.16.3 We suggest later in this chapter possible revised arrangements.[11]

15.17 We have referred[12] to the arrangements for the accommodation of the steward. During the archiepiscopate of Dr Carey, this position has just about been tenable because the steward has been Dr and Mrs Carey's daughter. Had it not been for that close family relationship, the arrangements would be totally unsatisfactory; and cannot be expected to continue into other archiepiscopates.[13]

Operational costs at Canterbury

15.18 The recurrent costs, rounded, met by the Commissioners in support of the Archbishop at Canterbury for the years 2000 and 2001, under the headings which we proposed in our First Report,[14] are as set out in the following table.[15] The figures:

a. exclude the costs of the Bishop of Dover's offices; and

b. reflect the net rental income derived from the two flats.

Description	2000 £	2001 £	Notes
A. Office and Support Staff Costs			
Stipend, pension contributions and employers' National Insurance contributions in respect of the Archbishop of Canterbury's Chaplain	10,000	11,000	(a)
Salary, pension contributions and employers' National Insurance contributions of the Archbishop of Canterbury's Private Secretary	20,000	21,000	
Office expenses	2,000	2,000	
Total A	32,000	34,000	
B. Administrative and Operational Costs			
Ordination expenses	nil	1,000	
Legal fees	16,000	17,000	
Total B	16,000	18,000	
C. Individual Working Costs			
Travel	1,000	1,000	
Official hospitality	8,000	11,000	
Total C	9,000	12,000	
D. Premises Expenses: Recurrent			
Heating and lighting	2,000	3,000	
Maintenance and repairs of premises and equipment (including maintenance contracts)	15,000	7,000	
Council tax and water charges	1,000	1,000	
Insurance	nil	nil	(b)
Steward's, deputy steward's and gardener's pay and pension contributions	27,000	29,000	(c)
Minor household and garden items	1,000	1,000	

Description	2000 £	2001 £	Notes
Depreciation	nil	nil	
Furnishings and equipment	1,000	nil	
Total D	47,000	41,000	
E. Premises Income: Recurrent			
Rents receivable	(9,000)	(9,000)	
Total E	(9,000)	(9,000)	
F. Premises Expenditure: Capital	nil	nil	
Total F	nil	nil	
G. Summary			
A. Office and Support Staff Costs	32,000	34,000	
B. Administrative and Operational Costs	16,000	18,000	
C. Individual Working Costs	9,000	12,000	
D. Premises Expenditure: Recurrent	47,000	41,000	
E. Premises Income: Recurrent	(9,000)	(9,000)	
F. Premises Expenditure: Capital	nil	nil	
TOTAL	£95,000	£96,000	

Notes:
(a) one-half of full time post.
(b) premises covered by the Commissioners' block policy.
(c) the posts of deputy steward and gardener are part-time.

15.19   The premises expenses for the years 1995 to 1999 are as follows:

	1995 £	1996 £	1997 £	1998 £	1999 £
Expenditure: Recurrent					
Heating and lighting	7,000	9,000	8,000	9,000	9,000
Maintenance, repairs and decorating	38,000	30,000	25,000	33,000	41,000
Steward's, deputy steward's and gardener's pay, pension contributions and employer's National Insurance contributions	26,000	23,000	23,000	29,000	29,000
Council tax, water charges and other recurrent running expenses	6,000	3,000	4,000	1,000	1,000
Furnishing, equipment	1,000	2,000	1,000	3,000	nil
Minor household and garden expenses	nil	1,000	1,000	nil	nil
Totals	£78,000	£68,000	£62,000	£75,000	£80,000
Income					
Rents receivable	£(5,000)	£(5,000)	£(4,000)	£(6,000)	£(12,000)
Capital expenditure	nil	£4,000	£24,000	£22,000	£25,000

The Archbishop and the Bishop of Dover

15.20.1   The Archbishop is, *de iure*, the diocesan bishop of the Diocese of Canterbury.

15.20.2   Progressively most of the responsibilities have been entrusted to the Bishop of Dover. When Bishop Richard Llewellin was consecrated as Bishop of Dover, Dr Carey conferred on him the title of Bishop in Canterbury. This was an honorary title, which had no legal significance. A similar title was conferred on Bishop Llewellin's successor, Bishop Stephen Venner. Bishop Venner understandably uses the title widely,[16] although in this report, for clarity, we use his formal title of Bishop of Dover.

15.20.3 Dr Carey delegated, by revocable Instrument of Delegation, his legal powers as diocesan bishop first to Bishop Llewellin and subsequently to Bishop Venner. A copy of the Instrument of Delegation to Bishop Venner is set out at Appendix D. The delegation relates only to diocesan functions and expressly excludes metropolitical functions. The Hurd Report recommended [17] that this should be taken a stage further, so that the delegation should be permanent, albeit reversible. We have proceeded on the assumption that there will continue to be a delegation of diocesan powers: whether that delegation is, as at present, by separate instrument, or in the more permanent form suggested in the Hurd Report, does not in itself have resourcing implications.

15.21.1 The Bishop of Dover is resourced in a hybrid manner.

15.21.2 As a *de iure* suffragan bishop, he lives in a house owned and provided by the Diocesan Board of Finance. This is the usual arrangement for a suffragan bishop.

15.21.3 The Bishop of Dover does not himself have a suffragan.

15.21.4 However:

a.   the Bishop of Dover receives a stipend at the rate applicable to a diocesan bishop;[18] and

b.   the Commissioners fund the provision for the Bishop of Dover of a chaplain [19] (whereas generally they do not fund the provision of a chaplain for a suffragan bishop [20]).

15.21.4 Furthermore, the Bishop of Dover is *ex officio* (but without voting rights) a member of the House of Bishops [21] of the General Synod.

15.22.1 Dr Carey's presidency at, or participation in, services in the Cathedral are much valued, and in acting in this way he is often performing both the role of archbishop, and so a spiritual leader of the nation, and that of the diocesan bishop. He has also conducted regular teaching missions within the diocese, made pastoral visits to diocesan clergy, and chaired some senior staff meetings. Broadly, it can be said that Dr Carey has an active role within the diocese, but that all the functions which require the exercise of legal powers are discharged by the Bishop of Dover.

15.22.2 Such an arrangement has the inherent potential for confusion. The confusion is not with regard to the extent of the delegation of legal powers – that is clear from the terms of the instrument of delegation – but with regard to the scope of pastoral and practical activities which fall outside the scope of a formal instrument of delegation.

15.23.1 The relationship between the Archbishop and the Bishop of Dover will no doubt continue to evolve. It may be that it will continue much along the present lines. It may be, at the furthest extreme, that as some have suggested in due course the Bishop of Dover will become legally and for all other purposes the diocesan bishop of the Diocese of Canterbury.

15.23.2 The essential requirement is for clarity in the relationship between the Archbishop and the Bishop of Dover and so of the expectations which the Church and the community have of each of them in relation to the diocese. Whatever the understanding between the Archbishop and the Bishop of Dover, it should be recorded. Fundamentally, the issue is whether the Archbishop should continue in some real and not merely formal sense to be the diocesan bishop of the diocese, or whether, following the model of the Presiding Bishop of the Episcopal Church of the United States of America, he should no longer have diocesan responsibilities. The Hurd Report recommended [22] the former. To depart from it would involve a very major change in ecclesiology which should certainly not be determined by resourcing considerations.

15.23.3 It is also to be kept in mind that a real involvement in the diocese constitutes a support *for* the Archbishop.

The Archbishop of Canterbury

15.24.1 In whatever manner the relationship between the Archbishop and the Bishop of Dover develops, we have no doubt that the Archbishop should continue to have a base at Canterbury. There is a particular significance for the Church of England, for the nation and for the Anglican Communion as a whole, of the Cathedral at Canterbury and of the place of the Archbishop in it.

15.24.2 At the present time, in several respects the Old Palace represents a gross under-utilization of resource. We do not regard it as proper for the current arrangements to continue. However, provided that the changes which we propose are implemented, we have no doubt that the historical connection should be preserved and that the Archbishop's base in Canterbury should continue to be in the Old Palace.

Episcopal working offices

15.25.1 For so long as both the Archbishop and the Bishop of Dover have responsibilities and functions in relation to the Diocese of Canterbury, there is an axiomatic need for close coordination between them. It would be unfortunate, for example, if, as a consequence of uncoordinated planning, the Archbishop and the Bishop of Dover were both to visit the same part of the diocese at about the same time. Likewise, it would be unhelpful if both the Archbishop and the Bishop of Dover were to seek to give uncoordinated pastoral care to the same member of the clergy or laity.[23]

15.25.2 Furthermore, if the post of Archbishop's Canterbury Chaplain is made redundant, but the Archbishop continues to have a Private Secretary at Canterbury, he or she will need local guidance.

15.25.3 We therefore **recommend** that:

a.   the working offices of the Archbishop at Canterbury and those of the Bishop of Dover should be merged to provide a combined archiepiscopal and episcopal office;

b.   the Archbishop of Canterbury's Private Secretary should continue to be a member of the Archbishop's personal staff, but located in that combined office; and

c.   although the primary role of the Archbishop's Canterbury Private Secretary would be to deal with matters of particular concern to the Archbishop, he or she should also be available to assist with other work in the office.

15.25.4 We do not take the view that the fact of there being a combined episcopal office would blur the separate and distinctive roles of the Archbishop and the Bishop of Dover.

15.25.5 We have had no evidence that a combined office would save any secretarial staff post, but we consider that it would lead to greater operational efficiency. It would also assist in enabling the post of the Archbishop's Canterbury Chaplain to be made redundant.[24]

15.25.6 The Archbishop receives and sends many communications which are confidential and which often relate to his roles other than that of the *de iure* diocesan bishop. We have not seen (and have not asked to see) a sample of those communications, but we believe that satisfactory arrangements could be made within a combined office to preserve that confidentiality.[25]

Residence of the Bishop of Dover

15.26.1 Where should the Bishop of Dover live? As noted previously,[26] at present he does not live in the Old Palace, but elsewhere in a house provided by the Canterbury Diocesan Board of Finance. In the next section of this chapter we consider possible conversion works to the Old Palace: should they make provision for the Bishop of Dover as well as the Archbishop to reside in the Old Palace?

15.26.2 In our view such a step would involve a change in the balance between the Archbishop and the Bishop of Dover, and it could lead to some blurring in the perception of their separate roles. We therefore **recommend** that while this possibility should be kept in mind, the Bishop of Dover should only reside in the Old Palace if as a matter of policy (and not resourcing) that is thought appropriate.

Conversion of the building?

15.27.1 We understand from very preliminary work which the Commissioners' agent has done that it should be physically possible to convert the existing building so that it provides:

a.   a self-contained flat, together with a study, for the Archbishop;

b.   a second significant residence in a self-contained wing;

c.   as at present, the chapel;

d.   also as at present one or more state or official reception rooms;

e.   adequate offices for archiepiscopal and episcopal administration;

f.   a self-contained flat for the steward; and

g.   one or more flats available for letting.

15.27.2 The residence in the self-contained wing could be occupied by the Bishop of Dover, if that was thought appropriate, or it could be made available for letting.

15.27.3 It would clearly be necessary for both the Archbishop and, if he is to reside on the property, the Bishop of Dover to have available facilities for accommodating overnight official guests. In our view it should be left open to be decided at the detailed design stage what accommodation for overnight official guests should be provided.

15.27.4 A conversion of the building on these lines would involve the loss of all or most of the accommodation which is at present available for ordination candidates. However, particularly now that the International Study Centre, which has its own residential facilities, is open, we have little doubt that, with proper planning, ordination candidates could be accommodated within or near to the precincts of the Cathedral.

15.28 Because the Old Palace is a listed building, sensitive and, possibly, lengthy discussions with the local planning and other authorities would be required before such conversion works could take place, but we hope that the requirements of the authorities could be satisfied.

15.29.1 We have not attempted to cost the conversion works and, indeed, before the requirements of the planning authorities are known, there would be little point in doing so. However, as the broadest indication – it is nothing more – it might be that the cost of such a project would be of the order of £900,000 exclusive of VAT.

15.29.2 Were the Bishop of Dover to live in the property, the Canterbury DBF would be able to sell the house in which he at present resides, and we would hope that it would be willing to apply the proceeds of sale towards the cost of the conversion.

15.29.3 If the Bishop of Dover were not to live in the property, a further part would be available for letting, and part of the cost of conversion would be recoverable from the rental income.

15.30.1 We **recommend** that:

> a.   the Commissioners should carry out a detailed appraisal of a conversion programme on the lines to which we have referred in paragraph 15.27;

b. the appraisal should be on the alternative bases that the Bishop of Dover (i) would and (ii) would not reside in the property;

c. in the course of the appraisal the Commissioners should hold discussions with:

  i. the planning and heritage authorities;

  ii. the Dean and Chapter, in view of the option which relates to the property; and

  iii. in case the Bishop of Dover were to reside in the property, the Canterbury DBF;

d. the programme should be fully costed; and

e. the income which would be derived from the parts of the property available for letting should be carefully assessed.

15.30.2 We propose later in this chapter[27] that strategically the precinct should be considered as a whole. Accordingly, we **recommend** that the appraisal should also take account of other accommodation within the precinct so that the conversion programme would have regard to the wider needs.

15.30.3 In conjunction with the appraisal, the Commissioners would no doubt take account of the present restrictions on their legal powers to which we refer later.[28]

Other recommendations with regard to the building

15.31 We also **recommend** that the chapel should be brought into daily use. This would easily follow if the conversion resulted in the chapel being conveniently within a common area rather than one intended for the exclusive use of the Archbishop.

15.32.1 We further **recommend** that the state or official reception and meeting rooms should be available for use, in the following order of priority:

a. by the Archbishop; but when not required by him

b. by the Bishop of Dover; but when not required by him

c. by others within the Church, such as the Dean and Chapter of the Cathedral and diocesan officers.

15.32.2 So far as not required to meet those prior claims, the rooms should be available for daily letting to third parties on commercial terms, or, in the case of charities, on concessionary terms.

15.32.3 Such a scheme should not inhibit the use of these rooms by the Archbishop, because almost always the occasions on which he wishes to use them are known many months in advance.

The precinct as a whole

15.33.1 We understand that, at present, the Old Palace, the Cathedral and its properties (including the International Study Centre), and the King's School are not only separately owned but are also separately managed.

15.33.2 We recommend that the management of each part of the precinct should have regard to the other parts. We have recommended[29] that the Dean and Chapter should be among those who are able to have some use of the state rooms in the Old Palace. Conversely, when ordination candidates and other official visitors are to be received by the Archbishop (or the Bishop of Dover) it might well be possible for them to be satisfactorily accommodated elsewhere within the precinct.

The Commissioners' powers

15.34.1 At present, the Commissioners only have power to make the Old Palace available to the Archbishop as a see house.[30] It is the view of the Official Solicitor that they do not have power to make it available to the Archbishop in any other capacity; and to the extent that it is not used a see house, the Commissioners would be required, subject to the option, to treat the property as an investment.

15.34.2 We recommend that, perhaps as part of legislation promoted to deal with other recommendations in our First Report, the Commissioners should seek powers which would enable them to carry out whatever conversion programme ensued from the appraisal which we have proposed.[31]

Diocesan review of episcopal accommodation

15.35 In our First Report, we recommended,[32] among other things, that:

> a. there should by a review within each diocese of the living and working accommodation to be provided for bishops in the diocese;

b.   there should be the opportunity to exchange an existing see house for another; and

c.   the ownership of the see house (or any replacement see house) should ultimately be transferred to the Diocesan Board of Finance.

15.36   We repeat the recommendation for a review in relation to the Diocese of Canterbury. However, we do not consider that the Canterbury DBF should have the right to ask for the Old Palace to be exchanged for another property. Such a right would be inconsistent with the option and inappropriate if the conversion programme is carried out.

15.37   The Old Palace is, and will continue to be, unique, whether or not the conversion programme which we have proposed is carried out. In addition to the Commissioners, the Archbishop, the Bishop of Dover, the Dean and Chapter (as the holders of the option as well as the owners of other parts of the precinct and controllers of the main access to the property) and the Canterbury DBF (if it contributes to the cost of the conversion works) would all have legitimate interests.

Ownership of the Old Palace

15.38.1   We accordingly **recommend** that in due course:

a.   a separate trust should be established in respect of the property. All interested parties would be represented on that trust; and

b.   that trust should be responsible for the maintenance of the property and its use.

15.38.2   The trust would be on the lines which we indicated in Chapter 6, but without there being a trading arm.

chapter 16

The Archbishop of Canterbury and the Anglican Communion

Introduction

16.1   The Archbishop of Canterbury is the linchpin of the Anglican Communion. To be a member of the Anglican Communion a Church must be in communion with the see of Canterbury. Without the Archbishop of Canterbury the Communion would not exist.

16.2   Progressively, and particularly since the archiepiscopate of Archbishop Geoffrey Fisher (1945–1961), the involvement of the Archbishop in the Anglican Communion has increased. This increased involvement has happened without a clear overall strategy to guide the balance which the Archbishop is to maintain between on the one hand the affairs of the Church of England and on the other hand the affairs of the Anglican Communion generally.

16.3.1   This chapter is in two parts. The first part deals at some length with the nature and structure of the Anglican Communion and of its organizations; the Archbishop's relationship to them; and the financial context so far as the Church of England is concerned. The second part deals with the specific resourcing needs of the Archbishop in relation to the Anglican Communion and our recommendations with regard to them.

16.3.2   This chapter does not deal with the individual Churches, other than the Church of England, which are members of the Communion; and the recommendations relate only to those matters which affect the Church of England generally and the Archbishop in particular.

Terminology

16.4.1   It may be helpful at the outset to note two expressions which are used in relation to the Anglican Communion, namely:

    a. 'Provinces'; and

    b. 'Primates'.

16.4.2 The use of these expressions can cause confusion because both of them bear meanings within the Church of England which are different from those which they bear elsewhere in the Communion.

16.5 *'Provinces'*

16.5.1 By 'Province' is meant a group of three or more dioceses which can be regarded as comprising a Church in organizational terms and which have a common constitution. A Province can transcend linguistic, national or cultural boundaries, but the members have in common those elements of doctrine and practice which enable them to be united in a community of worship.[1]

16.5.2 The whole of the Church of England is considered to be a single Province in the context of the Communion, notwithstanding that for other purposes the Church of England comprises the separate Provinces of Canterbury and York.[2]

16.6 *'Member-Churches'*
We consider later[3] the concept of membership of the Anglican Communion, and show that the Communion is generally regarded as comprising Provinces and certain smaller Churches with are referred to as extra-Provincial bodies. Although the expression 'Member-Church' is not used for formal purposes in relation to the Communion, for convenience in this chapter we use the expression to denote each of those Provinces and extra-Provincial bodies which are members of the Communion.

16.7 *'Primates'*

16.7.1 Within the Communion the expression 'Primate' is used to denote the senior bishop of a Province irrespective of the title of his office within that Province. Within the Province he may indeed be known as the 'Primate', or by some variant such as 'Primus', or by some other title, such as 'Presiding Bishop'.[4]

16.7.2 For the purposes of the Communion, there can be only one Primate of a Province, irrespective of the titles or standing of the most senior bishops within the Province. Accordingly, although, as a matter of English law, both the Archbishop of Canterbury and the Archbishop of York are Primates, it is the Archbishop of Canterbury alone who is regarded within the Communion as the Primate in relation to the Church of England.

The Anglican Communion and its organizations

16.8.1 In considering the Anglican Communion, it is necessary to draw a distinction between:

    a.   the Communion itself and the Provinces or *Churches* which comprise it; and

    b.   the central *organizations* of the leaders or members of those Churches.

16.8.2 The organizations are:

    a.   the Anglican Consultative Council;

    b.   the Lambeth Conference; and

    c.   the Primates' Meeting.

The Anglican Communion

16.9.1 The Communion may be briefly described as a fellowship of self-governing Churches which share traditions born of history, theology and worship, and which are in communion with the see of Canterbury.

16.9.2 As will be seen,[5] the Anglican Communion does not have a constitution and, accordingly, no definitive marks of membership, but more fully it can be said that the Communion comprises the Churches:

    a.   which satisfy the fundamental conditions that:

        i.   they wish to belong to it;

        ii.   they are in communion with the see of Canterbury;[6] and

        iii.   they share or adhere to Anglican origins and traditions; and

    b.   they are recognized as belonging by:

        i.   having the right to appoint one or more members of the Anglican Consultative Council (or being represented on the Council through the Archbishop);[7]

        ii.   their bishops[8] being invited to the Lambeth Conference; and

iii.   their Primate being invited to the Primates' Meeting.[9]

16.9.3   The membership of the Anglican Communion is not closed. New Provinces can be formed out of existing Provinces; and further Churches can become Member-Churches by meeting the criteria.

Catholic and Reformed

16.10.1 The Member-Churches of the Anglican Communion have their roots in the life of the Church of England whose traditions are characteristically described as both 'Catholic' and 'Reformed'. By that is meant that the loyalty of the Church of England is both (a) to the universal, or 'catholic', tradition which stems from the Church of the Apostolic Age, and (b) to the insights of the Reformation. For these reasons, the Church of England has maintained its commitment to the threefold form of the Ordained Ministry, to the Apostolic and Nicene Creeds, and to the principal sacraments of Baptism and Holy Communion. Equally, it has emphasized the central authority of Scripture; the place of lay people in the ministry and governance of the Church; and the place of the continuing guidance of the Holy Spirit.

16.10.2 These commitments were articulated in the Thirty Nine Articles of Religion of 1562, and published as an appendix to subsequent editions of the Book of Common Prayer. The Articles remain a definitive description of what the Church of England understands by a tradition that is both Catholic and Reformed.[10]

Historical origins

16.11.1 The Member-Churches have a historical connection with the British Isles. They owe their specific Anglican identity to the expansion following the Reformation of the Church of England and other Episcopal Churches in Great Britain.

16.11.2 There were two phases of this expansion. The first phase started in the seventeenth century and accompanied the colonization in the United States, Australia, Canada, New Zealand and South Africa.

16.11.3 The second phase began in the eighteenth century, when missionaries from Great Britain and Ireland worked to establish churches in Asia, Africa and Latin America.

16.11.4 A few Member-Churches have no actual historical connection with Great Britain, but have chosen to adhere to these traditions.[11]

16.12   The Communion is 'Anglican' because of these shared traditions and these historical connections with the Church of England and the British Isles.

Theology

16.13.1 Member-Churches hold certain fundamental beliefs and practices in common, the basis of which are Scriptures, Creeds, Sacraments and the Historic Episcopate. There is also a common tradition of worship whose roots are in the Book of Common Prayer, but which has developed and been adapted in a variety of ways in the Member-Churches.

16.13.2 In 1888 four Articles (known as the 'Lambeth Chicago Quadrilateral') were approved by the Lambeth Conference as stating from the Anglican standpoint the essentials for a reunited church. These form a summary of the theological basis of Anglicanism. Their text is as follows:

A   'The Holy Scriptures of the Old and New Testaments, as "containing all things necessary to salvation", and as being the rule and ultimate standard of faith.'

B   'The Apostles' Creed, as the Baptismal Symbol; and the Nicene Creed, as the sufficient statement of the Christian Faith.'

C   'The two Sacraments ordained by Christ himself – Baptism and the Supper of the Lord – ministered with unfailing use of Christ's Words of Institution, and of the elements ordained by him.'

D   'The Historic Episcopate, locally adapted in the methods of its administration to the varying needs of the nations and peoples called by God into the Unity of his Church.'

Communion with the see of Canterbury

16.14.1 Each of the Member-Churches is said to be 'in full communion with the see of Canterbury'. However, this expression is used imprecisely and with different shades of meaning. We consider first the concept of communion with 'the see of Canterbury' and then the specific connotation of 'communion' in that context.

16.14.2 The expression communion with 'the see of Canterbury' imparts elements both of the official and the personal. In origin, the use of the expression appears to have been derived from acts of successive

Archbishops of Canterbury, in their corporate capacity, in recognizing the valid constitution of the Churches. In this respect the emphasis is on the official, or corporate, person of the Archbishop.

16.14.3 On the other hand, the expression also denotes sacramental fellowship with the Archbishop, with the implicit understanding that that fellowship is with a living person.

16.14.4 The former meaning, which denotes the corporate capacity, is the essence. That this is so is demonstrated by the position which pertains when there is an interregnum in the archbishopric of Canterbury. Even although there is no individual in office as Archbishop of Canterbury, the communion with the Archbishop in his corporate capacity continues. It follows that that communion continues without any further act of recognition or acknowledgement being required when a new Archbishop takes up office.

16.14.5 Communion with the 'see' of Canterbury does not refer to the Diocese of Canterbury. We have previously noted [12] that 'see' denotes office, and all the powers, rights and responsibilities which go with it. In the case of the Archbishop of Canterbury, these are much wider than the Diocese of Canterbury.

16.14.6 In our view the communion is one which is with the Archbishop of Canterbury in his corporate capacity, but which is personified by communion with the individual who is at any particular time the Archbishop.

16.15 However, in some parts of the Anglican Communion, although the same expression is used, the significance of the Archbishop, in both the corporate and personal senses, is diluted. In these circumstances, the expression has come to be used in the more general sense of asserting that a Member-Church has been properly and validly constituted and that it is in good standing within the Communion.

Communion

16.16.1 Churches can only be in full communion where the recognition of each other is mutual.

16.16.2 In general it can be said that the marks of full communion between two Churches are that:

a.   one Church recognizes the validity of the ordination of the ministers of the other, so that a minister of one Church can canonically officiate within the other;

b.   accordingly, sacraments offered by ministers of one Church are of the same nature and have the same significance as those offered by ministers of the other; and

c.   members of one Church are entitled without special permission to participate in the sacraments offered within the other.

16.17.1 There are, however, two major exceptions to this general statement. The first is that where a woman has been ordained as a bishop within one Member-Church, and another Member-Church does not recognize the ordination of women as bishops, then a woman ordained as a bishop in the first Church is not able to exercise public episcopal ministry within the second church. Furthermore, a man or a woman ordained by a woman bishop in the first Church would not be recognized in the second Church as being in valid priestly orders.

16.17.2 Secondly, even where there is no question as to the canonical validity of the ordination of a minister, he or she will need to satisfy any local legal requirements before officiating.[13]

'The Instruments of Unity'

16.18.1 It is said that the Communion has four 'instruments of unity', namely:

a.   the Archbishop of Canterbury; and

b.   three organs or organizations, namely:

i.   the Anglican Consultative Council;

ii.   the Lambeth Conference; and

iii.   the Primates' Meeting.

16.18.2 Before examining the role of the Archbishop in relation to the Communion, we consider these three organs, and then, in the light of them, the concept of membership of the Communion.

The Anglican Consultative Council

16.19.1 The Anglican Consultative Council is a legal entity which was established in 1969. It is an unincorporated association which is registered as a charity with the Charity Commission for England and Wales.

16.19.2 As will be seen,[14] the Council has a standing committee. The members of its standing committee are the trustees of the Council for the purposes of the Charities Acts. For convenience of asset holding, the members of the standing committee for the time being are incorporated.[15]

16.19.3 Consideration is currently being given to the incorporation of the Council as an English company limited by guarantee. It would also be registered as an English charity.

16.20 The objects of the Council are prescribed by its constitution. The objects which are stated[16] first are:

    a.   'to facilitate the cooperative work of the Member-Churches of the Anglican Communion'; and

    b.   'to share information about developments in one or more provinces of the Anglican Communion with the other parts of the Communion and to serve as needed as an instrument of common action'.

16.21.1 The Archbishop of Canterbury is the president of the Council. He is *ex officio* a member of all committees of the Council.

16.21.2 The members of the Council are:

    a.   the Archbishop of Canterbury;

    b.   either one, two or three persons appointed by each of the Provinces which are Member-Churches; and

    c.   certain coopted and other persons.

16.21.3 The members of the Council select from their own number a chairman and vice-chairman.

16.22.1 Much of the business of the Council is conducted by a Standing

Committee of nine members appointed by the Council, including the chairman and vice-chairman of the Council.

16.22.2 The Secretary General[17] of the Anglican Consultative Council is the secretary of the Council and of the Standing Committee.

16.22.3 The Standing Committee conducts joint meetings with the Standing Committee of the Primates.[18]

16.23.1 The Council provides, in the form of the Anglican Communion Office, the secretariat for the central organs of the Communion.

16.23.2 The Council also conducts its own activities. These are primarily in the fields of communication and of ecumenical affairs and relations, but it also promotes mission and evangelism within the Communion.

The Lambeth Conference

16.24 The Lambeth Conference is an assembly of bishops of the Member-Churches of the Anglican Communion. The first conference was held in 1867. In the past the pattern has varied, but it is now usual for the Conferences to be held every ten years, the last being in 1998. Nearly 800 bishops attended the 1998 Conference, with a separate programme, led by Mrs Carey, for over 650 spouses. Many advisers also attended.

16.25 The Archbishop of Canterbury presides over the Lambeth Conference.

16.26.1 There is no constitution of the Lambeth Conference. It is not a separate legal entity. Attendance is by invitation of the Archbishop of Canterbury and it can vary. For example, by contrast with attendance at the 1988 Conference, Dr Carey invited suffragan, as well as diocesan, bishops of the Church of England to attend the 1998 Conference.

16.26.2 It is open to successive Archbishops to decide whom they will invite and considerations of size and expense may dictate a change. However, there is at present an expectation that, except perhaps where there are exceptional circumstances, all bishops within the Communion who are in active episcopal diocesan work will be invited to attend subsequent Conferences.

The Primates' Meeting

16.27   Since 1979 the 38 Primates[19] have met about once in every two or three years under the chairmanship of the Archbishop of Canterbury.

16.28   The Primates' Meeting, which also is not a separate legal entity, has no constitution. Primates attend the meeting by invitation of the Archbishop of Canterbury. In practice, the Archbishop normally invites all Primates unless in any particular case there is a very strong reason for not doing so.

16.29   There is a Standing Committee of the Primates' Meeting, usually comprising five primates, under the chairmanship of the Archbishop of Canterbury.

16.30   One of the functions of the Standing Committee is to act jointly with the Standing Committee of the Anglican Consultative Council in deciding whether to admit new Member-Churches as bodies which are entitled to appoint members of the Anglican Consultative Council.

Membership of the Anglican Communion

16.31   As stated earlier,[20] the Anglican Communion is a group of self-governing Churches which share common traditions, adhere to a common theology and follow common worship. The Communion has no constitution. It is not a legal entity, and it probably has no juridical existence.

16.32   Because there is no written constitution, there are no formal membership rules. However, as we indicated above[21] there are marks of membership which generally apply.

16.33.1 The most helpful starting point when considering evidence of membership is that the Province has the right to appoint one or more members of the Anglican Consultative Council. However, this test does not apply in all circumstances.

16.33.2 First, extra-Provincial bodies do not have that right, although, in practice, members of those Churches may be coopted to the Council, and even if that is not the case, the Churches are represented on the Council through the Archbishop.

16.33.3 Secondly, in the case of a new member there can be a delay between when the other conditions are satisfied (which would generally be regarded as marking membership of the Communion) and when the procedures of the Anglican Consultative Council have been followed to the point at which it is formally recognized that they are entitled to appoint members of the Council.

16.33.4 Thirdly, there might be a delay in the reverse direction. This is hypothetical, but suppose, for example, that because of schism an Archbishop felt obliged to declare that he was no longer in communion with a Member-Church; or, indeed, a Member-Church declared that it was no longer in communion with the Archbishop. It seems that thereupon that Church would cease to be regarded as a member of the Communion even though it might be some months thereafter that its right of appointing members of the Council was formally removed.

16.34 At the present time the Communion comprises 38 Provinces and 8 extra-Provincial bodies.[22] It has been estimated[23] that these Provinces and other bodies have in aggregate more than 70 million adherents in 161 countries, but these figures are not verified.

Authority

16.35.1 As has been noted, the Anglican Consultative Council has rules which determine which Provinces have the right to appoint members of it. Those decisions affect membership of the Communion and have binding legal effect. The Council also has power to make decisions in the conduct of its own affairs.

16.35.2 Subject to that, none of the organs of the Communion has the power to make decisions which are binding on the Member-Churches, and the organs do not, therefore, have coercive authority. However, the organs have come to have persuasive authority, and it may be that that authority is increasing.[24]

The Anglican Communion Office

16.36.1 The organs of the Communion are serviced by what is widely known as the Anglican Communion Office. The principal officer is the Secretary General of the Anglican Consultative Council who heads a Secretariat of about fifteen members.

16.36.2 The Office is located in Waterloo Road, London SE1, which is within about 20 minutes walk from Lambeth Palace.

16.37   We consider later[25] the possibility that the office might be relocated to Lambeth Palace.

The Anglican Observer to the United Nations

16.38.1 We have mentioned[26] the activities of the Anglican Consultative Council in the fields of Communications, Ecumenical Affairs and Relations, and Mission and Evangelism. We refer here to the Anglican Communion Observer to the United Nations. The Observer's office has Category II Consultative status with the United Nations Economic and Social Council. The Observer thereby has access to the United Nations Secretariat, and is able to represent the concerns of the Anglican Communion to the United Nations from a theological and biblical perspective.

16.38.2 The Secretary General of the Anglican Consultative Council is the line manager of the Observer.

16.38.3 The Observer is based in New York, and is provided with an office by the Episcopal Church of the United States of America.

16.38.4 The Observer is funded partly by the Anglican Consultative Council and partly as a result of various other endeavours of the present Archbishop of Canterbury.

The financial context

16.39   After this brief survey of the nature and composition of the Anglican Communion, and of its central organs, we turn to the financial context and deal:

> a.   in outline with the overall financial position of the organs of the Anglican Communion;

> b.   also in outline with the support given by the Compass Rose Society, a body which we describe later;

> c.   with the costs incurred by the Church of England in relation to the Communion generally; and

> d.   in greater detail with the costs which are incurred by the Archbishop in relation to the Anglican Communion.

Finance: the Anglican Consultative Council

16.40.1 The Anglican Consultative Council operates what is described as the Inter-Anglican Budget. The Member-Churches of the Communion[27] are asked to contribute to this budget broadly according to their means. In origin, these contributions were intended to cover the basic costs of the Secretariat and of the meetings of the central organs of the Communion.

16.40.2 In recent years, however, these contributions have proved to be insufficient, and they have been supplemented by donations from the Compass Rose Society.[28] However, the Member-Churches continue to be the major funding source.

16.40.3 In addition to contributions from Member-Churches and donations from the Compass Rose Society, the Anglican Consultative Council receives some, comparatively minor, income from investments and from other sources.

16.41.1 From these sources the Council has to fund:

    a.   its own recurrent activities; and

    b.   the meetings of itself and the other central organs.

16.41.2 These meetings take place according to different cycles. The Council meets every three years; the Lambeth Conference every ten years; and the Primates according to an irregular pattern which is not yet finally settled.

16.41.3 The recurrent funding is required to meet the costs of the Secretariat, the costs of the Council's Communications, Ecumenical and Mission activities, and to make a contribution to the cost of the Anglican Observer at the United Nations.

16.41.4 From its core income, the Council meets the cost of these recurrent activities and makes provision to cover the costs of the meetings.

Financial statements

16.42 Until 1999, the Council prepared its financial statements in relation to each calendar year. It decided to change its accounting period to one ending on 30 September, and so in respect of the year

2000 it prepared 9 month accounts for the period which ended on 30 September 2000. The financial statements for the year which ended on 30 September 2001 are not available to us as we write this report.

16.43   The financial statements of the Council are complex. In addition to reflecting the Council's recurrent annual activities, the financial statements deal with specific reserves which are maintained for meetings and also with funds which it receives and disperses for specific projects within the Communion.

16.44   For the *nine months* which ended on 30 September 2000 the key figures for its recurrent annual activities were:

Income	£
Contributions from Member-Churches	763,424
Donations from Compass Rose Society[29]	145,661
Investment income	18,200
Other donations and miscellaneous income[30]	33,876
	£961,161

Expenditure	
Recurrent activities	654,142
Provision for meetings	267,365
	921,507
Transfer to General Reserve[31]	39,654
	£961,161

16.45.1 Of the amount of contributions from Member-Churches which were requested by the Council in respect of the nine months which ended on 30 September 2000, just over 10% was unpaid. For the most part the underpayment was due to the financial inability of the Member-Churches to pay.

16.45.2 The figures in respect of that nine month period for the contributions payable by the Church of England, the Episcopal Church of the United States and the totals are:

	January to September request £	Received £	Unpaid £	Total received in period £
England	249,382	249,000	382	249,000
United States	241,409	252,701	nil	252,701
All Member- Churches	837,441	760,987	88,784	763,424

16.46 The corresponding full year figures for 2000 and the budgetary figures for the four subsequent years are:

Church	2000 actual £	2001 budget £	2002 budget £	2003 indicative budget £	2004 indicative budget £
England	332,000	345,800	359,700	374,100	389,100
United States	342,345	334,800	348,200	360,000	374,400
All Member- Churches	1,013,932	1,128,400	1,174,800	1,217,800	1,266,700

Finance: The Lambeth Conference

16.47.1 In principle:

a.   a fee is payable in respect of each bishop who attends the Lambeth Conference;

b.   a fee is payable in respect of each spouse of a bishop who attends; and

c.   the travelling expenses of each bishop and each spouse of a bishop are payable.

16.47.2 The fees and the travelling expenses are payable by the bishop or by his diocese. The fees in respect of the 1998 Conference were £1,250 for each participant.

16.47.3 Many bishops and their spouses from economically disadvantaged parts of the Communion need bursary assistance. This is provided from the proceeds of a Communion-wide appeal, to which dioceses of the Church of England contribute on a voluntary basis.

16.48 The major expenses of the Lambeth Conference are funded:

    a.   by the Anglican Consultative Council from the annual provisions which it makes;

    b.   by the delegate fees for the participants; and

    c.   by donations solicited for the purpose, including donations from the dioceses of the Church of England. Much of the donated income is used for the bursary fund.

16.49.1 In addition, the Commissioners support the Conference. In relation to the 1998 Conference the Commissioners:

    a.   seconded (and continued to pay for) a member of their staff to act as the Conference Manager;

    b.   paid one half of the salary of the manager's assistant who was employed for the purposes by the Anglican Consultative Council;

    c.   paid the costs of accommodation and facilities at the Conference for the staff of the Archbishop of Canterbury (where other Primates were accompanied by staff, their Churches were expected to cover the costs of those staffs);

    d.   paid for a Garden Party at Lambeth Palace; and

    e.   met the Archbishop of Canterbury's incidental expenditure.

16.49.2 These direct costs which were incurred by the Commissioners in respect of the 1998 Lambeth Conference amounted to £836,722.

16.50 In addition, travelling and subsistence costs incurred by bishops of the Church of England and, where applicable, their wives in attending the Conference, together with the conference fees, were paid by the Commissioners.

16.51.1 The Anglican Consultative Council reviews internally the financial out-turn in respect of each decade. Its latest review, which is for the period from 1 January 1990 to 31 December 1999, covers the preparation for the 1998 Conference, the Conference itself, and its immediate aftermath.

16.51.2 The review considers separately the income and expenditure in respect of:

a. the bishops' programme;

b. the spouses' programme; and

c. a Lambeth Conference Fund, which is essentially the bursary fund.

16.51.3 The ten-year summary shows the following figures:

	Bishops' Programme £	Spouses' Programme £	Conference Fund £	Total £
Income	2,729,340	836,658	1,347,489	4,913,487
Expenditure	2,661,315	735,663	785,122	4,182,100
	68,025	100,995	562,367	731,387

16.51.4 Subject to certain adjustments, the unexpended balances are carried forward for application towards the expenses of the next conference.

16.52   It is important to note that these figures are extracted from annual accounts of the Council. The figures are, therefore, included in, and are *not* in addition to, those published in the annual accounts.

Finance: The Primates' Meeting

16.53.1 The costs of the Primates' Meetings were intended to be covered by the annual provisions made by the Anglican Consultative Council from the Inter-Anglican Budget.[32]

16.53.2 However, these meetings are now held more frequently than was previously the case, and the expenses incurred in respect of the latest meetings were higher than anticipated.

16.53.3 As we write this report, the funding of Primates' Meetings is under consideration.

The Compass Rose Society

16.54.1 The Compass Rose Society has its origins in an initiative of Dr Carey in 1994. Its members are a group of individuals, parishes and dioceses who support the mission and ministry of the Anglican Consultative Council and the Communion more generally. The Society raises funds to support both the work of the Anglican Consultative Council and also specific projects within the Communion.

16.54.2 The Society's slogan is 'Helping the Anglican Communion Unite the World Through Compassion'.

16.55.1 The Society is an unincorporated association with no formal constitution, although in 2001 it was decided to establish an international board.

16.55.2 At the present time the Society has members in the United States, Japan, Hong Kong, Canada, Uruguay and Switzerland.

16.55.3 The members of the Society hold an Annual Meeting in London, including working and social sessions with the Archbishop at Lambeth Palace.

16.55.4 The Society also arranges occasional familiarization visits to different parts of the Communion.

16.56 In 1997 members of the Society in the United States incorporated a non-profit corporation under the laws of the State of Texas with the name The Anglican Communion Compass Rose Society Inc. This corporation is a tax-exempt body for United States tax purposes.[33]

16.57.1 Funds raised by the Society are applied:

> a.   in part to support the work of the Anglican Consultative Council and, in particular, its communications work; and

> b.   in part to support specific projects within the Communion.

16.57.2 Funds from sources in the United States may be applied directly by the US corporation for specific projects, in which case they are not reflected in the accounts of the Anglican Consultative Council. Other funds for specific projects are received by the Council, as restricted funds, and are applied by the Council for those projects.

16.57.3 In the period from 1 January 1999 to 30 September 2001 members of the Society provided:

a. about £725,000 for the work of the Anglican Consultative Council;

b. about £575,000 for specific projects within the Communion; and

c. £150,000 as an endowment fund for the communications work of the Council.

Church of England Financial Support for the Communion

16.58 We turn now to the financial support from the Church of England for the Anglican Communion. It falls into two broad categories, namely:

a. annual recurrent expenditure; and

b. expenditure related to the Lambeth Conference.

16.59.1 There are two forms of annual recurrent expenditure, namely:

a. the Church of England's contribution to the Inter-Anglican Budget; and

b. expenses incurred by the Archbishop of Canterbury specifically in relation to the Communion.

16.59.2 The Church of England's contribution to the Inter-Anglican Budget is paid by the *Archbishops' Council*. As has been seen,[34] the contribution for 2001 was £345,800 and for 2002 it is budgeted to be £359,700. These contributions can be regarded as being mainly paid indirectly by the dioceses.[35]

16.59.3 The *Commissioners* pay the direct costs incurred by the Archbishop of Canterbury in his role as President of the Communion. We detail those later.[36]

16.60.1 Funds provided by the Church of England in relation to the Lambeth Conference fall into four main categories.

16.60.2 First, the Archbishops' Council pays various incidental costs of the Lambeth Conference and, at present, it accrues £5,000 a year for this purpose.

16.60.3 Secondly, the delegate fees[37] payable in respect of bishops in active episcopal ministry in the Church of England, who attend the Lambeth Conference, and the fees in respect of their spouses are paid by the Commissioners directly. The travelling and associated costs incurred by the bishops and their spouses are treated as operational costs and in the first instance paid from the bishops' local accounts. They are subsequently reimbursed by the Commissioners.

16.60.4 Thirdly, the Commissioners also meet part of the costs of the Lambeth Conference. The main items of expenditure borne by them in respect of the 1998 Conference were described above.[38]

16.60.5 Fourthly, dioceses contribute to the Conference bursary fund.[39]

The Archbishop's operational costs in relation to the Communion

16.61 As we have stated, the direct recurrent costs incurred by the Archbishop in relation to the Anglican Communion are paid by the Commissioners. Principally, these are the costs of travel by the Archbishop and his personal staff on the business of the Communion, and the stipendiary and salary costs of his staff engaged on this aspect of his work.

16.62.1 The main items of direct expenditure are:

	1999 (actual) £	2000 (actual) £	2001 (budget) £
Stipends, employer's National Insurance contributions and pension contributions of the Archbishop's Anglican Communion Officer and the appropriate proportion of such costs in respect of his Assistant	23,960	24,774	43,000 (estimate)
Salaries, employer's National Insurance contributions and pension contributions of secretaries and clerical staff supporting the Archbishop's Anglican Communion Officer and the appropriate proportion in relation to the support of his Assistant	24,420	32,768	39,800 (estimate)
Office overhead expenditure, postage and communications charges	11,373	19,483	23,000 (estimate)
Overseas travel of the Archbishop and his staff in relation to the Communion	73,030	91,889	81,300
Totals	£132,783	£168,914	£187,100

16.62.2 These figures relate only to the marginal costs. We have not attempted to allocate any part of the Archbishop's stipend, general operational costs or premises expenses to his work in relation to the Communion: these figures therefore significantly understate the economic cost.

The financial considerations generally

16.63 We have referred to the financial contributions by the Church of England to the Anglican Communion in general and in relation to the Archbishop in particular solely in order that the position may be made known. It is not part of our purpose to maintain that the amounts are too large (or too small).

The Ecclesiology of the Anglican Communion

16.64 Against this structural and financial background, we refer to certain broad considerations and then the role of the Archbishop of Canterbury in relation to the Communion.

16.65.1 For the purposes of our First Report we defined[40] 'ecclesiology' as 'the principles which underlie the structure and organization of the Church of England and the roles of its office holders, both ordained and lay, including their respective rights, duties and obligations'.

16.65.2 In the work which led to the First Report our approach was to reflect with particular care and caution before making any recommendations which, if implemented, might lead to a change in ecclesiology in this sense.[41]

16.65.3 The ecclesiology of the Church of England was not prescribed by a great master plan. It evolved and because many issues of ecclesiology are matters of balance – of influence, responsibility and authority – it will continue to evolve.

16.66.1 In the same way it can be seen that there is emerging an ecclesiology of the Anglican Communion. Many of the attempts which have been made to describe the nature of the Church of England can, with little adaptation, be applied to the Communion.[42]

16.66.2 It is not for us to attempt a treatise on the ecclesiology of the Anglican Communion, but aspects of it include:

a.   the relationship of the Archbishop of Canterbury with the Anglican Consultative Council and the other central organs of the Communion;

b.   the relationship of the Archbishop with the Provinces of the Communion; and

c.   the role of the Archbishop in relation to the Communion in the Canterbury setting on which we comment at the end of this chapter.

The Archbishop and the Secretary General

16.67.1 The Archbishop might be described as having a semi-detached relationship with the Secretary General of the Anglican Consultative Council.[43]

16.67.2 On the one hand, one of the roles of the Secretary General is to support the Archbishop in relation to the Communion.[44]

16.67.3 On the other hand:

a.   the Secretary General is not a member of the Archbishop's personal staff in the sense that he is not one of the principals at Lambeth Palace;

b.   the Secretary General is based in the Anglican Communion Office, which is physically separate and some way away from Lambeth Palace;

c.   the Secretary General is not accountable to the Archbishop and the Archbishop is not his line manager; and

d.   the Archbishop has his own Anglican Communion Officer who is a member of his personal staff.

16.68   Structurally, this looks like a recipe for dysfunctionality, if not disaster. However, we are told that in practice at the present time the relationship between the Archbishop and the Secretary General works well. We discern, however, that this appears to depend to a large extent on good personal chemistry between the present Archbishop and the present Secretary General. The structure is not one which encourages a cohesive relationship and the relationship will alter with each change of Archbishop or Secretary General.

The Archbishop's staff and the Secretariat

16.69.1 The relationship between the Archbishop and the Secretary General is paralleled by that between the respective members of the Archbishop's personal staff, whom he can direct, and other members of the Secretariat, whom he cannot.

16.69.2 The risk of uncoordinated activity is perhaps even greater at this level, requiring constant vigilance on the part of all concerned to ensure that there is proper harmonizing of their work.

The Archbishop of Canterbury and the Anglican Communion

16.70.1 The Member-Churches of the Communion recognize the Archbishop of Canterbury as the principal archbishop of the Communion.[45]

16.70.2 As has been seen,[46] he is regarded as one of the four instruments of unity. In practice, with varying degrees of emphasis, this relates both to his personification of the see of Canterbury and to the roles which he performs.

16.71.1 The Archbishop of Canterbury is:

a.   the President of the Anglican Consultative Council;

b.   a member of all its committees;

c.   the President of, and invitor in relation to, the Lambeth Conference;

d.   the Chairman of, and invitor in relation to, the Primates' Meeting; and

e.   the Chairman of the Standing Committee of the Primates' Meeting.

16.71.2 Although, formally, there is no such office, in this report we refer to the Archbishop as 'President of the Anglican Communion' to encompass all of the roles which he has in relation to the Communion.

16.72.1 The Archbishop of Canterbury has no general metropolitical jurisdiction over the Member-Churches of the Communion. They are generally autonomous and self-governing, and metropolitical jurisdiction is determined by their own constitutions.

16.72.2 However, in a small number of cases the Archbishop does exercise metropolitical jurisdiction. This is by virtue of provisions in the constitutions of the particular Churches, and not by virtue of his Presidency of the Communion.

16.73.1 The Archbishop does much of his work as President of the Anglican Communion at Lambeth Palace, where his specialist staff is based. He also has an important Anglican Communion ministry which he exercises at Canterbury.[47]

16.73.2 The Archbishop makes a number of visits in each year, either specifically in his capacity as President of the Communion or otherwise to individual Provinces.

16.73.3 The present Archbishop estimates that about 30% of his total time has been occupied on the business of the Communion.

16.74.1 There is nothing remotely resembling a job description for the Archbishop in relation to the Anglican Communion.

16.74.2 Our attempt at the main elements of such a description would be:

    a.   to strive to maintain the unity of the Communion;

    b.   to provide guidance and support for Member-Churches of the Communion;

    c.   to encourage and support the bishops within the Communion;

    d.   to preside at and lead the planning for the Lambeth Conference;

    e.   generally to encourage the efficient and harmonious operation of the organizations of the Communion, particularly the cooperative work of its Member-Churches; and

    f.   to be the principal representative of the Communion to third parties.

16.75 It is the first of these elements which is the most onerous. Much of the burden of these responsibilities comes down to the preservation of unity. Just as any bishop is to be an instrument of unity, so the Archbishop of Canterbury is to be an instrument of unity writ large. The Member-Churches of the Communion have their common characteristics, but it seems almost inevitable that with such diversity very substantial differences of opinion will emerge. Issues concerning the ordination of women to the priesthood and then to the episcopate, and deep divisions of conviction about the ordination of practising homosexuals and about the possibility of single sex marriages are notable examples. Irregular episcopal ordinations and lay eucharistic presidency are also becoming major issues.

16.76.1 To some extent work of the Archbishop in relation to the Communion is responsive to developments within it.

16.76.2 Subject to that, the Archbishop's ministry is self-directing. In general, he decides: in which disputes he will intervene; which projects he will support; and which visits to Member-Churches he will make. Although in a general sense the Archbishop may be answerable to his fellow Primates and other bishops in the Communion, he has no formal accountability to any body for what he does.

16.77 In our First Report we referred[48] to the responsibilities imposed on, primarily, diocesan bishops without their having the corresponding legal authority to enable those responsibilities to be discharged. There is a clear parallel with the Archbishop in relation to Communion. He is under the heaviest moral responsibility to strive to maintain unity, but has virtually no legal or metropolitical authority to achieve it. He has to act by persuasive (but not binding) moral influence. This factor alone makes a heavy time commitment almost inevitable.

Specific resourcing issues

16.78 We now consider the resources the Archbishop needs in order to perform his role as President of the Communion and how, consistent with the availability of funds, he can best be supported.

16.79 The specific resourcing issues which relate to the Archbishop in the context of the Anglican Communion are:

    a.   the quantum and source of financial support;

    b.   the location of the Anglican Communion Office;

c.   the inter-relation between the roles of members of the Archbishop's personal staff and those of the Secretariat;

d.   communications and the media;

e.   the Archbishop's visits in his capacity as President of the Communion; and

f.   the Archbishop's ministry in relation to the Communion at Canterbury.

Quantum of financial support

16.80.1 It is for the Church Commissioners and the Archbishop's Council, and not us, to decide, as a matter of policy, what part of the income from central funds[49] of the Church of England should be deployed for the purposes of the Anglican Communion, and we do not express any view on whether or not the present level is appropriate.

16.80.2 We do, however, consider that whatever amount is to be applied for those purposes should be decided as a separate matter; and that the way in which that amount is spent should be clearly identified.

16.80.3 We recommend that:

a.   in calculating the amount to be devolved to the Archbishop by way of block-grant, there should be included a specific amount for his work in relation to the Communion;[50] and

b.   particularly as that amount would not be hypothecated,[51] the actual expenditure by the Archbishop on the purposes of the Communion should be separately identified.[52]

The Commissioners' powers

16.81.1 The Commissioners regard the costs incurred by the Archbishop of Canterbury in relation to the Anglican Communion and that part of the costs of the Lambeth Conference which they meet as falling within the general operational costs of the see of Canterbury. The Commissioners have no separate legal power to support the Anglican Communion or its central organizations.

16.81.2 In view of our recommendations that a specific amount in relation to this aspect of the Archbishop's ministry should be included in the formula, and our recommendation that the amount spent by the

Archbishop on the purposes of the Communion should be separately identified, we **recommend** that, as part of legislation to be promoted to implement recommendations in our First Report, the Commissioners should seek express powers to continue their support in these ways.

Location of the Anglican Communion Office

16.82.1 We discuss in another chapter[53] the utilization of space within Lambeth Palace. The question arises whether, in the event of adequate space becoming available, the Anglican Communion Office should be relocated to Lambeth Palace.

16.82.2 There would be clear operational advantages in doing so, particularly because the Secretary General would no doubt in practice have greater or easier direct contact with the Archbishop and the senior members of his staff; and because there would be much greater opportunity for face-to-face contact between members of both staffs.

16.82.3 Such a move might also be helpful to the Anglican Consultative Council.[54]

16.83.1 In our view whether the Office should be relocated to Lambeth should be decided on policy and not resourcing grounds.

16.83.2 We are told that at least some primates welcome the degree of 'semi-detachment' of the Archbishop from the Secretary General and the Secretariat, and might regard with anxiety any apparent move to increase the influence of the Archbishop over the Secretariat.

16.83.3 Furthermore, if the Anglican Communion Office were to move to Lambeth Palace, and at some time thereafter, for whatever reason, that arrangement was not considered to be appropriate, the removal of the Office *from* Lambeth could easily convey an unfortunate message.

16.83.4 At the present time, the Archbishop has the necessary (but varying)[55] degrees of independence from Church House and the Anglican Communion Office. A move of the Anglican Communion Office to Lambeth Palace would disturb that balance.

16.84 We **recommend** that:

a. relocation or otherwise of the Office should be decided as a matter of broad policy, and not on resourcing grounds. The policy issues should be determined first; and

b.   as a corollary, the Anglican Communion Office should not be relocated to Lambeth Palace merely because, if this occurs, space becomes available.

Staff

16.85   The Secretariat of the Anglican Consultative Council has a staff of about fifteen. The Archbishop has on his personal staff his own Anglican Communion Officer, a part-time Deputy Officer, and their own secretarial support. Is there a duplication of roles?

16.86.1 Although there may be a *perception* of duplication, we are satisfied that their roles are different.

16.86.2 In the first place, much of the work of the Secretariat of the Anglican Consultative Council is related to the central organs of the Communion, whereas much of the work of the Archbishop's Anglican Communion Officer is concerned with the Archbishop's direct dealings with other Primates and the Provinces.

16.86.3 In the second place, one of the roles of the Archbishop's Anglican Communion Officer is to make arrangements for the Archbishop's visits within and on behalf of the Communion, and there will continue to be a need for that role to be performed by someone. We are satisfied that that could not be done by the Secretary General consistent with his other responsibilities.

16.86.4 The appropriate staffing arrangements are related to the location of the Anglican Communion Office. For so long as it continues to be other than at Lambeth Palace we **recommend** that:

a.   the Archbishop should continue to have his own staff to support him in dealing with the Communion affairs; and

b.   the exact size of that staff should be considered by the Chief of Staff.

We also **recommend** that if the Office is relocated to Lambeth Palace,[56] the issue should be re-examined.

The Archbishop's visits

16.87   When the Archbishop travels in his capacity as President of the Anglican Communion he is accompanied by his Anglican Communion Officer. On some occasions he has also been accompanied by his Press Secretary. We refer to that later.[57]

16.88   When the Archbishop is travelling primarily in his capacity as President of the Communion, he may well also be travelling in one or more of his other capacities.

16.89.1   The travel and associated accommodation and incidental costs of the Archbishop and those travelling on his behalf have increased by 300% during the period from 1990 to 2000.[58] This includes, but is not restricted to, visits in relation to the Anglican Communion. It is to be expected that the longer an Archbishop is in office the greater will be the demands on him to travel.

16.89.2   We have made recommendations earlier[59] about travelling costs.

16.90   We recommend that visits made by the Archbishop in his capacity as President of the Communion should be subject to the same post-visit evaluation as we have recommended[60] in the case of other visits.

Communications and the media

16.91   A further question about possible duplication of staff arises with regard to communications and the media. The Secretariat has its own Director of Communications. The Archbishop has his Press Secretary. Both might need to be involved in the Archbishop's visits within the Communion, and with other aspects of his work in relation to the Communion. Does this indicate a duplication of roles?

16.92   The functions are different, and we have not detected duplication, although those concerned must work closely together.

16.93   We recommend, however, that were there to be, for other reasons, a relocation of the Anglican Consultative Office to Lambeth Palace, there should then be considered the possible formation of a joint communications and press office.

16.94.1 More specifically with regard to the Archbishop's visits, much may happen during the course of a visit which deserves to be made known to a wider audience. Yet it is unrealistic to expect the Archbishop's Press Secretary both to be able to support the Archbishop and to deal with pressmen and broadcasters while also gathering material to be used thereafter in the interests of the Archbishop and the wider Church.

16.94.2 We accordingly **recommend** that where the Archbishop travels wholly or mainly in his capacity as President of the Communion, and the circumstances so permit, account should be taken of the need to serve the roles both of supporting the Archbishop and of gathering material. This might be achieved by the Archbishop being accompanied both by the Press Secretary (who, as now, would travel at the expense of the Commissioners and which expenditure in future would be funded through the block-grant) and by the Director of Communications of the Council (who would travel at the expense of the Anglican Consultative Council). The matter would need to be decided separately in relation to each visit because, apart from the issue of actual cost, it would be necessary to avoid any perception of undue total cost.

The Archbishop, the Communion and Canterbury

16.95.1 Apart from making visits and attending meetings overseas, most of the work which the Archbishop does in his capacity as President of the Anglican Communion is done at Lambeth Palace. It is there that the members of his personal staff who are concerned with the Communion are based.

16.95.2 However, in a deeper sense, Canterbury rather than Lambeth Palace is the focus of the Communion. There is a unique symbolism for the Communion in the Archbishop of Canterbury in his Cathedral. For the members of the Communion the presence of the Archbishop in his Cathedral demonstrates far more vividly than any intellectual analysis what is meant by being in communion with the see of Canterbury.

16.96 The connection between the members of the Communion and Canterbury has been enhanced by the recent opening of an International Study Centre in the precincts of the Cathedral.[61] The centre is an enterprise of the Dean and Chapter and was funded by American Friends of the Cathedral. Up to 40 people can stay in the centre. The centre is managed by the Dean and Chapter, who intend to make it available for study, meetings and conferences in relation to the Communion as much as it is required for such purposes. As this report is being printed, the Primates' Meeting is taking place in that centre.

16.97   To enable the Archbishop to exercise his ministry in Canterbury to the fullest extent is one of the principal reasons why we have recommended[62] that the Archbishop should continue to have a base at the Old Palace in Canterbury.

An Anglican Communion bishop at Lambeth

16.98.1 The Hurd Report recommended[63] that there should be established a post at episcopal level at Lambeth, funded by the Anglican Communion, to act as the Archbishop's right hand in Anglican Communion affairs. Such a bishop would wherever practicable deputize for the Archbishop in Anglican Communion affairs and help to coordinate support with the Anglican Communion Office. The Hurd Report expressly[64] left open whether such a bishop should become the Secretary General of the Anglican Consultative Council; or should be in addition to, but superior to, the Secretary General; or should be in addition to, but parallel with, the Secretary General.

16.98.2 We have the greatest sympathy with the objective of seeking to reduce the workload of the Archbishop on Communion affairs. We can see some advantages in such an arrangement.

16.98.3 The broader policy and ecclesiological aspects of such an appointment go outside our terms of reference, but from a resourcing viewpoint we **recommend** caution. If the bishop were based at Lambeth Palace, the relationship between him and the Chief of Staff would be of some delicacy, particularly as we take the view[65] that the Chief of Staff should manage all staff at Lambeth Palace. We are also concerned that the same mistake would be made as has been made with the concept of the Bishop at Lambeth as that post is presently constituted, namely that a person in episcopal orders would be doing a non-episcopal job. On balance, we would prefer to see the Archbishop being supported in a different way.

chapter 17

The Lambeth Palace Library

Introduction

17.1   In this chapter, we consider the present position with regard to the Lambeth Palace Library and make recommendations, particularly in relation to the Library as a resource for the Archbishop.

17.2   We refer in this chapter to:

a.   the books, papers and other objects in the Library as 'the Collection';

b.   those parts of Lambeth Palace in which the Collection is housed as 'the Library Buildings'; and

c.   the overall undertaking of holding, curating and making the Collection available for consultation as 'the Library'.

History

17.3.1   The Library was founded in 1611 when Archbishop Bancroft bequeathed to his successors as Archbishop of Canterbury his extensive personal collection of books on divinity. This bequest was accompanied by the earnest exhortation that succeeding Archbishops of Canterbury should look to the preservation of the library with care and diligence and ensure that it was utilized 'to the service of God and his Church, to the Kings and Commonwealth of his Realme, and particularly of the Archbishops of Canterbury'.

17.3.2   Ever since its foundation, the Library has been referred to as the personal library of the Archbishops of Canterbury, albeit that the Collection is not now owned by them, even in their corporate capacity.[1]

17.3.3   The ownership of the Collection became vested in the Ecclesiastical Commissioners in 1866,[2] and became vested in the Church Commissioners in 1948.[3]

17.3.4   Prior to 1866, the cost of maintaining the Collection was met from the income of the estates of the see of Canterbury.[4] Since 1866 the cost has been met by, originally, the Ecclesiastical Commissioners and, latterly, the Church Commissioners.

The Collection

17.4   The Library is the main special library in London for material on the history and affairs of the Church of England. It also serves as an archives repository and research centre for the archiepiscopal and provincial (but not diocesan) records of Canterbury, as well as records of a similar character. For present purposes, it is significant that, apart from those records, the Collection is one on the Church of England rather than specifically the Archbishops.

17.5   In addition to a large number of manuscripts, the Collection includes over 200,000 printed books, of which 40,000 were published before 1700.

Usage

17.6.1   The Library had 1,630 reader visits in 1999, 1,893 in 2000 and 1,812 in 2001. Overall there has been an upward trend in the number of reader visits, particularly so since 1990 when it was 1,234.

17.6.2   The staff of the Library answers about 3,000 written enquiries a year, as well as dealing with telephone enquiries.

17.6.3   The Library has extensively published its archival and manuscript holdings in microfilm, and the Library enables individual readers to consult the Collection at a distance by supplying them with microfilm or other copies.

17.6.4   About 50 monographs are published each year which depend for primary research on the Collection.

17.6.5   The Library began in 1994 a project for the preparation of an electronic catalogue of its printed books and it is beginning the electronic cataloguing of its archives and manuscripts. As they are produced, these catalogues are made available through the Library website which was launched in April 2000. The website currently receives about 300,000 hits a year and when the cataloguing is complete, it is expected that this figure will rise to about 500,000 a year.

17.6.6   Generally it can be said that the local clientele of the Library is small and much the greater part of the use of the Collection is at a distance.

Other books and records in Lambeth Palace

17.7   The Collection does not include the working books of the Archbishop and his staff which have been acquired at the expense of the Commissioners, notwithstanding that they belong to the Commissioners. Likewise, it does not include the books which the Archbishop or members of his staff own personally.

17.8.1   Papers which are created by an Archbishop and members of his staff are stored[5] within Lambeth Palace separately from the Library. There is an archivist on the Archbishop's staff.

17.8.2   Following various weeding processes, the papers relating to each archiepiscopate are transferred to the Library where they are catalogued and become part of the Collection. The records become open to public inspection under the thirty-year rule.

Management structure

17.9   The management and funding arrangements in relation to the Library are worthy of Byzantium. They involve:

    a.   the Commissioners;

    b.   the trustees of The Lambeth Palace Library Trust; and

    c.   the Library Committee.

The Commissioners

17.10.1 The Commissioners, who are the owners both of the Collection and of the Library Buildings (and who are the primary funders of the Library), are the determiners of most issues of policy. This is a role which they actively discharge, primarily, but not exclusively, on matters which have financial implications. They do this partly at meetings of the Board of Governors and partly by appointing trustees of The Lambeth Palace Library Trust as well as a member of the Library Committee.

17.10.2 Although the Commissioners are the determiners of most aspects of policy, the trustees of The Lambeth Palace Library Trust determine policy with regard to staffing.

The Lambeth Palace Library Trust
17.11.1 The Lambeth Palace Library Trust is an unincorporated charitable trust.

17.11.2 The trustees of the trust have two separate functions. The first is to run the Library and to implement the Commissioners' policy for it. They conduct this activity with funds provided by the Commissioners and, although they do so as principals, in some respects the position of the trustees is similar to that of managing agents for the Commissioners.

17.11.3 The second function of the trustees is to act as substantive trustees in investing and deploying funds raised for the Library, primarily from sources other than the Commissioners.[6] Since October 2000 in respect of this second function the trustees have been registered with the Charity Commission as a separate charity.

The Library Committee
17.12.1 The Library Committee is a committee of the trustees, but includes one member nominated by the Commissioners and one by the British Library.

17.12.2 The Library Committee is responsible for the general management of the Library, and for oversight of the Librarian.

The Friends of Lambeth Palace Library
17.13.1 There is in addition a separate charitable body known as The Friends of Lambeth Palace Library. It has an executive committee whose members are the trustees of that body for the purposes of the Charities Acts.

17.13.2 The Friends of Lambeth Palace Library is a body which exists primarily to raise funds to assist in the acquisition of books and manuscripts. This body plays no part in the management of the Library.

Management: summary

17.14 The policy-making and management structure can be illustrated as follows:

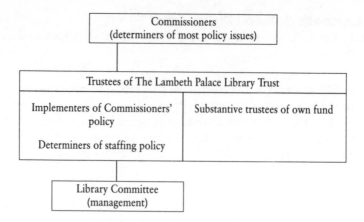

Funding

17.15.1 The Commissioners are solely responsible for: the maintenance of the fabric of the Library Buildings; their internal and external repair and decoration; the cost of insurance; and heating, lighting and cleaning. Neither the trustees of The Lambeth Palace Library Trust nor the Library Committee are involved in these aspects.

17.15.2 The Commissioners directly discharge the costs of dealing with these matters as part of the overall premises expenses.

17.16.1 The trustees of The Lambeth Palace Library Trust draw up and agree with the Commissioners an annual budget to cover staff and other operational costs.

17.16.2 The Commissioners pay the agreed amount to the trustees, who disburse it. Although the trustees are one of the National Church Institutions,[7] and are the persons with legal responsibility with regard to the payments which they make, the amounts which the Commissioners provide are not accounted for as payments made to the trustees, and the disbursement of these funds is not accounted for as being made by the trustees, but the Commissioners' accounts are prepared as if the ultimate payments were made directly by the Commissioners.

Correspondingly, the accounts of the trustees reflect neither the receipt nor the payment of these amounts, nor are they reflected in notes to the accounts.

17.17   The funding arrangements can be illustrated as follows:

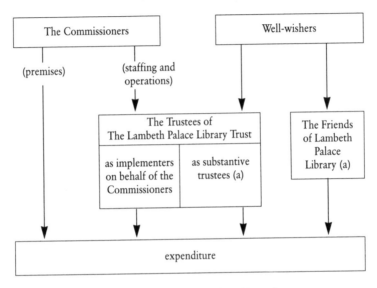

Note (a): the application of these funds is considered later.[8]

Staff
17.18   The trustees of The Lambeth Palace Library Trust, as one of the National Church Institutions, are the managing employers of the staff employed in the Library.

17.19.1 The present staff establishment is:

a.	the Librarian and five other professional librarians or archivists	6
b.	an archives assistant	1
c.	a conservator	1
d.	a Library assistant	1
e.	a Library secretary	1
		10

The salary costs of these members of staff are paid by the Commissioners.

17.19.2 In addition, there is a member of staff working on the computerization programme. The Trustees of the Lambeth Palace Library Trust meet the salary costs in respect of that post from the proceeds of an appeal which they made in 1994. A further member of staff is engaged on a new programme for the digitalization of plans of Church buildings. The costs of that post are met from a grant from the National Heritage Lottery Board.

The Library Buildings

17.20 The following parts of Lambeth Palace comprise the Library Buildings:

> a.   Morton's Tower,[9] the gatehouse to the palace, in which a large part of the Collection is housed, together with a well-equipped conservation studio, offices used by the Librarian and his staff, and a meeting room;

> b.   the Great Hall, the reading room and three strongrooms, which are within the main palace building; and

> c.   the Archbishop's Papers Room, which is situated under an archway between Morton's Tower and the main palace building.

17.21 These buildings generally are unsuitable for Library purposes. The movement of items from one building to another is inhibited in bad weather. There are both fire and water damage risks in Morton Tower, and the temperature and humidity controls in some of the strongrooms are below standard.[10]

The need for additional and improved space

17.22.1 The Library faces a major challenge. In addition to dealing with the matters referred to in the previous paragraph, the Library no longer has adequate space to house the Collection. Furthermore, following an inspection in March 2001, the Historical Manuscripts Commission stated that unless by 2003 the Library put forward plans to bring storage accommodation up to acceptable levels, the Commission would no longer accredit the Library. Accreditation is a pre-condition to the receipt of funds from many grant-making bodies.

17.22.2 The Commissioners, the Archbishop and the Trustees are presently considering the possibility of constructing an underground storage facility beneath the main courtyard of Lambeth Palace, although no decision has been taken on this and there is no settled policy. The likely cost is somewhat in excess of £5 million at current values. It is hoped to cover the cost by donations from external sources.

17.22.3 In order to carry out the project, not only would the funds have to be raised, but also it would be necessary to overcome a legal difficulty. Although the Commissioners have power to *maintain* the buildings in which the Collection is housed they have been advised that they have no legal power to *construct* a building or to incur capital expenditure for such purposes. We refer to this aspect later.[11]

Non-financial value

17.23.1 We are not ourselves qualified to comment on the value of the Library and it is not within our terms of reference to attempt to do so. However, the Historical Manuscripts Commission has referred [12] to the 'outstanding reputation of the Library in curatorial and scholarly circles', and others have paid tribute to the value of its work. We have no reason to doubt that value.

17.23.2 It has also been represented to us (otherwise than by those connected with the Library) that the Church of England should treasure its written and printed heritage as it does its buildings. That assertion is also outside our terms of reference, but we do not dissent from it.

17.24.1 Overall:

a.   it is for the Commissioners to decide the future of the Library; and

b.   no doubt in reaching that decision, the Commissioners will have regard to the view of the Archbishop's Council.

17.24.2 We recommend later [13] a change in the law so that the Commissioners will have greater freedom of action.

Cost

17.25.1 No accounts are prepared showing the total cost of the Library (although separate accounts are prepared for The Lambeth Palace Library Trust and The Friends of Lambeth Palace Library [14]). We **recommend** that overall accounts should be prepared, partly as an essential condition for management and partly so that the true cost of the Library can be identified.

17.25.2 It may be that the reasons for the absence of overall accounts include the facts that the Commissioners pay directly the running costs of the premises;[15] and that the staff and operational costs are not reflected in the Trustees' accounts.[16]

17.25.3 We regard this absence of accounts as unsatisfactory, and as a factor which does not encourage an attitude of overall financial control (although we are not suggesting abuse).

17.25.4 The position is far from transparent.

17.26 Based on information supplied to us by the Commissioners, the direct cost to the Commissioners of the Library in the years which ended on 31 December 2000 and 31 December 2001, rounded to the nearest £1,000, and net of contributions from third parties is as follows:

	2000 (detail) £	2000 £	2001 (detail) £	2001 £
Office and support staff costs		263,000		299,000
Operational costs:				
Equipment and furniture purchase and replacement	13,000		8,000	
General running expenses	25,000		17,000	
Conservation and binding	60,000		68,000	
Purchase of books	13,000		13,000	
Computerization	28,000		26,000	
Other operational costs	3,000		2,000	
	142,000		134,000	
Use of common services (such as Human Resources and communications) charged to the Library	23,000	165,000	25,000	159,000
Maintenance and repairs of Library Buildings	25,000		23,000	
Insurance	17,000	42,000	17,000	40,000
Improvements to Library Buildings		14,000		14,000
		£484,000		£512,000

17.27.1 This materially understates the recurrent economic cost of the Library. The figures do not attempt to attribute to the Library a full proportion of the general overhead expenditure in relation to Lambeth Palace as a whole, such as the cost of security and the upkeep of the grounds; the figures do not take full account of the value of the residential accommodation provided for the Librarian;[17] and they do not include any notional charge for the use and occupation of the Library Buildings.

17.27.2 We understand that the rental value of the Library Buildings while they are put to their present use is in the region of £200,000 per annum.[18] Accordingly, when there are taken into account the direct costs specified in paragraph 17.26, the rental value of the Library Buildings, and the other matters to which we have referred in paragraph 17.27.1, it is seen that the true economic recurrent cost to the Commissioners of the Lambeth Palace Library is of the order of £750,000 to £800,000 per annum. These figures are without taking into account subventions from third parties.

The Commissioners' accounts

17.28 We observed in our First Report that we regard it as misleading for the costs incurred by the Commissioners in relation to the Lambeth Palace Library to be brought into account in their statutory accounts under the heading of 'bishops' working costs'.[19] We refer to this later.[20]

Other funds

17.29.1 At present, the trustees of The Lambeth Palace Library Trust apply income from their own fund primarily for the Library's computerization programme.[21] The Friends of Lambeth Palace Library make grants for purchase and conservation.

17.29.2 The amounts spent by these bodies were:

	2000 £	2001 £
Trustees of The Lambeth Palace Library Trust	41,902	50,806
The Friends of Lambeth Palace Library	28,700	21,375

Use of the Library Buildings

17.30.1 On a non-financial aspect, we note that there is no written instrument between the Commissioners and the trustees which governs the terms on which the trustees are permitted to have the use of the Library Buildings.

17.30.2 We are not aware that this has caused significant problems, except with regard to the extent to which the Library Buildings, particularly the Great Hall, are to be available for non-Library purposes. We also refer to this later.[22]

The Archbishop and the Lambeth Palace Library

17.31.1 We turn now to the relationship of the Archbishop to the Library. We have noted that it is generally referred to as the Archbishop's Library. Formally, the roles of the Archbishop in relation to the Library are:

> a. as Chairman of the Church Commissioners and as Chairman of the Board of Governors of the Church Commissioners,[23] the formulators of policy;
>
> b. as Chairman of the trustees of The Lambeth Palace Library Trust;
>
> c. as appointor (after consultation with the other Commissioners) of the majority of the other trustees of The Lambeth Palace Library Trust;
>
> d. as appointor of the members of the Library Committee; and
>
> e. as President (but not trustee) of The Friends of Lambeth Palace Library.

17.31.2 To different degrees, most of these roles impose a time commitment on the Archbishop.

17.31.3 Apart from these formal relationships, there is the practical relationship between the Archbishop and his staff and the Library, to which we refer later.[24]

17.32.1 We readily recognize that the maintenance of the Collection and affording public access to it can properly be regarded as being part of the ministry of the Archbishop to the nation and, increasingly, also to those in other countries.

17.32.2 We are, however, very doubtful whether it is properly regarded as a major resource *for* the Archbishop. We would be surprised if the Archbishop or members of his staff used the Library as a source of reference more than, say, once a month (and no doubt if the Collection were housed elsewhere most of the reference materials could be made available on short notice). In a different sense, the Library is a resource to the Archbishop, in that he is readily able to show distinguished visitors some of the treasured items in the Collection. However, our assessment is that the Library gains more from the Archbishop's association with, and interest in, it, than he gains from having the Collection immediately available to him.

17.32.3 Our terms of reference do not ask us to assess the value of the Library to the Church, the nation and the international community, but to look at the Library as a resource for the Archbishop. Looked at from this narrow perspective, we do not consider the value of the Library to the Archbishop justifies its cost; and likewise from the narrow perspective it occupies space which could be used in better ways to support the Archbishop.

The issues

17.33 Turning to more specific issues, for our purposes the main issues with regard to the Library are those relating to:

  a.   its location;

  b.   its cost; and

  c.   its relationship with the other parts of Lambeth Palace.

Location

17.34.1 It is possible that the Library would suffer if it ceased to be at Lambeth Palace. If it were located elsewhere, it is highly likely that the amount of time which the Archbishop spent in relation to it would diminish, and the significance of it being, in some sense, 'the Archbishop of Canterbury's Library' would lessen. Furthermore, we would expect that a lessening of the involvement of the Archbishop would in some respects make fund-raising on behalf of the Library more difficult.

17.34.2 Nevertheless, we are not convinced that the Library should remain on the Lambeth Palace site. It may be convenient for members of the public as well as the Archbishop for the Library to be in Central London, but it is not essential.[25] From the viewpoint of users, physical location will become less important as electronic access increases. There must be attractions in the Library being in a purpose-built building elsewhere, whether or not in conjunction with the Church of England Records Centre. Some potential donors might be more willing to contribute if the Collection is to be housed in modern purpose-built accommodation.

17.35.1 We **recommend** that the Commissioners should conduct an immediate review of the housing and conservation of the Church of England's documentary heritage and the provision of access to it for members of the Church and the public generally. That review should:

    a.   be focused on the Library, recognizing that it is an important part but by no means the entirety of that heritage. The review should, therefore, have regard to other relevant collections;

    b.   examine the courses of:

        i.   continuance of the Library at Lambeth Palace;

        ii.   relocation to another site on a stand-alone basis;

        iii.   relocation to another site, where the Collection would be maintained jointly with those of one or more other bodies;

    c.   examine the respective financial implications of those courses, including the return which could be derived from an alternative use of the Library Buildings; and

    d.   include a specific review of the opportunity for Government and quasi-governmental, as well as private, grant-aid.

17.35.2 We further **recommend** that the review should examine ways of increasing access to the Collection by a wider section of the public in addition to specialist readers.

17.35.3 The review should also take account of the present severe restrictions on the Commissioners' powers to which we refer in paragraph 17.37.1 and our proposals in paragraph 17.37.2 for enlarging them.

17.36.1 In conducting such a review, we would expect the views of the other National Church Institutions to be sought, as well as those of other relevant bodies, such as the British Library.

17.36.2 We have been mindful of the difficulties in which the Library might be placed in consequence of such a review, and we have reflected carefully before making our recommendations. We hope that the outcome of the review would be that:

  a.   the Collection would be kept together, but perhaps as part of a larger collection; and

  b.   the Collection would be housed elsewhere than at Lambeth Palace but in much more satisfactory physical conditions than at present.

Legal powers
17.37.1 The Official Solicitor has told us that:

  a.   although the Commissioners have power to maintain the Collection, they do not have power to incur capital expenditure on housing it;[26] and

  b.   even the power to maintain the Collection applies only while it is housed at Lambeth Palace.[27]

17.37.2 We **recommend** that at the same time as promoting the legislation which would be required to implement other recommendations which we have made, the Commissioners should seek a general power to deploy the Library in such a manner as they think fit in the overall interests of the Church of England.

Cost and its disclosure
17.38   We have indicated[28] the present cost of the Lambeth Palace Library and explained that the decision about the quantum of funds to be made available for the purposes of the Library is a matter for the Commissioners.[29]

17.39.1 Irrespective of the amount which is provided, we **recommend** that the Library should be regarded as a separate cost centre.

17.39.2 Accordingly, we consider that provision for the Library should not be included in the block-grant which we have recommended[30] should be made to the Archbishop.

17.40 We further **recommend** that:

> a. in their statutory accounts, the Commissioners should identify the cost of the Library (wherever it is situated); and
>
> b. that cost should be disclosed[31] as a separate item, and not attributed to bishops.

Relationship with other parts of Lambeth Palace

17.41.1 There is a lack of clarity in the relationship between the Archbishop and the trustees of the Lambeth Palace Library Trust so far as concerns the running of Lambeth Palace.

17.41.2 Everyone else[32] who works within Lambeth Palace is *de facto* an employee of the Archbishop.[33] The Librarian and his staff are *de facto* employees of the trustees.[34] The Librarian is not a member of the Archbishop's personal staff and he is not one of the principals[35] at Lambeth. Various efforts are made to make the staff within the Library feel that they are one with the others who work within the palace, but our assessment is that despite those efforts, for the most part the staff consider themselves to be, and are regarded as, working in a largely separate unit.

17.42.1 There is also a lack of clarity about the use of the Library Buildings. We observed in our First Report[36] that it is not the practice for there to be a licence between the Commissioners and diocesan bishops with regard to see houses, and although Lambeth Palace is not a see house,[37] similarly there is no licence between the Commissioners and the Archbishop. This has much potential for confusion and leaves open the extent to which the Archbishop can control the use of the Library Buildings. Were the trustees to be tenants of the Library Buildings the Archbishop would, in principle, not have such a right.[38] On the other hand, the Archbishop clearly does have such a right with regard to the remainder of the palace.

17.42.2 Such uncertainty, which is part of the larger question of the extent of the authority of the trustees, is unsatisfactory.

17.43   We **recommend** that for so long as the Lambeth Palace Library is located within Lambeth Palace:

> a.   the Librarian should also be a member of the Archbishop's personal staff;[39]
>
> b.   he should therefore fall within the purview of the Chief of Staff whom we have proposed;[40] and
>
> c.   it should be for the Archbishop, or the Chief of Staff on his behalf, to determine the use of all space within the palace, but having regard to the requirements of the Library.

Concluding observation

17.44   Some of our recommendations might be thought to suggest a diminution in the standing of the Library. That is not the purpose of them, and we repeat that we are in no way casting doubt on the value of the Library.

Part IV:
The Archbishop of York

chapter 18

The needs and resources of the Archbishop of York

Introduction

18.1   In this chapter we consider:

a.   the roles and workload of the Archbishop of York;

b.   the context in which he performs those roles;

c.   the resources which are presently provided for the Archbishop;

d.   possible changes in the Archbishop's roles; and

e.   the resourcing implications of those changes.

The roles of the Archbishop of York

18.2   The offices[1] held by the Archbishop of York are those of:

a.   Archbishop;

b.   Diocesan Bishop of the Diocese of York;

c.   Metropolitan; and

d.   Primate.

18.3   As Archbishop, the Archbishop of York is a spiritual leader of the Church and nation. He is a member of the House of Lords[2] and, after the Archbishop of Canterbury, the most senior Lord Spiritual.

18.4.1   The Archbishop of York is the diocesan bishop of the Diocese of York. There are three suffragan sees[3] in the diocese, and in addition, one Provincial Episcopal Visitor[4] is, formally, a suffragan bishop in the diocese.

18.4.2   The present Archbishop of York, as diocesan bishop,[5] has conferred on the suffragan bishops, but not to the exclusion of himself, certain powers, including those relating to ordination and patronage, but he has not made an exhaustive delegation of his powers as diocesan.

18.4.3   The Archbishop, as diocesan, has a close relationship with the Diocesan Office. The Diocesan Secretary, who, by decision of the Archbishop, bears the title of Chief Executive Officer of the diocese, regards himself as being directly accountable to the Archbishop. He is formally accountable to the Chairman of the York DBF.

18.5   As Metropolitan, the Archbishop of York has canonical jurisdiction over the fourteen dioceses which comprise the Northern Province. He does not have metropolitical jurisdiction over any Churches overseas.

18.6.1   The Archbishop of York is Primate of England[6] and as such shares with the Archbishop of Canterbury the leadership of the Church of England.

18.6.2   The Archbishop of York shares the chairmanship of the Archbishops' Council. In practice, but not by virtue of office, the present Archbishop usually chairs meetings of the Board of Governors of the Church Commissioners and the standing committee of the House of Bishops.

18.6.3   The Archbishop leads the Church of England in its relationship with other Churches in the Porvoo Communion.[7] This does not involve a major commitment of his time.[8]

Workload and time

18.7   The Archbishop's workload is demanding. Each Archbishop orders his schedule in his own way. Dr Hope regards his working day (weekday or weekend) as beginning at 6am and as ending on some days at about 6pm and on others at about 10.30pm. He attempts to keep some days and some evenings clear, but, we surmise, by no means with complete success.[9]

18.8   Dr Hope estimates that he spends broadly one-third of his own time on each of (a) diocesan affairs (b) provincial affairs and (c) primatial and archiepiscopal affairs. A somewhat greater proportion of the time of some members of his staff is spent on diocesan affairs.

Relationship with the central structures of the Church of England

18.9.1   There are three areas of relationship which affect the context in which the Archbishop performs his ministry. The first is the Archbishop's relationship with the central structures of the Church of England.

18.9.2   We have referred[10] to the Archbishop of Canterbury as having, and needing to have, a certain degree of independence from such structures. This is because the Archbishop of Canterbury, as President of the Anglican Communion, may need to hold a balance between the Church of England on the one hand and other Churches within the Anglican Communion on the other. We have also shown[11] that, in order to exercise leadership, the Archbishop of Canterbury may wish to take a line on matters on which there is no concluded General Synod view.

18.9.3   The Anglican Communion considerations do not apply to the Archbishop of York and his work in relation to the Porvoo Communion does not require him to have any independence from the structures of the Church of England.

18.9.4   Potentially the Archbishop of York might need a degree of independence in order to be able to exercise a national leadership role, although, so far as we have been able to establish, this need has not arisen in recent years.

Relationship with the Commissioners

18.10.1   The second relationship is with the Commissioners. The Archbishop of York is both (a) in practice the Chairman of the Board of Governors of the Church Commissioners and (b) dependent on the Commissioners for almost[12] all of the resources provided for him. However, no evidence whatever has been adduced to us to suggest that this apparent conflict of interest gives rise to any difficulty.

18.10.2   This is because the relationship between the Archbishop and the Commissioners with regard to the provision of resources is broadly the same as that which applies in the case of other diocesan bishops and, accordingly, detailed decisions as to resourcing are taken by the Bishoprics and Cathedrals Committee of the Commissioners, of which the Archbishop is not a member. The observations which we have made[13] in relation to the Archbishop of Canterbury apply also to the Archbishop of York.

18.10.3 The absence of difficulty is no doubt also due in part to the notable restraint which Dr Hope exercises in seeking resources, but as the natural demand for resources grows so the potential for difficulty increases.

Relationship with the Archbishop of Canterbury

18.11.1 The third relationship is with the Archbishop of Canterbury. By way of background, we have described in a previous chapter[14] the similarities and dissimilarities in the roles of the two Archbishops.

18.11.2 The position changes from time to time, but for resourcing purposes, the major differences are that:

> a.   the Archbishop of York is in the fullest sense the diocesan bishop of his diocese, whereas the Archbishop of Canterbury is not;

> b.   the Archbishop of York's official overseas commitments are small: those of the Archbishop of Canterbury are substantial; and

> c.   the Archbishop of York works solely from Bishopthorpe, whereas the Archbishop of Canterbury has a dual site operation and works from both Lambeth Palace and the Old Palace, Canterbury.

18.12   Two particular aspects of the relationship between the Archbishops concern us, namely cohesion and the division of archiepiscopal and primatial roles.[15] On the first aspect, that the two Archbishops – and their staffs – should work closely together, keep each other in their confidence, and to the very greatest extent speak with one voice is axiomatic, and we do not need not comment on it further.

18.13.1 We do, however, comment on the second aspect, namely the division of archiepiscopal and primatial roles. There are established procedures whereby a diocesan bishop is able formally to delegate powers to a suffragan. There is no procedure for the formal division of the national roles between the Archbishop of Canterbury and the Archbishop of York, and there is no body which has standing authority to allocate responsibilities between them.

18.13.2 It is for the Archbishops and not for us to suggest how these roles should be allocated. However, we have recommended[16] that the allocation should be reviewed near to the beginning of the archiepiscopates of either of the Archbishops. Both Archbishops will wish to know exactly what each expects of the other. Without encouraging formality where it is not essential, we **recommend** that the division of responsibilities should be recorded in writing, and that where one function is to be primarily performed by one Archbishop, then the extent, if any, of the circumstances in which the other Archbishop will have a role in that function should be made entirely clear.

Present resources

18.14.1 We turn now to the main resources which the Commissioners provide for the Archbishop of York. They can be summarized as:

    a.   private residential accommodation at Bishopthorpe;

    b.   working accommodation at Bishopthorpe;

    c.   a personal staff, of which we give details in the next chapter;[17]

    d.   working accommodation for the staff;

    e.   reception and meeting rooms;

    f.   a chapel;

    g.   IT and other equipment for the Archbishop and his staff;

    h.   facilities for the provision of hospitality;

    i.   accommodation for overnight official guests;

    j.   a car and a driver; and

    k.   funds to enable the Archbishop and his staff to travel.

18.14.2 The Archbishop also has the use of a small flat at Lambeth Palace, although this is provided by arrangement with the Archbishop of Canterbury and not on the initiative of the Commissioners.

18.14.3 The Archbishop has had modest support from the York DBF.[18] In addition, he has had *pro bono* support, such as the services of his Special Adviser[19] as well as advice on human resources and IT matters.

Composite provision of resources

18.15.1 As metropolitan, the Archbishop is provided with the specific resources of the services of the Vicar-General and the Provincial Registrar.[20]

18.15.2 Subject to that, the resources are provided to the Archbishop irrespective of the capacity in which he utilizes them. Thus, for example, the senior members of his staff may be engaged at different times during the day on diocesan, provincial or national affairs.

Observations on present resources

18.16.1 For reasons which we give in a subsequent chapter,[21] we are satisfied that, in principle, it is right for the Archbishop to continue to reside in and work in Bishopthorpe.

18.16.2 As will be seen, the Archbishop's private residential accommodation is totally unsatisfactory.[22]

18.16.3 The members of the Archbishop's staff are well-knit, but almost certainly in the medium term the size of the staff will need to be enlarged.[23]

18.16.4 However, subject to these points, looking at the position broadly as the Archbishop's role is currently conceived, both the nature and quantum of the resources provided for him at Bishopthorpe are about right.

Styles of ministry and national roles

18.17.1 We consider now two possible areas of change in an Archbishop of York's ministry. An Archbishop of York will be subject to a tension between the interests of the diocese and province on the one hand and the interests of the Church as a whole on the other. Dr Hope has placed emphasis on his diocesan and provincial ministry and we have no doubt that that has been greatly valued.

18.17.2 Some other Archbishops of York in the past have placed, and in the future may place, greater emphasis on a national role, perhaps accompanied by a reallocation of some national responsibilities.

18.18.1 If an Archbishop of York is to place more emphasis on a national role, he will need further staff support. We deal with that in the next chapter.[24]

18.18.2 In our view it should not be assumed that an increase in the size of the Archbishop of York's staff would necessarily increase the total resources made available to both Archbishops taken together. It might be possible to achieve this by a reallocation of resources between them.

18.18.3 If there is to be any reallocation of roles, we **recommend** that particular regard should be paid to the time and direct cost implications. Bishopthorpe is about 200 miles from London. It takes over, sometimes well over, 3 hours for the Archbishop to travel from Bishopthorpe to Church House, London. It would not be unusual for Dr Hope to make about 30 official return journeys to London each year. Great care is needed to keep the number of such journeys and, therefore, the cost in time and money, to a minimum, although we appreciate the difficulties in planning a number of meetings, sometimes involving many other people, so that optimum use is made of the Archbishop's time.

18.18.4 To keep as low as possible the number of journeys is one of the reasons why we have recommended[25] that the Archbishop should continue to be provided with overnight accommodation at Lambeth Palace.[26]

The Hurd Report

18.19 The second respect in which the Archbishop of York's ministry might change is if recommendations in the Hurd Report are implemented. The recommendations are that:

a.   the Archbishop of York should have an advanced national role;[27]

b.   he should take a greater part in the overall governance of the Church of England by, for example, taking the lead archiepiscopal role in General Synod and usually chairing meetings of the Archbishops' Council;[28]

c.   he should take on a greater share of representative attendance at State events;[29]

d.   he should represent the Church of England at Meetings of Primates in the Anglican Communion;[30] and

e.   to enable these additional duties to be undertaken, he should reduce his commitments within the Diocese of York.[31]

18.20   The first two of these recommendations cover matters which we considered in the previous section, and we have no further comment on them.

18.21   We support the third recommendation, so that, save in exceptional circumstances, both Archbishops would only occasionally need to attend the same national or State events.

18.22   In relation to the Anglican Communion, we think it unlikely that it would be acceptable to the other Primates of the Anglican Communion for the Archbishop of Canterbury to preside and for the Archbishop of York to represent the Church of England at the Primates' Meeting. Furthermore, we have had no evidence that the Church of England has been disadvantaged by the Archbishop of Canterbury being both the President and the representative of the Church of England.

18.23   We accept that, with the Archbishop's existing workload,[32] any material increase in national responsibilities would involve some reduction in the Archbishop's commitments within the Diocese of York – however unwelcome that would be.

Other prospective changes

18.24.1   On a more detailed point, as in the case of the Archbishop of Canterbury, we expect that the Archbishop of York will be required, in his metropolitical capacity, to spend more time in dealing with disciplinary matters if the Clergy Discipline Measure 2000 is enacted.[33] It seems likely that there would be an increase in the time which would be taken up by the Archbishop in dealing with appeals against disciplinary decisions.[34]

18.24.2   Provided, however, as we assume will be the case, that there will continue to be adequate support from the Provincial Registrar, so far as we can judge, this increase in workload should not require additional resources other than, perhaps, some additional administrative support, but this would need to be reviewed in the light of experience.

18.25   The observations which we have made[35] about communications equipment for the Archbishop of Canterbury apply also in principle to the Archbishop of York.

18.26　　We are not aware of any other likely developments in the Church of England during the next ten years in the ministry of the Archbishop, in any of its aspects, which will have resourcing implications, except those which affect all bishops.[36]

chapter 19

The Archbishop of York's staff

Introduction

19.1.1   The Archbishop of York has traditionally run a tight ship at Bishopthorpe. He has done so with a small, committed and cohesive staff. The members of the staff know their own responsibilities, but they are willing to go outside their own areas of responsibility and to help out each other when the occasion requires.

19.1.2   In this chapter we consider the Archbishop's staff and make recommendations with regard to it.

Location

19.2.1   The preliminary question is whether Bishopthorpe should be retained, and should continue to provide the working accommodation for the Archbishop's staff.

19.2.2   For the reasons given in a later chapter,[1] we consider that, in principle, Bishopthorpe should be retained, and should continue to provide the residential and working accommodation for the Archbishop. We consider that the Archbishop should have his personal staff with him in his immediate surroundings, and we therefore **recommend** that his staff should continue to work at Bishopthorpe.

Staff offices

19.3   The staff offices are located together in the main palace building. They provide ease of access for face to face contact, and we **recommend** that in this respect the present arrangements should continue.

Atmosphere

19.4.1   Three aspects of the working atmosphere at Bishopthorpe stand out. First, it may be thought that the smaller the staff the easier it is to engender a sense of loyalty. Whether or not that is so, loyalty to the Archbishop is present at Bishopthorpe in abundance. We discern this as being loyalty both to the Archbishop personally and to the office of Archbishop.

19.4.2   Secondly, the Bishopthorpe precincts are not enclosed. Although there are notices that the property is private, those who are minded to do so are able to walk[2] or drive into the grounds without challenge. The openness of the physical setting gives a sense of accessibility. Indeed, part of the grounds is specifically set aside for public use.

19.4.3   Thirdly, Bishopthorpe is in a village, not a large built-up area. That, together, perhaps, with the physical distance from the location of the other National Church Institutions,[3] contributes to a sense that those working in the palace must to a large extent be self-reliant.

The present establishment

19.5   Without purporting to indicate formal line management, the present establishment at Bishopthorpe can be illustrated as follows:

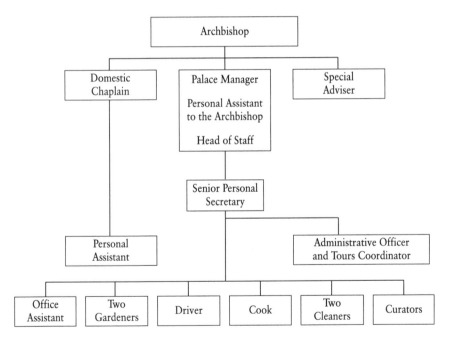

19.6   The following points are to be noted:

19.6.1   The Domestic Chaplain has a full-time post, of which at present half of the time is as the Archbishop's Chaplain and the other half as the Diocesan Director of Ordinands. His salary and associated costs are shared between the Commissioners and the York DBF;

19.6.2 The post of Palace Manager was originally that of the Archbishop's Personal Assistant. That is still very much part of the role, but it has been developed and the post-holder now also holds the titles of Palace Manager and Head of Staff. For convenience, in this report we refer to the post-holder as the Palace Manager;

19.6.3 The present Special Adviser is a retired Chaplain-General who provides his services *pro bono* for two days a week. He works with the Domestic Chaplain and the Palace Manager[4] in supporting the Archbishop with regard to his responsibilities to the wider Church and to the secular world;

19.6.4 The Archbishop's driver attends to other duties when he is not driving the Archbishop. On some occasions the Archbishop drives himself;

19.6.5 The two curators, a husband and wife, provide a wide range of duties as custodians,[5] caretakers, and general assistants. They are not remunerated, but are provided with accommodation on a house-for-duty basis.

19.7 Other than the Archbishop, there is no bishop at Bishopthorpe and, apart from the Domestic Chaplain and the Special Adviser, there is no other ordained member of the staff.

19.8 The history of continuity in post is good. The following table shows whether the posts are full-time or part-time and the length of service of the post-holders:

	Full- or part-time	Approximate length of service
Domestic Chaplain	Effectively part-time	4 years
Palace Manager	Full-time	13 years
Special Adviser	2 days	4 years
Senior Personal Secretary	Full-time	14 years
Personal Assistant to the Domestic Chaplain	Part-time (28 hours)	13 years

	Full- or part-time	Approximate length of service
Administrative Officer and Tours Coordinator	Full-time	10 years
Office Assistant	Part-time (16½ hours)	3 years
Head Gardener	Full-time	25 years
Assistant Gardener	Full-time	13 years
Driver	Full-time	4 years
Cook	Part-time (25 hours)	12 years
Cleaner (public rooms)	Part-time (16 hours)	15 years
(offices)	Part-time (3 hours)	3 years
Curators	as required	1 year

19.9.1 At one time the Archbishop of York had a chaplain and a secretary, together with a significant domestic and gardening staff. Since then the pattern has been to reduce the number of domestic staff, and increase the number of administrative staff to the present level of three full-time and three part-time posts.

19.9.2 The pattern has also been one of a progressive increase in the level of staff responsibility and, accordingly, some upward re-grading of posts. In part this has been as a result of delegation by Dr Hope to his staff of various matters, such as the procedural aspects of appointments, and in further part it has been due to increased opening of the palace.[6] The trend is more widespread among members of the Archbishop's staff, so that, for example, the head gardener is now responsible for all aspects of planning the garden.

19.9.3 Each Archbishop has his own wishes for his staff. Our assessment is that the staff at Bishopthorpe have adapted well to changed expectations and circumstances. We **recommend** that the present arrangements for the Archbishop to have a personal staff at Bishopthorpe should continue.

The Palace Manager

19.10.1 The Palace Manager acts as a personal assistant to the Archbishop. She makes arrangements for the Archbishop's visits; manages his diary; makes arrangements for post-consecration receptions;[7] and liaises with other bishops, members of the clergy, members of General Synod, staff of the Archbishops' Council, of the Commissioners, and of the Archbishop of Canterbury, as well as diocesan personnel and members of the general public. The Palace Manager is often the first point of contact for public and media enquiries. She is responsible for the smooth running of the Archbishop's office, and the palace in general. She manages the local expenses account.[8]

19.10.2 Significantly for the purposes of this report, the Palace Manager is also charged with ensuring value for money in all aspects of the work of the palace, and developing existing and new income streams, such as the use of part of the palace for conferences. We refer further to this aspect of her work in a later chapter.[9]

Press and communications

19.11.1 It will have been noted that the Archbishop's staff does not include a press officer, public affairs officer, or communications officer.

19.11.2 The Archbishop previously had on his staff a part-time media adviser who worked approximately two days a week. When that adviser formed his own company, the Archbishop entered into a contract with that company for the supply of that person's services as Press Officer. Those services are used primarily in respect of national issues with which the Archbishop is concerned. The adviser is based in London.

19.11.3 The York DBF has fairly recently appointed a Diocesan Communications Officer, but his work is very largely discrete to the diocese, and he is asked to assist the Archbishop only to a very limited extent. The Diocesan Communications Officer does not in any way also act as the Archbishop's Communications Officer.[10]

19.11.4 The Archbishop does not make extensive use of the services of the Communications Unit of the Archbishops' Council.

19.11.5 For diocesan issues, or wider issues if the Press Officer is not available, the Palace Manager liaises with the press.

19.11.6 These arrangements appear to work to the satisfaction of Dr Hope, but we do not regard them as entirely satisfactory. We **recommend** that there should be a press officer (to be responsible for all media relations) or, perhaps, a public affairs officer, as a member of the Archbishop's personal staff: this will be essential if an Archbishop of York takes on an enhanced national role.[11]

Research

19.12.1 It is also noteworthy that there is no Research Assistant on the Archbishop's staff. The Special Adviser assists the Archbishop in maintaining some current research materials, and his Domestic Chaplain may also assist him with research from time to time. However, the Archbishop himself conducts most of his own research.

19.12.2 Dr Hope does not complain about this, but we **recommend** that he should be provided with research assistance. We hope that our recommendation[12] for the devolution to the Archbishop of funds by way of block-grant will give sufficient flexibility for this to be provided.

Observations on the present position

19.13.1 We commented[13] at the outset of this chapter on the cohesion of the members of the Archbishop's staff and their mutual cooperation.

19.13.2 There are two further general observations. First, as has been shown,[14] most of the members of the Archbishop's staff are long-serving and experienced. With the benefit of that experience, they are able – just – to cope with the present workload. It would be otherwise with less experienced staff: hence succession planning is important. There is no slack.

19.13.3 Secondly, there is scope for increased use of electronic communication. The Archbishop has his personal email address, but apart from that there is only one email terminal in the office. Incoming email messages are printed out, and hard copies distributed within the palace in the same manner as incoming letters or faxes. We **recommend** greater use of information technology within the Archbishop's office,[15] but we doubt whether that would materially alleviate the workload.

19.14 More generally, we regard the present size of the Archbishop's staff as just adequate to support his present style of ministry, but that it would be inadequate if an Archbishop were to take on an enhanced role.

A Chief of Staff?

19.15.1 We turn now to possible future requirements. The Hurd Report recommended[16] that the Archbishop of York should have an enhanced national role. Quite apart from that recommendation, it may be that future Archbishops of Canterbury and York will agree between them[17] a different allocation of archiepiscopal and primatial responsibilities.

19.15.2 Although there are no plans to this effect, it is also possible that, at some time in the future, there might be a re-location of the Diocesan Office of the Diocese of York to Bishopthorpe.[18]

19.15.3 Furthermore, proposals which we make later[19] envisage a substantial increase in the income-generating activities to be conducted within the palace.

19.16.1 In these circumstances it would be necessary to re-examine the staffing structure within the palace, and it may well be appropriate to appoint a Chief of Staff. Without predicting the outcome of such a re-examination, it might involve a re-grading of the post of Palace Manager and a re-allocation of responsibilities.

19.16.2 The management responsibilities of a Chief of Staff would be much less than those of the corresponding officer whom we recommended[20] should be appointed for the Archbishop of Canterbury. Furthermore, so far as we can predict, the sensitivities of the office of Chief of Staff to the Archbishop of York would be less than those of the Chief of Staff to the Archbishop of Canterbury.

19.16.3 Accordingly, if there is to be a Chief of Staff at Bishopthorpe, we do not consider that the post would be ranked as highly as that at Lambeth Palace. Nevertheless, good cooperation between the two would be of primary importance – we regard close liaison with the Archbishop of Canterbury's staff as being a major responsibility of a Chief of Staff – and to encourage this both officers would need to be of sufficient calibre for them to have mutual respect.

A Finance Officer?

19.17.1 We applaud the fact that it is part of the responsibilities of the Palace Manager to ensure value for money and to develop income streams. In a later chapter[21] we make recommendations which are designed to encourage income generation.

19.17.2 We do not, however, propose the appointment of a finance officer at Bishopthorpe[22] as we expect that the Palace Manager would continue to be able to perform that role. However, as we note in the next section, if the extent of the financial activities greatly increases, it would need to be considered whether any further staff assistance should be provided.

Income generation

19.18.1 The Administrative Officer and Tours Coordinator assists with conference bookings, coordinating tours of the palace, receptions, Open Days and dinners, and handles the proceeds of sale of palace goods. She also prepares for audit the Events Account.[23] She estimates that these activities occupy about 35 per cent of her time.

19.18.2 If there is to be a substantial increase in income-generating activities, there would be a requirement for increased capacity in this post. The cost of that increase would need to be budgeted into the programme.[24]

Catering

19.19.1 The Archbishop's cook works for four mornings a week. She prepares lunch and (in advance) some weekend meals for the Archbishop – for which he pays – but she spends most of her time catering for official hospitality provided by the Archbishop and, increasingly, catering for those using the conference centre[25] or those attending buffet lunches and receptions.[26]

19.19.2 The cook prepares lunch and dinner for parties of up to 40 people, or buffet meals for up to 70. For the larger events, she is assisted by another member of staff, while the curators may act as stewards and wait, and the Archbishop's driver acts as a wine waiter. It is an attraction for some visitors to Bishopthorpe to know that they are being looked after by members of the Archbishop's personal staff.

Housekeeping

19.20 There is no housekeeper on the Archbishop's staff. Housekeeping is dealt with by the Palace Manager during working hours. Where official guests stay overnight at Bishopthorpe, they are looked after outside working hours by the Archbishop personally.

Gardens

19.21   The grounds at Bishopthorpe[27] are maintained by two gardeners. That arrangement works efficiently and cost effectively, and we do not suggest any change to it. No doubt the Chief of Staff would look at the options as and when the gardeners retire.

Relationship with other National Church Institutions

19.22.1 The Archbishop's staff at Bishopthorpe is largely self-contained. In part, this is due to the distance from the other National Church Institutions, all of which are in London. In part, it is due to the fact that it is often easier and quicker to deal with matters locally than through central organs of the Church. We do not suggest that there is a positive policy for the Archbishop to have an independent operation at Bishopthorpe, or for other National Church Institutions not to involve his staff, but the relationship with the staff of some other National Church Institutions could be closer.

19.22.2   We have no doubt that one of the functions of a Chief of Staff, if appointed, at Bishopthorpe, would be to establish and maintain a close, and collaborative, working relationship with the staff of the Archbishop of Canterbury, of the Archbishop's Council and of the Commissioners. We have referred previously to the close relationship which should be established with the Archbishop of Canterbury's Chief of Staff, the Secretary General of the General Synod and the Secretary of the Church Commissioners.

Non-duplication

19.23   A further consequence of the staff at Bishopthorpe being largely self-contained is that there is no duplication – or perceived duplication – of functions performed at Bishopthorpe with those performed in other National Church Institutions.

Human resources

19.24.1 The Archbishop of York (in his corporate capacity) is one of the National Church Institutions[28] and so he is one of the common employers of all staff employed within those institutions. He is the managing employer of his personal staff.[29]

19.24.2 As one of the National Church Institutions, the Archbishop is able to take advantage of the services provided by the Human Resources

Department of the Archbishops' Council. A proportionate part of the cost, calculated according to use, of that Department is attributed to the Commissioners, and accounted for by the Commissioners as part of the Archbishop's operational costs.

19.25.1 Put at its simplest, the HR Department:

> a.   superintends a regime for the appointment of members of staff who will serve in any of the National Church Institutions; and

> b.   provides advice on a wide range of human resource issues.[30]

19.25.2 The Archbishop would be expected to follow the standard procedure in the event of vacancies on his staff, but from a narrow perspective there seems to be little merit in his so doing. In practice, it is most unlikely, for example, that someone who is working for one of the other National Church Institutions, which are all in London, would wish to re-locate to Bishopthorpe.

19.25.3 From a broader perspective, however, the Archbishop, as a leader of the Church as a whole, will wish to lead by example. However, we **recommend** that modified arrangements for the appointment of staff should apply so that external advertisement could proceed concurrently with internal advertisement.

19.26.1 The Archbishop makes little use of the advisory services provided by the HR Department, preferring where possible to obtain *pro bono* local advice.

19.26.2 We support the principle of meeting some resourcing needs by *pro bono* support.[31] In all instances, however, it must be of a nature on which, for his own protection, the Archbishop can rely.

Employment

19.27.1 In our First Report, we recommended[32] that the secretaries of bishops in a diocese should be employed by the Diocesan Board of Finance of that diocese, albeit that bishops should be fully involved in the selection process.

19.27.2 We made that recommendation:

a. so that the bishops would not themselves have to deal with complex issues of employment law;

b. so that DBFs would, from a pool of staff experienced in Church administration, be able to provide cover on a temporary basis;

c. so that movement of staff between a diocesan office and the bishop's office would be facilitated;

d. so that anomalies in the terms and conditions of a bishop's staff and those employed in the diocesan office and elsewhere in the diocese could be progressively eliminated; and

e. so that, if difficulties arose between a bishop and a member of his staff, the member of staff could, without disloyalty, raise that matter with the officer within the DBF who is responsible for human resources issues.

19.27.3 Some of those factors, particularly the first, might be thought to apply to the Archbishop of York's staff, but we consider that the size and nature of his staff and the expertise available to him are such that the arrangement which we recommended in the case of other bishops should not apply to the Archbishop. We would be very reluctant to see the discontinuance of an existing arrangement which clearly works well. Accordingly, while the staffing structure remains as it is at the present time, we **recommend** that there should be no change to the present employment arrangements.

19.28.1 Two circumstances might, however, occur, on the happening of either of which the position would need to be re-examined. First, we **recommend** that if the diocesan office of the Diocese of York should become located on the Bishopthorpe estate,[33] then there should be a common employment arrangement for all staff. We leave open to be decided at the time whether the Archbishop's staff should continue to be employed[34] under the current arrangements or whether they should be employed by the DBF.

19.28.2 Secondly, we propose later a possible ownership structure for Bishopthorpe. Within that structure, there would be separately employed staff and it would be necessary to consider how their employment arrangements would relate to those of the Archbishop's staff.

chapter 20

Financial management and control at Bishopthorpe

Introduction

20.1.1 In this chapter we consider the arrangements for financial management and control at Bishopthorpe, and we make recommendations with regard to them. We also refer to relevant recommendations on financial affairs which are made in other chapters of this report.

20.1.2 At the end of the chapter, we summarize the amounts which the Commissioners have provided in the years 2000 and 2001 in support of the Archbishop of York.

20.1.3 As a general principle, we consider that Bishopthorpe should be a separate cost and accounting centre.

Present position: operational costs

20.2 With some variations, the present arrangements with regard to the payment of operational costs and premises expenses which apply to the Archbishop of York are the same as those which apply to other bishops.[1] This accords with the Archbishop being in the fullest sense the diocesan bishop of the Diocese of York.

20.3.1 A budget for operational costs[2] is drawn up in discussion between the staff of the Bishoprics and Cathedrals Department of the Commissioners on the one hand and the Archbishop and his staff on the other.

20.3.2 The salary and office equipment costs are paid directly by the Commissioners and debited to the central account in their books.

20.3.3 The Commissioners remit amounts quarterly[3] to a local bank account which is administered by the Archbishop's Administrative Officer. From this account the other, smaller, operational costs are paid.

20.3.4 The operational costs which are paid in these ways cover not only those incurred by the Archbishop in his capacity as diocesan bishop, but also those incurred by him in his capacities as metropolitan, primate and archbishop.

20.3.5 The Archbishop's Administrative Officer prepares and sends to the Bishoprics and Cathedrals Department quarterly details of the expenditure made from the local account.

20.3.6 On the basis of that information and details in their own records, the Bishoprics and Cathedrals Department prepares reports which are sent to the Archbishop's staff.

20.3.7 The Bishoprics and Cathedrals Department monitor during the course of a year financial performance against budget.

20.3.8 The Archbishop's staff have some, but only limited,[4] opportunity also to monitor performance against budget.

Premises expenses

20.4.1 In relation to premises expenses, a rolling programme of maintenance and repairs, and of any essential capital works, is formulated. It is intended that this programme will be based on quinquennial inspections, but at the time when this report is being written only the first of these inspections is due to be carried out. The programme is costed and agreed between the Commissioners' agent[5] and the Bishoprics and Cathedrals Department. The anticipated cost is included in the Commissioners' housing budget.

20.4.2 Payments for works carried out to implement the programme are made by the Commissioners direct and debited to the housing account in their books.

20.4.3 A budget for the other premises costs is drawn up between the Archbishop's staff and the Bishoprics and Cathedrals Department.

20.4.4 Amounts are remitted by the Commissioners to a separate local bank account quarterly. Other premises expenses are paid from that account.

20.4.5 Financial performance against budget is reviewed by the

Bishoprics and Cathedrals Department on an *ad hoc* basis, but not by the Archbishop's staff.

20.4.6   As will be seen,[6] an important exception to the principle that the Commissioners meet the cost of premises expenses is that certain works are paid for from income generated within the palace.

Overseas travel

20.5   It would be open to the Archbishop to charge the cost of official overseas travel[7] to the Commissioners' overseas travel account,[8] but in recent years it has been the practice of the Archbishop to treat these travelling expenses as ordinary operational costs.

Metropolitical resources

20.6   The only separate resources which the Archbishop has in his capacity as metropolitan are the services of the Provincial Registrar and the Vicar-General. Their fees are externally prescribed[9] and are paid directly by the Commissioners.

Financial management

20.7.1   We have noted,[10] and welcomed, the fact that the Palace Manager has, among her other responsibilities, those of:

a.   managing the financial aspects of the Archbishop's work;

b.   ensuring value for money in all aspects of activities within the palace; and

c.   enhancing income from existing sources and developing new sources of income.

20.7.2   Although the expression is not used, the Palace Manager is in effect also the Financial Controller of the palace.

Events account

20.8.1   We describe in the next chapter action which has already been taken and which is proposed to be taken to generate income from the palace.

20.8.2   The income which is raised is credited to a separate bank account. Accounts of income derived from events are prepared and audited.

20.8.3   From the proceeds of the income parts of the palace[11] have been renovated and equipment has been purchased for other income-generating activities.[12]

Charitable and other funds

20.9.1 There is no charitable trust established for the support of the Archbishop.

20.9.2 In 2000, there was severe local flooding and the Archbishop established a highly effective fund for the alleviation of those affected by it. That fund is administered by a member of his staff.

20.10 As in the case of most other diocesan bishops, the Archbishop has a discretionary fund, which is also administered by a member of the Archbishop's staff and disbursed on his instructions.

20.11 No money from these funds is used to meet any part of the Archbishop's operational costs or premises expenses, and it is not necessary for us to consider them further.

Devolution

20.12 We have recommended in an earlier chapter[13] that most of the funds provided by the Commissioners should be devolved to the Archbishop by way of block-grant. We have recommended[14] that there should be a block-grant to the Archbishop for the provision of resources for himself as diocesan bishop and for the other bishops of the Diocese of York, and a separate grant for the Archbishop in his other capacities.

20.13 We have also recommended[15] that an Archbishop's Resources Group should be established in order, among other purposes, to assist in the local provision of resources.

Palace accounts

20.14.1 We consider that the financial aspects of the Archbishop's work and of the other activities carried on within the palace should be considered as an entirety. This will be particularly so as the amount of generated income increases, and it will be even more so if funds are block-granted by the Commissioners.

20.14.2 In the light of these factors, we **recommend** that management accounts should be prepared within the palace to show its total financial operations. These accounts should show:

a. total expenditure;

b. the sources of funding for that expenditure (the Commissioners and self-generated income); and

c. the notional cost of parts of the property which are occupied by members of staff rent free.

Commissioners' financial support

20.15 The following table, which uses the expense categories which we recommended in our First Report,[16] shows, rounded, the Commissioners' financial support for the Archbishop of York during the years which ended on 31 December 2000 and 31 December 2001:

Description	Year ended 31 December 2000		Year ended 31 December 2001	
	Amount	Note	Amount	Note
(1)	(2) £	(3)	(4) £	(5)
A. Office and Support Staff Costs				
Stipend, pension contributions and employer's National Insurance contributions in respect of Archbishop's Chaplain and payments to part-time media adviser	34,000		35,000	
Salaries, pension contributions and employer's National Insurance contributions in respect of lay administrators and secretaries	88,000		99,000	
Exceptional staff costs	nil		1,000	
Staff Sub-total	122,000		135,000	
Office expenses	21,000		20,000	
Office equipment	nil		3,000	
Office furniture	nil		nil	
Miscellaneous	3,000		2,000	
Total A	146,000		160,000	
B. Administrative and Operational Costs				
Ordination expenses	nil		nil	
Patronage expenses	nil		nil	

Description	Year ended 31 December 2000		Year ended 31 December 2001	
	Amount	Note	Amount	Note
(1)	(2) £	(3)	(4) £	(5)
Training expenses	nil		2,000	
Legal fees	19,000	a	20,000	a
Removal and resettlement expenses of clergy members of staff	nil		nil	
Common services	9,000		37,000	
Total B	28,000		59,000	
C. Individual Working Costs				
Cars	7,000	b	7,000	b
Driver's pay	16,000		17,000	
Other travel within the United Kingdom, including petrol, and subsistence	10,000		10,000	
Hospitality	7,000		8,000	
Total C	40,000		42,000	
D. Premises Expenditure: Recurrent				
Heating, lighting and cleaning	8,000	c	11,000	c
Maintenance works, decoration and agents' fees	37,000		22,000	
Salaries and pension contributions of gardeners and domestic staff	42,000		45,000	
Council tax, water charges and garden equipment	10,000		nil	e
Insurance	nil	d	nil	d
Minor household and garden items	8,000		5,000	
Furnishings, equipment and restoration of portraits	1,000		nil	
Depreciation	nil		nil	
Total D	106,000		83,000	

Description	Year ended 31 December 2000		Year ended 31 December 2001	
	Amount	Note	Amount	Note
(1)	(2)	(3)	(4)	(5)
	£		£	
E. Premises Income: Recurrent				
Rents receivable	(8,000)		(9,000)	
	(8,000)		(9,000)	
F. Premises Expenditure: Capital				
General improvement works including agents' fees	39,000		19,000	
Transfer of part of kitchen garden	(8,000)		nil	
Total F	31,000		19,000	
G. Summary				
A. Office and Support Staff Costs	146,000		160,000	
B. Administrative and Operational Costs	28,000		59,000	
C. Individual Working Costs	40,000		42,000	
D. Premises Expenditure: Recurrent	106,000		83,000	
E. Premises Income: Recurrent	(8,000)		(9,000)	
F. Premises Expenditure: Capital	31,000		19,000	
TOTAL	£343,000		£354,000	

Notes:
(a) This figure excludes the fees paid to the Provincial Registrar.
(b) The lease payment of a car is paid as a lump sum on the commencement of the lease and is recorded in the Commissioners' accounts in the year in which it is incurred. The figures shown here are the portions of that amount spread over the period of the lease.
(c) The Commissioners account for these items as operational (or working) costs.
(d) Insurance cover is effected under the Commissioners' block policy, and no part of the premium is readily attributable to the Archbishop.
(e) This figure is shown as nil because in the year the Commissioners received a substantial credit for water charges for one of the associated properties which has been netted-off against the Council tax and other charges.

Publication

20.16   We recommend[17] that:

a.   details of operational costs should be disclosed together with other bishops' costs; and

b.   unless and until there is also disclosure by the Commissioners of premises expenses, these expenses should also be disclosed, if necessary by note to the Commissioners' statutory accounts.

chapter 21

Bishopthorpe Palace and its grounds

Introduction

21.1.1 In this chapter we consider Bishopthorpe Palace and its grounds, as a place for the Archbishop and his immediate family to live in, and as a place for the Archbishop and his personal staff to work in.

21.1.2 Many of the recommendations in this chapter are subject to:

a. the result of the first formal quinquennial inspection;[1] and

b. the outcome of the appraisal which we recommend.[2]

History

21.2 Bishopthorpe first became the home of Archbishops of York in 1241. With the exception of the Commonwealth period (1649–60), the palace has been in continuous use as a residence for the Archbishops since then.

Description

21.3 The palace and its associated buildings have grounds which comprise about 9 acres (3.6 hectares).

21.4.1 The buildings comprise:

a. main palace building, including a major wing on the north side;

b. between the road and the main palace building, a clock tower which bestrides the accessway;

c. between the road and that clock tower a converted coach block, together with a building, converted to a dwelling, known as The Brew House and currently occupied by the Archbishop's Chaplain; and

d. a house used by the Head Gardener.

21.4.2   Within the main palace building, there are:

    a.   accommodation for the private residential use of the Archbishop;

    b.   studies for the Archbishop and his chaplain;

    c.   offices for other members of his personal staff;

    d.   a chapel;

    e.   state rooms, being the Great Hall and the Drawing Room;

    f.   the main kitchen (on a floor below the Great Hall);

    g.   four double and one single official bedrooms;

    h.   two flats;

    i.   on the ground floor of the north wing, rooms which have been converted for use as a conference centre; and

    j.   also in the north wing, a self-contained flat known as 'the Ramsey flat'.

21.4.3   The basement of the main palace building is susceptible to flooding in severe conditions.

21.5   The former coach block has been converted into two flats.

21.6.1   The grounds, which are open, are bounded on the east by the River Ouse on which public boats ply. The grounds are in part susceptible to flooding and they do not provide privacy.

21.6.2   There are car parking areas within the grounds.

Adjacent properties

21.7.1   The Commissioners also own in the vicinity:

    a.   about 7 acres (2.8 hectares) of tenanted farmland, which are not managed as part of the Bishopthorpe estate;

    b.   two allotments;

    c.   a cricket field; and

    d.   two houses in the village of Bishopthorpe. They are let, although one is in need of considerable refurbishment.

21.7.2 We have recommended[3] that property in the vicinity of an archiepiscopal palace should be strategically managed with it.

Listing
21.8 The main palace building is listed Grade I as a building of architectural and historic interest and it is in a Green Belt. It is likely to be designated as being within a flood area.

Ownership and status
21.9 The palace is owned by the Commissioners, having been vested in them[4] as part of the process whereby all the former episcopal and archiepiscopal estates were transferred to the Commissioners.

21.10 The palace is the see house of the Archbishop of York.

Public access
21.11.1 Members of the public are invited to use and enjoy part of the grounds.

21.11.2 Apart from that the palace and its grounds are not open to the public as of right, but the grounds are opened on specific occasions and members of the public may see the grounds and the state rooms when they are participating in tours of the palace or attending receptions or other events.[5]

Maintenance costs
21.12.1 The cost of some refurbishment work has been met from income generated within the palace. As an example, in 2001 the Great Hall was decorated at a cost of £3,379, of which £1,500 was met from such income.

21.12.2 The Commissioners' expenditure in respect of the palace and the grounds in the years which ended on 31 December 2000 and 31 December 2001 has been stated in the previous chapter.[6]

Maintenance and repairs
21.13 The Commissioners employ a professional firm as see house agents.[7] That firm superintends the upkeep of the buildings and their grounds.

21.14.1 There is no direct labour force employed to look after the fabric of the buildings.[8] Such minor works as are necessary are carried out by local contractors under arrangements made by the Palace Manager. The Commissioners' agent makes arrangements with contractors for more major works to be undertaken.

21.14.2 The Archbishop's driver deals with minor matters about the property when he is not engaged on driving.

21.15.1 The Commissioners have recently[9] instituted a programme for the quinquennial inspection of see houses, and the carrying out of a programme of maintenance and other works based on that inspection.

21.15.2 The first such inspection of Bishopthorpe is due to be made later in 2002. Our recommendations made in the remainder of this chapter are subject to reconsideration[10] in the light of the inspection report when it is available.

Grounds

21.16 Two gardeners keep the grounds in a good state. The grounds comprise a small area of formal garden and a much more extensive area of largely natural woodland.

Capital and rental values

21.17.1 The property is carried in the books of the Commissioners at £1.[11]

21.17.2 We have not commissioned a valuation of the property,[12] but we have proceeded on the assumption that having regard to the cost of maintenance, and the constraints on altering the building and changing its use, the property has a present net value of not less than £3 million.

Retention or disposal

21.18 The fundamental question is whether the Commissioners should retain Bishopthorpe, or dispose of it and provide alternative accommodation for the Archbishop and his staff.

21.19.1 The Archbishop has a very small[13] personal staff and even if there is some increase in the size of the staff,[14] it is likely still to be small. It does not require a building of anywhere near the size of the main palace building (even without taking into account the other buildings) to provide proper residential accommodation for the Archbishop and his family[15] and working accommodation for his staff.

21.19.2 Furthermore, although the working accommodation for the Archbishop and his staff is satisfactory, as will be seen,[16] the residential accommodation provided for the Archbishop is not.

21.19.3 In addition, parts of the building, particularly those set aside as official bedrooms, are grossly under-utilized.[17]

21.20 On the other hand:

a. there is potential for a more intensive use of the property;

b. the property is a resource for the diocese, the Archbishop having encouraged its use for parish and diocesan 'quiet days';[18]

c. we recognize the value of historical continuity and the unique sense of place which attaches to the property; and

d. if the property were to be put on the market for sale, perhaps for use as a hotel, because of the high conversion costs which a purchaser would incur and the annual maintenance costs to which he would be liable thereafter, it is unlikely that the proceeds of sale net of relocation costs would be substantial.

21.21 We have not carried out a detailed evaluation, and we recommend later in this chapter that this should be done. Subject to the outcome of that appraisal, we **recommend** that the Commissioners should retain the property provided that:

a. proper residential accommodation is provided for the Archbishop;

b. existing measures to generate income from the property are enhanced; and

c. all parts of the buildings are put to effective use.

21.22 We consider in turn each of these aspects in the following paragraphs, and mention the possibility of the relocation of the diocesan office to Bishopthorpe.

The Archbishop's private residential accommodation

21.23.1 It might be supposed that a wing of the palace is set aside for the private use of the Archbishop, or, at the least, that he has the use of a good flat in the building. Neither is the case.

21.23.2 The Archbishop has a bedroom and bathroom. One goes down some steps and along a corridor to a small room which forms his sitting room. Come out of that room, cross the corridor, and there is a kitchen and breakfast area. Yet that corridor is the means of access to the Great Hall from the main kitchen. If the Great Hall is being used, staff must, therefore, go right through the Archbishop's private quarters. There is nothing separate or segregated about these quarters, and there is no sense of privacy.

21.23.3 This lack of privacy may not have mattered nearly so much in previous times when there were very few events taking place within the palace. The holding of such events, even at their present level, makes the present arrangements totally unsatisfactory: no Archbishop, or his wife or children, should be expected to live in these circumstances.[19]

21.24.1 We **recommend** that:

> a. self-contained private residential accommodation should be provided, at least up to the standard which accords with the relevant guidelines[20] for see houses generally; and

> b. depending on the outcome of the appraisal which we recommend,[21] that accommodation should be formed either in the north wing of the main palace building or elsewhere within the curtilage.

21.24.2 We also **recommend** that a small part of the grounds should be segregated, and formed into a private garden for use by the Archbishop and his family.

Income generation

21.25 The present activities which generate income from the property are:

> a. residential lettings;

> b. conferences;

> c. tours and sales of incidental items to visitors; and

> d. receptions and dinners.

Residential lettings

21.26.1 One of the flats in the converted coach block is let to a Church worker. Apart from the Ramsey flat, to which we refer below, no part of the main palace building is let.

21.26.2 As noted[22] there are two houses in the village which are let.

21.27.1 In the 1980s part of the north wing of the main palace building was converted into a flat, and was for a time lived in by Archbishop Michael Ramsey in his retirement.

21.27.2 In 1997 this flat, now known as the Ramsey flat, was refurbished primarily as a place in which members of the clergy could stay for short periods, particularly when they are in need of recuperation or quiet.

21.27.3 The cost of decorating and refurbishing this flat was met from income from visits and donations.

21.27.4 Depending on the circumstances of the person using the flat, a small rent is payable. It is not, however, primarily intended as a source of income generation. We regard the provision of this flat as part of the Archbishop's ministry.

21.27.5 It may be that this small flat should be absorbed into the accommodation which we have recommended[23] should be provided for the Archbishop. In that event, we hope that an alternative small flat could be provided for use by clergy and others. We **recommend** that:

> a.   as the first priority, the Ramsey flat (or a replacement flat) should continue to be made available for use by clergy and others on non-commercial terms; and

> b.   if it is not required for such use, then it should be available for other very short-term letting on commercial terms.

21.28.1 We **recommend** that, depending on the outcome of the appraisal which we propose,[24] there should be a review of those who need to live on the site or in the Commissioners' houses in the village.

21.28.2 We further **recommend** that, apart from the Ramsey flat, and apart from accommodation provided for those who need to live on site, residential accommodation should be commercially let.

21.28.3 We also **recommend** that in the preparation of the overall palace accounts which we have proposed,[25] there should be brought into account the rental value of the accommodation which is provided rent free for members of the Archbishop's staff as part of their terms of service. At present, such accommodation is provided for the Archbishop's chaplain, the head gardener, the Archbishop's driver and the curators.

Conferences

21.29.1 Two rooms in the north wing of the main palace building were adapted and equipped for conference use in 2000. They have their own entrance. The larger room has a maximum capacity of 30, and the smaller a capacity of 15.[26] The rooms are easily served from the main building. There are ample on-site car parking spaces.

21.29.2 The cost of providing the conference equipment for these rooms was met from the income from events and receptions in 2000/01.

21.29.3 We refer later[27] to the marketing of these facilities.

Events and receptions

21.30.1 Dr Hope introduced a policy of making the palace available on commercial terms for receptions and other events in order to raise money for the maintenance of its fabric. The Great Hall and the Drawing Room are the parts of the building most suitable for this purpose. The Great Hall has a maximum capacity of 70 and the Drawing Room a maximum capacity of 50.

21.30.2 The Archbishop's staff provide buffet lunches and food for receptions.[28] Outside caterers are engaged for dinners.

Tours of the palace

21.31 Although the palace is not open to individual members of the public, tours of the state rooms and chapel of the palace and the grounds are available for parties of between 10 and 50. There is a mobile shop for visitors.

Marketing

21.32.1 The income-generating activities (other than residential lettings) have been initiated by the Palace Manager, to implement the Archbishop's policy. Despite having had no previous experience in this field, we applaud the Palace Manager for having identified and taken advantage of some of the potential for these activities.

21.32.2 We also applaud the sensitivity with which these activities are conducted, so that only to a minimal extent do they interfere with the work of the Archbishop, and so that they do not intrude into the atmosphere and ethos of the palace.

21.33.1 Provided, as we have recommended,[29] separate, self-contained, private accommodation is made available for the Archbishop, we consider that there is considerable scope for expanding these activities.[30]

21.33.2 Subject to the outcome of the overall appraisal which we propose,[31] we **recommend** that so far as is consistent with maintaining the atmosphere and ethos of the palace, and not interfering with its use by the Archbishop, income-generating activities should be substantially increased, and the appropriate staff should be engaged to enable this to be done.

Income generation generally

21.34 The initiative of the Archbishop and, under his guidance, the Palace Manager, in seeking to identify and develop methods of raising income from the palace while not interfering with the work undertaken in it or the ethos of the place has pointed the way forward. Depending on the outcome of the appraisal, it now seems right to take these activities into a higher league.

Appraisal

21.35.1 The Church faces a major issue with regard to Bishopthorpe, which involves national and local interests. As is shown elsewhere in this chapter, Bishopthorpe should not be left as it is. In part[32] it is unsatisfactory. In part[33] the full income-generating potential has not been exploited. Furthermore, we would not be surprised if the quinquennial inspection[34] revealed major potential repairing liabilities.

21.35.2 We **recommend** that there should be a detailed feasibility study of:

a.   the likelihood of obtaining consents to implement the recommendations which we make;

b.   the cost of carrying out these works;

c.   the likely income to be derived from the property as converted;

d.   the period over which the capital expenditure would be recovered; and

e.   the interest cost which would be sustained in the meantime.

21.35.3 We also **recommend** that, for comparison, the appraisal should cover:

a.   the amount which might be expected to be realized from a disposal of the property; and

b.   the cost of providing alternative residential and working accommodation for the Archbishop and his operational staff and of those additional members of staff who we consider will need to be employed.

21.35.4 We further **recommend** that the feasibility study should be conducted jointly by the Commissioners and the Archbishop (or his representative).

21.35.5 The feasibility study should include the prospective re-location of the kitchen within the main palace building and the increase in catering facilities which would be necessary to serve the increased number of people visiting and using the palace.

Effective use

21.36.1 There are two further issues with regard to the use of accommodation and which should be taken into account in the appraisal. The first is with regard to the official guest bedrooms.[35]

21.36.2 It is possible to accommodate up to about 10 overnight guests, although in recent years the norm has been for up to about 5 guests to be put up. In the last three years the number of occasions on which official overnight guests have been accommodated in the palace have been:

    1999: 13
    2000: 5
    2001: 4

21.37.1 There will need to be works of reconstruction in order to implement some of our other proposals, but we consider that no more than one or two official guest bedrooms need to be provided within the

palace. In times of peak demand, other accommodation could be
arranged in the vicinity.[36]

21.37.2 A major factor in furthering the use of the conference centre
will be whether or not overnight accommodation can be provided.[37] We
recommend that in the appraisal:

    a.   consideration should be given to allocating space in order to
provide that type of accommodation; and if that is not possible

    b.   consideration should be given to forming out of that space
one or more flats for residential letting.

21.37.3 If overnight accommodation is provided primarily for those
attending conferences, that accommodation could also be used for
overnight official guests when there is an exceptional requirement.

Diocesan and other offices

21.38.1 The second issue about the use of space at Bishopthorpe relates
to the possible relocation of the diocesan office of the Diocese of York.
Views may vary on whether a diocesan bishop should have his main place
of work in, or adjacent to, the diocesan office.[38] We observe, however,
that, without having made any detailed appraisal, it would appear that
within the palace and its grounds there is space to provide a diocesan
office for the Diocese of York. This might well involve the reallocation
of some of the space currently used for residential occupation.

21.38.2 In 1998 the Commissioners gave initial consideration to a
proposal to re-convert the coach block so that the diocesan office could
be relocated to it. In consequence of a decision by the York DBF that
proposal did not proceed, but we understand that this was not on the
ground that the premises were physically unsuitable.[39]

21.38.3 We **recommend** that the possibility of relocation of the
diocesan office to Bishopthorpe should be taken into account as part of
the overall appraisal. We would hope that were the diocesan office to be
relocated then the proceeds of sale of the existing diocesan office might
be applied towards the capital costs which would be involved in
implementing our proposals.

21.38.4 One material factor in considering any relocation of the
diocesan office would be the extent to which diocesan and other

meetings which presently take place in the existing diocesan office would need to be held in the conference rooms in the main palace building, and the consequent impact on income-generating activities.

Ownership

21.39 In our First Report, we made recommendations[40] which included discussions within a diocese of the needs of the working and living accommodation of all bishops in the diocese and the eventual transfer of the ownership of see houses to the Diocesan Board of Finance. We were influenced in making that recommendation by the fact that much (but not all) of a diocesan bishop's ministry was local to the diocese; and that there was often within DBFs expertise in property management.

21.40.1 There are other factors in relation to Bishopthorpe. First, we envisage that if it is to be retained by the Commissioners, there should be a major income-generating activity at Bishopthorpe. The nature of the activities at Bishopthorpe is unlikely to change and the scale of those activities is likely to be very different from those of other see houses.

21.40.2 Secondly, the nature of the work undertaken by the Archbishop results in part in Bishopthorpe having elements of a provincial office, and to a lesser extent, a national office – and this work may increase.[41]

21.41.1 Particularly if, as a result of the appraisal, income-generating activities are to increase, we **recommend** the creation of a Bishopthorpe trust. The arrangement would be similar to that which we have proposed for Lambeth Palace,[42] and would involve:

> a. the creation of a charitable company limited by guarantee;
>
> b. the objects of that company, and of any subsidiary, being to seek to generate sufficient income to meet all or most of the recurrent expenses (and in the event of surplus, to apply that surplus for other purposes in furtherance of the Archbishop's ministry); and
>
> c. the grant by the Commissioners to the charitable company of a lease of the property.

21.41.2 Such an arrangement should reduce significantly the amount of time and money which the Commissioners would need[43] to spend on the property while providing sufficient encouragement for local endeavour.

Methodology and evidence

Introduction

1   The First Report of the Review Group and this report are the product of one overall review of the needs and resources of bishops and archbishops. Much of the information obtained, and evidence received, for the First Report also informed this report. This appendix deals only with the additional information and evidence which was obtained specifically for this report.

Invitations

2.1   General invitations to give oral or written evidence were extended to:

    a.   The Archbishop of Canterbury and Mrs Carey;

    b.   The Archbishop of York;

    c.   all other bishops;

    d.   all other bishops' wives;

    e.   all members of the General Synod; and

    f.   all members of the staffs of the Archbishops of Canterbury and York.

2.2   A list of those who responded is given later in this appendix.

3.1   Invitations were extended to a number of others to give evidence on specific aspects of the review.

3.2   In all cases these invitations were accepted. Those who gave evidence are also noted later in this appendix.

Meetings of the Review Group

4   There was some overlap between the initial work on the second phase of the review and the concluding work on the first phase.

ppendix A

5   The main work on the second phase commenced in March 2001 and has involved:

12 plenary meetings of the Review Group;

1 two-day residential meeting;

8 visits by some or all of the members of the Review Group to the archiepiscopal palaces; and

54 occasions[1] on which oral evidence was given to the Review Group.

Oral evidence

6   Oral evidence was given by:

a.   The Archbishop of Canterbury and (on a separate occasion) Mrs Carey; and

b.   The Archbishop of York.

7   Oral evidence was also given by 21 members of the staffs of the Archbishops of Canterbury and York. In accordance with assurances of confidentiality which were given to them, they are not listed here.

8   In addition, oral[2] evidence was given, at our request, by the following:

a. The Revd Preb Dr Paul Avis	General Secretary of the Council for Christian Unity
b. Mrs Ruth Badger	Then Secretary of the Bishoprics and Cathedrals Department
c. The Revd Dr William Beaver	Then Director of Communications, the Archbishops' Council
d. Mr William Chapman	Prime Minster's Appointments Secretary
e. Miss Mary Eaton	Formerly the Archbishop of Canterbury's Private Secretary
f. The Rt Revd Colin Fletcher, OBE	Bishop of Dorchester, formerly the Archbishop of Canterbury's Domestic Chaplain

g. Mr Ewan Harper, CBE   Member of the See of Canterbury
                                    Review Group

h. Mr Howell Harris Hughes   Secretary of the Church
                                    Commissioners

i. The Lord Hurd of Westwell,   Chairman of the See of Canterbury
    CH, CBE   Review Group

j. Miss Sue Jones   Official Solicitor to the Church
                                    Commissioners

k. Mr David Kemp   Diocesan Secretary, Diocese of
                                    Canterbury

l. Mr Andrew Male   See Houses Officer, Bishoprics and
                                    Cathedrals Department

m. Mr Philip Mawer   Secretary General of the General
                                    Synod

n. Mrs Su Morgan   Director of Human Resources,
                                    Archbishops' Council

o. Mr R M Morris, CVO   Secretary, See of Canterbury
                                    Review Group

p. Mr Michael Nunn   Director of Finance and
                                    Administration, Anglican
                                    Consultative Council

q. The Hon Sir John Owen   Formerly Dean of the Arches

r. Dr Richard Palmer   Librarian, Lambeth Palace Library

s. The Revd Lesley Perry   Formerly the Archbishop of
                                    Canterbury's Press Secretary

t. The Revd Canon John Peterson   Secretary General, Anglican
                                    Consultative Council

u. Miss Carol Pym   Finance Officer, Bishoprics and
                                    Cathedrals Department

v. The Revd Canon John Rees   Provincial Registrar, Province of
                                    Canterbury, and Legal Adviser to
                                    the Anglican Consultative
                                    Council

w. The Revd Canon Jim Rosenthal   Director of Communications, Anglican Consultative Council

x. Mr Anthony Sadler   Archbishops' Appointments Secretary

y. Mr Colin Sheppard   Diocesan Secretary, Diocese of York

z. Mr Richard Scott   Church Commissioners' agent for Lambeth Palace and The Old Palace, Canterbury

aa. Dr Wendy Sudbury   Director, Church of England Records Centre

bb. The Rt Revd Michael Turnbull   Bishop of Durham

cc. The Rt Revd Stephen Venner   Bishop of Dover

dd. The Very Revd Robert Willis   Dean of Canterbury

Written evidence

9   Written submissions were made or evidence given by:

a. Mr C A Beck   Diocesan Secretary, Diocese of Sheffield

b. Mr Peter Beesley   Senior partner, Messrs Lee Bolton & Lee

c. Mr Ian Fawkner   Formerly Chairman, Rochester DBF

d. Mr Alastair Findlay   Chairman, Worcester DBF

e. The Rt Revd Colin Fletcher, OBE   Bishop of Dorchester, formerly the Archbishop of Canterbury's Domestic Chaplain

f. Mr Robert Higham   Secretary, Worcester DBF

g. The Rt Revd Christopher Hill   Bishop of Stafford

h. The Very Revd John Methuen   Dean of Rippon

i. Mr R M Morris, CVO   Secretary, See of Canterbury Review Group

j.	Mr Michael Nunn	Director of Finance and Administration, Anglican Consultative Council
k.	The Rt Revd Anthony Priddis	Bishop of Warwick
l.	The Revd Canon John Rees	Provincial Registrar, Province of Canterbury and Legal Adviser to the Anglican Consultative Council
m.	The Rt Revd John Saxbee	Bishop of Ludlow
n.	The Rt Revd Stephen Venner	Bishop of Dover
o.	The Very Revd Robert Willis	Dean of Canterbury

Other information

10   In addition to the foregoing, we were much assisted by information given to us *ad hoc* at our request by members of the staffs of the Archbishops, of the Commissioners and of the Archbishops' Council.

Index to observations on the Hurd Report

The following is an index to the observations contained in this report on those recommendations in the Hurd Report which relate to resources for the Archbishop of Canterbury.

Reference in the Hurd Report	Subject of Hurd Report Recommendation	Reference to paragraph(s) in this report
Ch 10, p.74, para. (h)	There should be a planning team to prepare for the hand-over from a serving Archbishop of Canterbury to his successor	8.10.1
Ch 7, p.54, para. (g)	The number of overseas official visits undertaken by the Archbishop of Canterbury should be restricted	9.19.4
Ch 10, p.73	The post of Bishop at Lambeth should be abolished	12.15
Ch 10, p.73, para. (a)	There should be appointed a Chief of Staff to the Archbishop of Canterbury	12.16.1
Ch 10, p.73, para. (c)	The Chief of Staff should manage all staff at Lambeth Palace	12.18
Ch 10, p.73, para. (d)	There should be a presumption that the Chief of Staff will be lay	12.27.1
ibid	The Chief of Staff should be fully remunerated	12.28.1
Ch 5, p.35, para. (c)	There should be a review of the administrative functions of the Archbishop of Canterbury as metropolitan.	appendix E
Ch 4, p.29, para. (a)	There should be a more permanent delegation of episcopal powers to the Bishop of Dover	15.20.3

Reference in the Hurd Report	Subject of Hurd Report Recommendation	Reference to paragraph(s) in this report
Ch 7, p.53, para. (d)	A bishop from elsewhere in the Anglican Communion should be appointed to serve at Lambeth Palace	12.19; 16.98.3
Ch 6, p.39	The Archbishop of York should have an increased national role	18.19.a; 19.15.1
Ch 6, p.41	The Archbishop of York should take a greater part in the overall governance of the Church of England	18.19.b
Ch 6, p.42, para. (d)	The Archbishop of York should take on a greater share in representative attendance at State events	18.19.c
Ch 7, pp.51, 54, para. (h)	The Archbishop of York should represent the Church of England at Primates' Meetings	18.19.d
Ch 6, pp. 41, 42, para. (c)	The Archbishop of York should reduce his commitments within the Diocese of York	18.19.e

Archbishops in the Anglican tradition

An historical, theological and practical note by the Rt Revd Peter Nott

Introduction

1.1   In Chapter 2 we noted the difficulties inherent in attempting precise definitions of the nature and role of Archbishops based on historical and theological factors. Nevertheless we have always emphasized the importance of this kind of reflection as a background to our practical work. So what follows is an examination of certain issues that we believe to be important and which have informed our work.

1.2   We are very grateful for the generous help and advice we have received from three people who have assisted us in this reflection: Lord Habgood (JH),[1] Professor Owen Chadwick (OC)[2] and Dr Rowan Williams (RW).[3] They have kindly given us permission to quote extensively from our correspondence with them.

History

2.1   The authority of an archbishop is related to the nature and history of the diocese of which he is the bishop.

> 'Although it is a common principle of much early Christian theology that all bishops are equal (Cyprian), the practical conviction that some were more equal than others established itself fairly early. Bishops of the larger towns and cities clearly held some kind of precedence in a district; by the mid-third century, it is evident that when councils were held, the bishop of the leading city in a region would be in the chair.' (RW)

> 'To be bishop of Alexandria where St Mark was believed to have come as founder, and which by reason of the dominance of the city in the province dominated the whole church in

Egypt, was a job different in kind from that of being bishop of some (other) place that was hardly more than a village.' (OC)

2.2   In England something similar happened.

'When Mercia dominated England with its capital at Lichfield the king turned the see of Lichfield into an archbishopric. Why did York survive as an archbishopric? Because it first organized the union of Celtic and Roman Christianity in the north of England and so had the needed near-apostolic aura and because the Northerners were determined not to be dominated by Londoners from Lambeth.' (OC)

2.3   With very few exceptions archbishops are always diocesan bishops, and the history of the see is important.

'The Pope may be a world evangelist – but he is only so because he is Bishop of Rome. The bishop of that diocese was responsible for putting order into the very first Christian congregations of the western world and the history is indispensable to his authority. [The Archbishop of Canterbury] may have world responsibilities but he only has them because he is the Bishop of the Canterbury diocese. His predecessor was responsible for putting order into the first Christian congregations in Anglo-Saxon England and that history still matters to his authority and office.' (OC)

'The Archbishop's relation to a particular diocese remains essential. A bishop may be consecrated to a territorial see, or to responsibility for some defined pastoral constituency, or to an oversight in mission work in some area. It is at best very doubtful whether he could or should ever be consecrated to an office that has no organic relation with particular congregations and a "ministerial community" of some kind. If a metropolitan's office were defined by being one among a college of episcopal pastors, it would be a major departure from ancient usage to remove direct pastoral charge from him.' (RW)

So our third adviser comments, succinctly,

'The fact that they are diocesan bishops themselves is … essential to their credibility.' (JH)

2.4　There were exceptions to the normal practice of linking the office of archbishop to a particular see. When certain sees were conquered by (usually Muslim) invaders, the Roman Church:

> 'maintained their claim to the diocese by calling the bishop *in partibus infidelium* – he was still the bishop of Ephesus but couldn't get there as the politics of the world went. In the late 19th century Pope Leo XIII changed the title to "titular bishops" – titles which were used occasionally as a way of elevating the stature of certain senior officials in the church.' (OC)

2.5　In more recent times it has been the practice of some churches in the Anglican Communion, such as the Canadian and American Episcopal churches, for Presiding Bishops to have no diocese. The Report of the Archbishops' Group on the Episcopate commented on these examples that:

> 'these variants raise questions about the relationship of episcope and pastoral ministry.'[4]

Nomenclature

3.1　There is little agreement about the original differences, if any, in the use of the terms 'archbishop', 'primate', and 'metropolitan'.

> 'The historical record suggests (that) there is no difference between an archbishop and a metropolitan as far as nomenclature goes. Despite the use of "primate" for some kind of sub-metropolitical figure in Roman Africa, there is no reason to suppose any sort of substantive terminological distinction here. Modern Anglican usage effectively makes a "primate" superior to a metropolitan (as in Canada, Australia or Nigeria); but this is simply a way of demarcating responsibilities.' (RW)

> 'The name (archbishop) was first used in the East to describe the occupants of eminent sees, otherwise called metropolitans or patriarchs or exarchs … During the sixth century the word *archiepiscopus* appears in the West to describe these more eminent churchmen, though not at first very common; more normal in Charlemagne's time and after.' (OC)

> 'All three titles ("archbishop", "metropolitan", "primate") simply refer to a bishop who, in virtue of his tenancy of a prominent see … presides as of right over a provincial synod (and in modern

usage over the synod of a group of "provinces" constituting a national or otherwise corporately self-governing church).' (RW)

3.2   A 'Province' is generally regarded as a group of dioceses. The first Lambeth Conference of 1867 recommended the formation of Provinces as federations of dioceses.

3.3   Despite a lack of clarity about differences in titles, (RW) nevertheless believes one can give a distinct meaning to the term 'patriarch' –

> 'a "patriarch" ... is a local metropolitan who convenes episcopal meetings across a number of smaller provinces with their own metropolitans.'

Functions

4.1   Historically, one of the principal functions of archbishops has been to preside at regional meetings of bishops and synods. By implication this includes the task of maintaining the unity of the church in the area (as is the function of every bishop), ensuring consistency in discipline and overseeing the appointment of bishops:

> 'He is president of the synod and, as such, has the responsibility of seeing that synodical decisions are implemented; and there seems to be a general assumption that he will guarantee good order in the province.' (RW)

> 'When the Council of Nicaea (325AD) formalized the conventions for calling provincial synods, it fixed the basic elements of metropolitical authority. The bishop of the provincial metropolis had the duty of convening such a synod twice a year. Fourth-century practice in many areas required the metropolitan's ratification of any synodical decision; some canonical texts prescribe that the ordination of bishops and the discipline of clergy must not be determined without the *gnome* of the metropolitan – a phrase which should probably be understood as referring to his formal ratification of a decision rather than his individual sentence.' (RW)

4.2   Some of these responsibilities were facilitated by means of visitations, both formal and informal, to the churches in the area of their archiepiscopate.

'Early in the fifth century, the right of a metropolitan to conduct some sort of visitation begins to be asserted in synodical texts, though it is difficult to work out exactly what this means. Essentially, it seems to be a matter of checking that canonical enactments are being observed and that there are no scandals requiring disciplinary attention, which are being ignored by a diocesan. Later in the West, the metropolitan's rights of visitation are linked with his status as representative of the Roman see, a status reinforced symbolically through the personal gift by the pope of the *"pallium"* to each new incumbent of a metropolitan see. By the end of the Middle Ages, some metropolitans – including the Archbishop of Canterbury – enjoyed the status of *legatus natus* of the pope, which conferred more directive powers than ordinary metropolitan jurisdiction. This authority was exploited in the English Reformation in order to further the new policies of Henry and Edward, and to limit the independence of dioceses and even Convocation.' (RW)

4.3   Archbishops have a representative function, which varies according to the relationship of Church and state in the country concerned. For example in Europe they have played a central role in the consecration of monarchs, though not always an uncontroversial one:

'Where there were monarchs they needed consecrating and swearing-in to reign morally. That duty was the archbishop's and it was a serious constitutional trouble when a new king tried to bring in somebody else whom he preferred. William the Conqueror could do it because he had seized the power at that moment to do what he liked and the sitting Saxon archbishop had a dim reputation not only with Norman invaders. The Holy Roman Emperor could only be crowned by the Pope and that made quite a weakness to the constitution of the Empire, because Popes were liable to refuse and eventually emperors did not bother to ask.' (OC)

The Archbishop of Canterbury

5.1   There is a counterpart to each of these historic functions in the ministry of the Archbishop of Canterbury in the present day. His presidential function is exercised in the Church of England as Chairman of the Archbishops' Council, House of Bishops and General Synod. In the Anglican Communion he is President of the Lambeth Conference and Chairman of the Primates' Meeting.

5.2   The representative role is a major aspect of the Archbishop's ministry, which has many facets. This includes his constitutional relationship to the monarchy, his role as spokesman for the Church of England and for Christians in general, his membership of the House of Lords, his chairmanship of Synods, the Lambeth Conference and his role in Ecumenical affairs.

5.3   He remains in addition the Bishop of the Diocese of Canterbury.

The Archbishop of York

5.4   The relationship between the Archbishop of Canterbury and the Archbishop of York is obviously crucial, and we are grateful for the benefit of the long experience of Lord Habgood, who has served as a senior bishop and archbishop with four Archbishops of Canterbury. There is clearly much more scope for the development of a shared ministry between the two archbishops. The Hurd Report is concerned with this subject,[5] but it does relate theologically, and hence practically, to the comments in our previous report concerning suffragan bishops and their relationship to diocesans.[6]

> 'The balance between Canterbury and York also needs careful attention, though obviously it must depend in part on personalities. Without defining responsibilities too closely, it would be useful to have suggestions about their allocation (between them), and to back this up with recommendations about relationships between their two staffs. My impression is that the Archbishop of Canterbury can become so oppressed by the weight of responsibility that it becomes difficult to let anything go. Consultation with those outside the immediate Lambeth circle tends to suffer, and the public image of the Church of England as a one-man band only adds to the pressures. I think the Archbishop of Canterbury can only be rescued from some of these pressures if there is an explicit policy that others, and particularly the Archbishop of York, should carry some of his responsibilities.' (JH)

> 'Ceremonial occasions, palace dinners etc are part of this national responsibility, but some of these occasions might be shared with the Archbishop of York. There is value in getting to know people in high places, but if (they) are to work more

closely together, more contacts at this national level for the Archbishop of York could actually be a help.' (JH)

The principle of teamwork

5.5.1 These responsibilities have become much heavier in recent years because of a combination of factors, including the great increase in synodical activity, the demands and opportunities of the media, ease of communication world-wide, as well as the necessity to respond to radical change in society and the Church. It is therefore clearly necessary for the Archbishops to work in active cooperation with a number of individuals and organizations. A commitment to teamwork is an essential quality for a modern archbishop if he is not to be overwhelmed by the weight of his responsibilities. In fact teamwork is at the heart of the meaning of episcopacy, which simply echoes the theological truth about the nature of ordained ministry, that it is collegial in essence.[7] This principle applies to the whole range of archiepiscopal functions:

5.5.2 It applies most obviously in the arrangements for the *Diocese of Canterbury* which, like many dioceses, has two suffragan bishops. Unlike other suffragans, the Bishop of Dover has most of the main powers of a diocesan bishop, and for much of the time acts as such. Nevertheless the Archbishop's position as Bishop of the Canterbury Diocese is carefully maintained, and it is never merely a nominal role.

> 'It is possible to sit fairly lightly to diocesan responsibilities if there is the will to use the immense opportunities provided by the office to concentrate on broader national issues. I am sure it would be a mistake to remove the Archbishop of Canterbury from all diocesan responsibility, though it can be kept to a minimum.' (JH)

5.5.3 His relationship with *other bishops* also underlines the principle:

> 'There is obviously some sense in which he reproduces on a larger scale some of the offices of the bishop in the diocese, but it is important to observe the limits of his sacramental authority in respect of other bishops. The principle of a theological equality between bishops is a significant way of affirming that the unity and fullness of the Church lies in the interconnections of local ecclesial life, not in a delegation from some centre of power nor simply in the agglomeration of all particular

churches – i.e. in a scheme that is neither papalist nor congregationalist. Anglicanism, like the Orthodox Churches, has always held to this as its ideal.' (RW)

'bishops everywhere ... are the elementary centre of unity, and bishop is superior to bishop only in rank (for example as archbishop or metropolitan).'[8]

'The See of Canterbury enjoys a primacy of honour, not jurisdiction.'[9]

'A primate exercises his ministry not in isolation but in collegial association with his brother bishops. His intervention in the affairs of a local church should not be made in such a way as to usurp the responsibility of its bishop.'[10]

'He must know, lead, and win the confidence of the diocesan bishops. This is essential if the style of corporate leadership that the Church of England professes is to be effective. This is all the more important at a time when the Church is divided on matters central to its life. Trust between the bishops and in their leadership is an absolute necessity if delicately balanced policies are to be carried through. It does not necessarily follow that the Archbishop of Canterbury has to chair all meetings of bishops, but his relationship with them is crucial.' (JH)

5.5.4   The issue of *staffing* – the teamwork and balance between Lambeth Palace or Bishopthorpe, and the General Synod, the Church Commissioners and more recently the Archbishops' Council – is one that is fraught with difficulties, and is clearly in need of reformation.

'The new Archbishops' Council may well have shifted the balance between Lambeth and Church House. It is a balance which I believe is crucial because the load which falls on the Archbishop of Canterbury, and hence the size of the staff he needs, depends on the degree to which he can rely on other bodies and individuals. The tendency over the past few decades has been for Lambeth to grow – very understandably in view of media pressures and the focus on the Archbishop of Canterbury as an individual. But in my time this led to a good deal of frustration in Church House at what were felt to be an unnecessary duplication of resources, and a lack of communication.' (JH)

'The need for a personal focus within the Church correlates well with the degree of public interest and media attention lavished on "top people". Like it or not, archbishops are the public face of the church, and they need to be equipped for this. I am not sure that this necessarily requires enormous staffs. Apart from secretaries my own staff consisted of a chaplain and a lay assistant who doubled as press officer, researcher and critic. Canterbury obviously needs more, but I think there is a lot of expensive and unnecessary duplication with Church House.' (JH)

5.5.5 Leadership of the *Anglican Communion* has become an increasingly heavy responsibility involving extensive travel and very full programmes of visits. Personal visits from the Archbishop of Canterbury and his wife mean much to the Church overseas, but one should not underestimate their cost, not least in terms of the sheer physical demands. There is also the demanding responsibility of holding together an international federation of churches of great cultural, national and theological diversity.

'Given that the Archbishop of Canterbury's role in the Anglican Communion is a personal one, there is no escaping it though I suspect there is scope for reducing the amount of overseas travel. Closer liaison with English bishops who have partnership arrangements with overseas dioceses might allow for some natural devolvement of responsibilities, though these would require tactful handling if they were not to be misinterpreted as an attempt by the Church of England to substitute for the Archbishop of Canterbury. Personal messages from the Archbishop and personal reports to him might usefully become a regular feature of such visits by other bishops. Another useful link might be through the World Council of Churches. When I was a member of its Central Committee I had opportunities for visiting Anglican and other churches in various parts of the world, and realize now that I could have made better use of these occasions. There needs to be some coordination.' (JH)

'As regards the Communion itself, I see little chance of it accepting a greater degree of central control, which means that it is going to have to continue to depend on personal links, of which the links between the primates and with the Archbishop of Canterbury himself are crucial.' (JH)

5.5.6 The Archbishop of Canterbury has a representative role in *ecumenical relations*, which is shared already to some degree, but which undoubtedly has scope for further delegation.

> 'High profile ecumenism, e.g. visits to the Pope, receptions for Patriarchs, and other major occasions, necessarily require the Archbishop of Canterbury's presence. But the donkey work of day-to-day ecumenism can be done by the Archbishop of York or a senior bishop – the more senior the better if the Church of England is to be seen to be committed to the various ecumenical bodies, and if the absence of the Archbishop of Canterbury is not to be interpreted as indifference. Whoever does this donkey work needs access to the Archbishop's own ecumenical advisers, as well as to the Synod's Council for Christian Unity.' (JH)

Reflection
5.6 Like all bishops, but to a much greater extent, and on a national and international level, the Archbishops have important and unavoidable ministries as spokesmen. They are the public face of the Church of England. But they are also often expected to speak, not only on behalf of Christians of all churches, but sometimes representing other religions as well, on certain moral and social issues. This raises the question of appropriate resources for this aspect of his ministry. What spiritual and intellectual resources do archbishops need, and how are they to be supplied?

> 'I believe it is immensely important to demonstrate that the most prominent Christian leader in this country has an intelligent, wide-ranging, and practical concern about the issues that matter to people, and can bring Christian insights to bear on them. Preparation for this kind of exercise needs to involve Church House expertise as well as his own staff and outside experts. There is a good example of such cooperation in a small group which meets two or three times a year to brief him on medical ethics, and which tries to look ahead to issues which are likely to arise in the near future. No doubt there are many other such groups, and I hope their use can be encouraged. But I find it significant that as a fellow archbishop I never really knew what resources of this kind there were.' (JH)

'He cannot avoid being the spokesman for, and representative of, the English churches in national and religious affairs. Whether he likes it or not the media will treat him as such. But this means that he needs time to read, think, and pray, and cannot afford to be a workaholic ... hordes of advisers and scriptwriters cannot rescue him if he is mentally and spiritually exhausted.' (JH)

5.7 There is an often unconsidered but potentially significant ministry for the Archbishops, by virtue of their offices, as (JH) notes:

'By bringing (these activities) under strict control he might be able to make better use of one of his major assets, the opportunity to meet, and bring together in a Christian context, people who are leaders in their own fields, and who would value an opportunity to share their concerns.'

5.8 It is appropriate that the most senior of our advisers should have the last word:

'A true archbishop, if godly and sensible and in a see with a history, is a piece of great weight on the Church's chessboard.' (OC)

Instrument of Delegation

The following is the text of the Instrument of Delegation by the Archbishop of Canterbury to the Bishop of Dover of powers as diocesan bishop of the Diocese of Canterbury

AN INSTRUMENT under Our hand executed in the Year of Our Lord One Thousand Nine Hundred and Ninety-nine in the Ninth year of Our Translation

WHEREAS by a resolution of the Diocesan Synod of the Diocese of Canterbury dated the Third day of July One Thousand Nine Hundred and Ninety-nine the Synod approved Our Delegation to **STEPHEN SQUIRES** by divine permission **BISHOP OF DOVER**

WE DO HEREBY DELEGATE to Our Well Beloved in Christ **STEPHEN SQUIRES** by divine permission **BISHOP OF DOVER** the episcopal functions set out in the Schedule hereto which functions may be discharged by him throughout Our said Diocese from the day written below for so long as he shall remain Bishop of Dover or until We otherwise order

AND WE declare that the references in such Schedule to any Measure shall be construed as references to that Measure as amended extended and applied by and under any other Measure or enactment including any other provision of the Measure in question.

THE SCHEDULE
1. Ordination to the Offices of Deacon and Priest
2. Administration of the Rite of Confirmation
3. Visitation of Parishes
4. Consecration of land and buildings
5. Licensing of buildings for public worship or for the publication of banns of matrimony and for the solemnisation of marriages

6. Subjection of unconsecrated churches and other ecclesiastical buildings to the faculty jurisdiction

7. Collation of benefices within our gift as Patron or by lapse

8. Appointment and formal admission of persons duly presented or appointed to any ecclesiastical office or benefice and administration of the oaths and declarations required on such admission

9. Acceptance of resignations

10. Appointment and Commissioning of Rural Deans

11. Licensing of Stipendiary Curates, Priests-in-charge, Extra-Parochial and other Ministers (and the variation and revocation of such Licences)

12. The Grant of Permission to Officiate

13. Admission to Office and Licensing of Readers and Lay Workers (and the variation and revocation of such Licences)

14. Authorization of lay persons for administration of the elements at the Holy Communion and for officiating at Morning and Evening Prayer

15. Directions in connection with the exclusion of persons from the sacraments

16. Approval of forms of service for local use either throughout the Diocese or in particular places of worship

17. Directions in connection with alternative forms of service

18. Dispensation from the obligation to hold services in Parish Churches or Centres of Worship

19. Directions as to Service required or not required to be held in churches other than Parish Churches or in buildings licensed for public worship

20. Rights and functions in connection with benefice property which belong to Us as Patron

21. The Chairmanship (in Our absence) of a board or committee of the Diocesan Synod

22. Functions under the Parsonages Measure 1938, the New Parishes Measure 1943, the Church Property (Miscellaneous Provisions) Measure 1960, and the Endowments and Glebe Measure 1976

23. Functions under the Churchwardens (Appointments and Resignation) Measure 1964 and the Church Representation Rules

24. Functions in connection with agreements made under the Sharing of Church Buildings Act 1969

25. Functions under the Incumbents (Vacation of Benefices) Measure 1977 – as amended

26. Functions under the Parochial Registers and Records Measure 1978

27. Functions under the Pastoral Measure 1983

28. Functions under the Church of England (Miscellaneous Provisions) Measure 1983

29. Functions under the Patronage (Benefices) Measure 1986

30. Functions under the Church of England (Ecumenical Relations) Measure 1988

31. Functions under the Diocesan Boards of Education Measure 1991

32. Functions under the Care of Churches and Ecclesiastical Jurisdiction Measure 1991

33. Functions under the Church of England (Miscellaneous Provisions) Measure 1992

NOTHING in this Deed of Delegation shall affect such of our functions as belong to us in Our Metropolitical capacity

IN TESTIMONY whereof We have hereunto set Our hand and the Archiepiscopal Seal of the Lord Archbishop of Canterbury is hereunto affixed this Eleventh day of September In the Year of Our Lord One Thousand Nine Hundred and Ninety Nine

Seal   ✠ George Cantaur

appendix E

Administrative functions of the Archbishop of Canterbury as Metropolitan of the southern province of the Church of England

The following is the main part of a Memorandum by the Joint Provincial Registrars and the Archbishop of Canterbury's Lay Assistant following a review conducted by them at the request of the Archbishop of Canterbury

Introduction

1.1   The Hurd Report recommended that the Archbishop of Canterbury should:

> '... consider instituting an immediate review of the administrative functions linked with the metropolitical and related roles. The review's brief should be – with the clear intention of removing obligations on the Archbishop – to identify their extent and practical incidence and recommend what changes of practice and law should be made to facilitate their further delegation'.

1.2   At the Archbishop of Canterbury's request, we have undertaken this further review. We have confined our attention to those matters falling within the scope of chapter 5 of the Hurd Report. We have also had in mind the following considerations, which were articulated at different stages to or by the Hurd Group, and which seemed to us to have particular relevance to the issues of metropolitical oversight which we have been asked to consider:

   a.   *Ecclesiology*: in the helpful passage in his own report on resourcing the bishops of the Church of England, Professor

Anthony Mellows notes the care and caution with which he approached 'any recommendations which, if implemented, might lead to a change in ecclesiology'.[1] We share his concerns.

b. *Personality*: a surprising amount of discretion may be exercised by successive Archbishops in the emphasis they give to different aspects of their archiepiscopal ministry. This is just as true in the purely metropolitical aspects of their work as it is (more obviously) in relation to their involvement with the wider Anglican Communion, the mission of the Church, the nation, or relationships with other denominations or faiths.

c. *'The top man syndrome'*: whether or not any formal appeal lies to the office of the Archbishop of Canterbury, so long as there *is* an office of the Archbishop of Canterbury, people will want to seek his views, complain to him, and ask for his help, since he symbolizes the public face of the Church of England at national level.

d. *Cost*: It is important that if any of this work is to be done at all, then the cost-effectiveness of doing it at a greater distance from the Archbishop should be taken into account, especially if the effect of delegation is to leave the Archbishop open to final appeal, whether formally or informally.[2]

1.3 We have also had in mind that the Hurd Group's recommendation is predicated upon there being a clear distinction to be made between the pastoral and administrative functions that belong to metropolitical oversight.[3] In our examination of individual aspects of the administrative work, we have found this distinction less easy to apply than might have been expected: for example, when letters are signed off by the Archbishop with an assurance that the recipient will be 'in my prayers' or 'in our prayers at Lambeth', we are very aware that this is not an idle cliché, but is carried through either in the Archbishop's own devotions, or in the regular worship which takes place in Lambeth Palace Chapel.[4] The setting in which metropolitical oversight takes place is pastoral, an aspect of the Archbishop's spiritual leadership of the Church of England and a model for his episcopal suffragans. The administrative functions which support that pastoral ministry are imbued with their own spirituality, albeit less obviously.

Individual administrative functions

2   Against that background, we will consider each of these metropolitical functions individually:

Episcopal appointments

3.1   Very properly, the Hurd Report begins this section of its analysis with the Crown Appointments Commission.

3.2   As a matter of ecclesiology, '... it is a general principle of Anglican canon law that metropolitans are in a legal position of superiority over the bishops of the provinces and are, as such, owed duty of obedience by these'.[5] The processes by which they are appointed inevitably, therefore, involve him administratively as well as pastorally. Those processes are carefully analysed in Baroness Perry's recent Report.[6]

3.3   A great deal of advice and administrative assistance is received by the Archbishop from *inter alios* his own Appointments Adviser (who prepares briefings and correspondence), his Adviser for Bishops' Ministry (who is involved in training of consecrands), the Principal Registrar (who deals with legal arrangements concerning the consecration of all bishops, and the confirmation of election of diocesan bishops), by the Archdeacon of Canterbury (who attends enthronements of diocesan bishops, on behalf of the Archbishop), and by the Bishop at Lambeth and the Archbishop's Chaplain (who have a 'back-stop' role, as well as coordinating the domestic and ceremonial aspects of the event).

3.4   As will be seen from the above summary, there is already extensive delegation of administrative functions; and the possibility exists for further delegation both in the selection process,[7] and in relation to pastoral and ceremonial functions (in Canon C.17.4).[8] The symbolism of the Archbishop absenting himself from, say, a consecration would however be significant. The coordinating and financial aspects of these processes have recently been the subject of careful review by a wider group, including the Church Commissioners' Bishoprics Department, and several recommendations of that group have already been implemented during the course of this year.

Visitations and visits

Visitations

4.1   The Archbishop of Canterbury is asked, from time to time, to conduct visitations, normally in connection with some wider controversy or perceived local scandal.

4.2   A right of formal visitation throughout the Southern Province belongs to the Archbishop's jurisdiction 'as superintendent of all ecclesiastical matters therein, to correct and supply defects of other bishops ...';[9] and during any such visitation, the Archbishop's jurisdiction would override that of all inferior Ordinaries, so enabling him to undertake 'all such acts as by law and custom are assigned to his charge in that behalf for the edifying and well-governing of Christ's flock ...'[10] There is no doubt that he has power to visit in this sense.[11] However, it is generally understood that such formal power of visitation has not been exercised for well over a hundred years, and would not be exercisable by custom in a number of parts of the Province of Canterbury, for example, the Diocese of London.[12]

4.3   If the Archbishop were to undertake a visitation of this sort today, the need for administrative support would be immense, and the legal implications, in particular, would need to be handled with great delicacy. In practice, any formal visitation might well be delegated to the Vicar-General or other legal officer, or (depending upon the nature of the visitation) to another Bishop of the Province as commissary for the Archbishop.[13]

4.4   Having said that, a certain amount of informal investigation of complaints does take place at the present time, and if pressed to give a legal justification, it would be the power of visitation that would be called in aid. Correspondence is received from complainants, and dealt with by the Lay Assistant in consultation with the Principal Registrar and, on occasions, the Vicar-General. Complaints are occasionally of a very serious nature, resulting in resignation of clergy or the imposition of pastoral discipline by inclusion on the Lambeth and Bishopthorpe Register. To an extent, this informal oversight may continue in practice as part of the Archbishop's metropolitical oversight, though the greater formality of the new clergy disciplinary framework will no doubt reduce the Archbishop's freedom of action in this regard, and consequently the extent of the administrative functions that support it.

Diocesan visits

5.1   Diocesan visits, of course, are conceptually quite different to formal visitations. Diocesan visits are entirely personal and pastoral in nature, are undertaken by agreement between the Archbishop and the diocesan bishops concerned, and the administrative arrangements that surround them are essentially local. Different archbishops will attach different degrees of importance to this aspect of their metropolitical role; and the difference of emphasis will vary not only between successive archbishops, but also between different periods of a single archiepiscopate, depending upon the changing needs of the dioceses and personalities of the diocesan bishops.

5.2   The effect of these visits upon the workload of staff at Lambeth Palace is not inconsiderable. When the Archbishop is away on a visit to another diocese in his Province, or another Province in the Anglican Communion, he needs to be kept informed at all times of the wider aspects of his work. Modern technology enables him to keep in contact with his support staff at the Palace and key officers in other places at all times, and wherever he is, unless he determines otherwise; it also means that the numbers of those travelling with him are kept to a minimum. We see little scope for change or further delegation in this sphere of his work, but emphasize the extent to which the style and extent of such visits is (in a non-perjorative sense) idiosyncratic.

Permissions and licensings

Preachers' licences

6.1   The Archbishop has power, as part of his metropolitical oversight, to license preachers to serve in any part of his Province.[14] Applications are few and far between, and are not encouraged. When they are received, they are considered by the Bishop at Lambeth and the Lay Assistant, and any licence is then drawn up by the senior clerk in the Principal Registrar's office. Only a very small number of preachers' licences have been granted in recent years, and several applications have been referred back to diocesan bishops in the diocese where the applicant lives, in the expectation that an appropriate licence from that bishop will enable the applicant to take advantage of the general provisions of Canon C8.2 (a).[15] Those who do receive permissions of this sort are usually individuals whose ministry the Archbishop particularly wishes to endorse, for example members of the *Springboard* team.

Overseas clergy permissions

6.2   Of greater significance is the Archbishop's role in granting permissions to overseas bishops and clergy to minister in his Province.[16] Important issues of principle may be involved;[17] but most applications are dealt with routinely, in the office of the Joint Provincial Registrar at Church House.[18] The Archbishop's direct involvement in this process is confined to signature of the licences. It seems ecclesiologically appropriate for this work to be undertaken in the Archbishop's name, and difficult to see how it could be further delegated than is already the case.

Service chaplains' licences

6.3   Similar considerations apply to the Archbishop's involvement with licensing of service chaplains and readers. It makes a good deal of sense for all chaplains in the services to derive their authority from 'the top man' in the Anglican church in the United Kingdom, whatever legal questions may exist about his authority to operate in provinces other than his own.

6.4   The licensing process for service chaplains is carried out by a clerk in the Joint Provincial Registrar's office at Church House,[19] and some similar provision would still need to be made, even if primary legislation were successfully introduced along the lines indicated above.

Prison service authorization

6.5   A bishop and an archdeacon are appointed by the Archbishop to oversee the chaplains in the prison service. The chaplains themselves are either licensed by the bishop of the diocese in which the prison is situated, under the Extra Parochial Ministry Measure, or undertake this ministry as an aspect of their existing parochial ministry. There is no significant administrative function, therefore, in relation to this aspect of the Archbishop's metropolitical oversight.

Faculties for ordination of divorcees

7.1   Mention should also be made of the Archbishop's role in granting faculties, jointly with the Archbishop of York, to enable candidates to be ordained despite any impediment arising from divorce.[20] The Clergy (Ordination) Measure 1990 was highly controversial, and reached the statute book only after being challenged in the courts (by four members of the General Synod), and after specific assurance had been given by the Archbishops to the Synod and

Parliament that the Archbishops would personally involve themselves in the process of authorization.

7.2 The administrative work is undertaken by the Lay Assistant, and by his counterpart in the Northern Province. Primary investigative work is undertaken at diocesan level, and when applications are received at Lambeth they are processed in groups, to minimize claims on the Archbishop's time.

7.3 Relocation and devolution of this process would be desirable, but very controversial.

7.4 A review group, which recently met to consider the operation of the process and to prepare fresh Directions and documentation for the Archbishops, concluded that primary legislation would be needed even to permit devolution of the process at diocesan level.

Clergy discipline

Lambeth and Bishopthorpe Register

8.1 In additional to the visitation powers noted above, the Archbishop has direct statutory involvement in the process of reader, lay worker, clergy and episcopal discipline, under various measures, notably the Ecclesiastical Jurisdiction Measure 1963, and appeals under Canons C12, E6 and E8.[21] In addition, the (non-statutory) Lambeth and Bishopthorpe Register is maintained in the Archbishops' names.

8.2 The Synod has legislated for the Register to be put on a statutory footing.[22] It should be noted that the new regime requires not only that the list be maintained by the Archbishops, but that it should be reviewed at regular intervals, probably every five years. The administrative work which will flow from this new statutory review process is not yet clear, and will need to be kept under review when the legislation is brought into effect. In this regard, work is being undertaken by the Archbishops' Pastoral Advisers' Group, who for many years have been given responsibility to meet with all on the Register who wish to avail themselves of their care. They recommend a more active role for the Archbishops in overseeing the rehabilitation and restoration to ministry of those under discipline. Whilst much of this work would be delegated to the Pastoral Advisers, bishops and other senior clergy in the dioceses, the coordinating and monitoring role of the Archbishops and their officers will require additional administrative support which would naturally belong with the maintenance of the Register itself.

Judicial role under Discipline Measures

8.3.1   At present, the Archbishop has direct involvement in a number of aspects of the procedure under the Ecclesiastical Jurisdiction Measure, notably with regard to those who have been convicted in the criminal courts or against whom certain findings have been made in matrimonial proceedings. Such cases are dealt with, on reference by diocesan bishops, by the Lay Assistant and the Principal Registrar, the latter paying particular regard to compliance with the Human Rights Act 1998. There are three or four such cases each year.

8.3.2   Under the new regime to be introduced under the Clergy Discipline Measure, some of this work will pass to the diocesan bishops, with advice from the Clergy Discipline Commission, funded from Synod resources. A new and more formal investigative operation will underpin much work that is currently undertaken informally. As noted earlier,[23] although the Archbishop's primary role in the disciplinary process under section 55 of the Ecclesiastical Jurisdiction Measure will be taken over by the bishops, a new tier of appeal will lie to the Archbishop from their decisions in such cases.[24] In the litigious climate into which we are moving, it is likely that some appeals, at least, will be pursued, especially given the untried nature of the new legislation.

8.3.3   The new structure has yet, of course, to pass into law and it will be some time before it is fully implemented and capable of assessment. It would be premature to offer any suggestions for its amendment, with a view to further reduction of the Archbishop's role, at this stage. *Under Authority*[25] assumes that the number of disciplinary cases, and the cost of the process, will increase.[26] Almost certainly, we envisage that complaints about bishops (which will need to be dealt with by the Archbishop) will increase in numbers as complainants become more aware of their rights.

Marriage licences and notarial functions

'Special' marriage licences

9.1   Under arrangements which pre-date the Reformation, the Archbishop of Canterbury has power throughout England and Wales to issue Special Licences for marriage in suitable cases.

9.2 This work is undertaken by the Faculty Office, under the general supervision of the Master of Faculties and her Registrar. It is time-consuming, and involves detailed legal knowledge, though the administration is dealt with by senior clerks of considerable experience. The direct involvement of the Archbishop is minimal, and usually confined to signature of documents. This involvement with matrimonial law does give him a direct influence over the Church's involvement in marriage issues nationally.

9.3 A General Synod paper introduced to the Synod for consultation at its sessions in November 2001 has been referred for further consideration, in the context of the Government's own review of marriage preliminaries.[27] This may result in significant changes to the church's involvement with marriage issues, including the Archbishop's direct jurisdiction. In the circumstances, it would seem inappropriate to make any recommendations in advance of the Government's own proposals becoming clearer.

Notarial functions

10 The Archbishop's role in notarial appointments (the appointment of Notaries Public) is clearly an anachronism, but the operation is self-financing and does not require any direct involvement by the Archbishop in day-to-day administration, all of which is dealt with by the Faculty Office.

Patronage

General

11.1 The right to present clergy for service in a benefice is important both legally and pastorally. An advowson (the right of presentation) is an incorporeal hereditament,[28] to be registered under the Patronage (Benefices) Measure 1986. Its transfer, whilst legally possible, is carefully controlled by due process under that Measure.

11.2 Pastorally, the links between parishes and patrons are strong, and often greatly valued by parishes. There is no reason to think that parishes would wish to sever their links with the Archbishop of Canterbury, which in some cases go back many hundreds of years. Some may protest vigorously against the dissolution of such a link. There is some evidence that the Archbishops themselves reciprocate this sense of 'belonging'.

11.3 Essentially, the Archbishop's patronage falls into three categories: those which derive from the diocese of Canterbury; those which come to him as registered patron from other dioceses, for historical reasons; and those which come to him from all parts of the Southern Province, through 'lapse' (that is the failure of the registered patrons to exercise rights of presentation within nine months from the date when a vacancy occurs).

Canterbury advowsons

12.1 In practice, the first category of patronage is dealt with by the Bishop of Dover, or the Diocesan Patronage Board in the diocese itself. The other two categories (the non-Canterbury registered advowsons, and those which come to the Archbishop by lapse) are dealt with by the Lay Assistant. There are approximately fifty non-Canterbury advowsons, of which on average two or three need to be filled each year; and the numbers of lapsed patronages varies considerably over the years. The numbers of benefices suspended under Part IV of the Pastoral Measure 1983, reflecting widespread pastoral reorganization already being undertaken and in contemplation throughout the Church of England, result in fewer cases being referred to the Archbishop than might otherwise be expected.

12.2 The work is undertaken by the Lay Assistant, with occasional reference to the Principal Registrar. Controversial cases may require direct and personal intervention, and if so this is provided by the Bishop at Lambeth in conjunction with the Lay Assistant (though with the Archbishop being kept informed, and giving guidance, in relation to any policy matters in such controversial cases, where there may be wider concerns).

Non-Canterbury advowsons

13.1 The non-Canterbury advowsons are anachronistic, and might be transferred to relevant diocesan patronage boards or bishops, over time. This would involve a considerable workload on the part of relevant support staff at Lambeth, since the strong local attachment by parishes to patrons is likely to come to the fore through the consultation procedure set out in the Patronage (Benefices) Measure. The combined effect of section 3 and section 39 of the 1986 Measure would be to require the consent of the Archbishop of York to every transfer, and it would be to the Archbishop of York that any Parochial Church Councils disaffected by the proposal would address their representations. In the circumstances, and in view of the administrative and legal tasks falling to the Archbishop of York in this regard, it would be prudent to seek his views, and to examine the administrative cost of the exercise, before attempting to undertake any wholesale transfer of these advowsons. It is not obvious that the amount of time freed up for the Archbishop would be worth the cost of the exercise, either financially or in terms of goodwill with the parishes concerned.

13.2   Alternatively, S.8 of the Patronage (Benefices) Measure already enables the Archbishop as registered patron to appoint some other person to act as his representative to discharge in his place the functions of a registered patron in respect of a vacancy.[29] This option, if generally adopted during a particular archiepiscopate, would enable an Archbishop to delegate this function without denying his successors the opportunity to choose personally to exercise patronage as a sign of pastoral oversight expressed through an administrative duty.

Lapsed patronage

14   As to lapsed patronage, it should be noted that the 1986 Measure provided a wholesale review of a rather more complicated regime, which had included different stages of lapse, with final lapse to the Crown as supreme patron.[30] We do not know what undertakings, if any, were given to the Crown or to Parliament at the time when this Measure passed into law. The function could no doubt be removed as an obligation upon the Archbishop, and passed over to a central patronage board constituted as part of the Archbishops' Council or of the Church Commissioners' Pastoral Department, but there may be an ecclesiological issue to be addressed, as well as cost implications. In our view, any change should be introduced as part of a further wholesale review of patronage in the Church of England, rather than piecemeal.

Appeal Courts and Visitatorial jurisdiction

Appeal courts

15.1   The Archbishop appoints the Judges of the Court of Arches and the Court of Ecclesiastical Causes Reserved, under the provisions of the Ecclesiastical Jurisdiction Measure 1963. He does not sit to hear cases personally, and all the work is dealt with by the Principal Registrar's office. In faculty cases, it is self-financing by the parties to the proceedings.

15.2   A review is currently being undertaken in relation to doctrinal, ritual and ceremonial disciplinary issues, and this may result in alteration to the structure as well as the operation of the Court of Ecclesiastical Causes Reserved.[31] If the new arrangements in this area should replicate those under the Clergy Discipline Measure, there could be an increased involvement for the Archbishop in the new process. Ecclesiologically, that would seem necessary and proper despite the potential for requiring additional support.

Archbishop as Visitor

16.1   By contrast, the Visitatorial jurisdiction is well-used, with two or three cases being referred each year to the Archbishop, from the institutions for which he is the Visitor. The Archbishop's involvement has historical origins in each case, and the extent of his authority is generally set out in the constitutions of the individual institutions.

16.2   When cases arise, the work is undertaken by the Provincial Registrar's office, with a standing arrangement whereby the Archbishop appoints the Vicar-General to act as his commissary. After an appropriate hearing, a report is submitted to the Archbishop with a recommendation which he adopts and a decision letter which he signs. The institution concerned is responsible for all the costs of the process.

16.3   The introduction of the Human Rights Act 1998 has resulted in a review of the entire Visitatorial jurisdiction in all public institutions, and there have been suggestions that all Visitors may be replaced by an Ombudsman, though these suggestions have yet to find their way into any legislative, or even agreed, form. It should be noted, however, that the Visitatorial jurisdiction has diminished, to an extent, over recent years, with significant aspects of the jurisdiction being removed from the Visitor by the Education Reform Act 1988.

16.4   To remove the jurisdiction altogether would involve an enquiry being initiated across the whole range of educational and other charitable institutions to which the Archbishop may be a Visitor (since the Archbishop's involvement is often unknown until a complaint or petition is received). The institution in question would then need to be asked to take steps to change its constitution, and the Archbishop would remain bound to deal with petitions coming in from that institution until its constitution had been altered. The process would be time-consuming, and possibly unpopular with the institutions concerned, many of whom may never have to call upon the Archbishop to exercise his jurisdiction, but may nevertheless value the historic symbolism of their connection with him ...

[*The authors of the report then make various recommendations to the Archbishop which are not reproduced here.*]

Andrew Nunn   **John Rees**
Lay Assistant to the   **Stephen Slack**
Archbishop of Canterbury   *Joint Provincial Registrars*

Notes

chapter 1

1   In the case of the Archbishop of Canterbury, Lambeth Palace and the Old Palace at Canterbury, and in the case of the Archbishop of York, Bishopthorpe Palace.

2   It will be seen (paras 2.28.1 *et seq*) that we regard the Archbishop of Canterbury as having several concurrent offices.

chapter 2

1   See further First Report, Chapter 2, and the article by Bishop Stephen Sykes printed as Appendix D to that report. Other recent examples of reflections on the theology of episcopacy include *Episcopal Ministry* (Report of the Archbishops' Group on the Episcopate) CHP 1990; and *Working with the Spirit* (Review of the operation of the Crown Appointments Commission) CHP 2001, especially the article by Bishop Michael Nazir-Ali on pp 104–112.

2   First Report, para. 2.5.1.

3   See, for example, paras 5.9.1 and 11.12.1 in relation to the Archbishop of Canterbury and para. 18.15.1 in relation to the Archbishop of York.

4   Or those holding two or all three of such offices.

5   There are certain exceptions, as in the case of a retiring archbishop of the Roman Catholic Church upon whom is conferred the honorary title of archbishop-emeritus.

6   In England, the Archbishops of Canterbury and York, as well as the Bishop of London, are by custom sworn as members of the Privy Council, and thereby also bear the second style of 'The Right Honourable'. This also applies to archbishops in some other Commonwealth countries where the archbishops are sworn as members of the Privy Councils of those countries.

7   No distinctive vestment was directed for an archbishop by any of the statutory Prayer Books of 1549, 1552 or 1662, or the Ordinal of 1550. By the rubric of 1552 archbishops and bishops were treated alike and were required to 'have and wear a rochet'. (A rochet is the episcopal surplice with large lawn sleeves.)

8   Canon C.17.1.

9   See Appendix C.

10 See First Report, paras 2.3.1 *et seq*.

11 Cyprian: *On the Unity of the Catholic Church V*, 251.

12 The word archiepiskopos was first used in the East to describe the occupants of eminent sees. It did not begin to be used in the West until the sixth century.

13 Although, in the case of 'metropolitan', with the occasional hark-back to *metropolis*: see Godolphin's Repertorium Canonicum 15.

14 The meaning of the word 'province' has also changed: see para. 16.5.2.

15 There is a direct comparison between on the one hand a diocesan bishop and his diocese and on the other an archbishop and his province. Just as a diocesan bishop is 'the chief pastor of all that are within his diocese' (Canon C.18.1) so an archbishop is the ultimate chief pastor of all that are within his province.

16 The Sovereign was not the *spiritual* superior of the archbishop.

17 Thus, the Archbishop of Canterbury has precedence immediately after the Royal Family and *before* the Lord Chancellor: House of Lords Precedence Act 1539, s.3. The Archbishop of York has precedence immediately *after* the Lord Chancellor: see Godolphin's Repertorium Canonicum 14.

18 Excluding the offices held by the Archbishop of Canterbury in the Church of England.

19 See paras 2.5.2a; 2.6.1.

20 Because there is no comprehensive definition of the rights, powers and obligations which attach to the corporation or of the expectations which attach to the office, it is likely that there are some differences between the two.

21 The former archiepiscopal estates were so held.

22 Hence, in relation to employment, each Archbishop in his corporate capacity is one of the National Church Institutions.

23 Formally a member of the Archbishop's staff is employed by all the National Church Institutions and managed by the Archbishop in his corporate capacity.

24 Unless, subject to employment law rights, there is a specific term to the contrary in the contract of employment.

25 Canon C.1.3, first part.

26 The requirement for confirmation on behalf of the province and the wider Church has been a requirement since the fourth century. It was restated in the Appointment of Bishops Act 1534.

27 A minimum of three bishops is required: Canon C2.

28 In the Form of Ordaining or Consecrating of an Archbishop or Bishop in the Book of Common Prayer. See also Canon C.1.3: 'According to the ancient law and usage of this Church and Realm of England ... the bishop of each diocese owes due allegiance to the archbishop of the province as his metropolitan.'

29 The form is: 'I [X] nominated to be Bishop [Suffragan] of the See of [Y] promise all due reverence and obedience to the Archbishop and to the Metropolitical Church of [Z] and their successors So Help Me God, through Jesus Christ.'

30 Canon C.17.2.

31 See Appendix E, para. 16.1.

32 Ibid. As 'Ordinary' he has originating jurisdiction, which is not dependent on delegation by any other person: Godolphin's Repertorium Canonicum 23.

33 The Measure has been passed by the General Synod but, as we write this report, has not been considered by Parliament. See further Appendix E, para. 8.3.2.

34 Both those who are and those who are not metropolitans.

35 Strictly, this meaning applies only for the purposes of the Anglican Consultative Council: see clause 3(a) of the constitution of the Council, and para. 16.7.1.

36 Within the Church of England there are two provinces, of Canterbury and York. For the purposes of the Anglican Communion, however, these two provinces are treated as constituting one province. In relation to the Anglican Consultative Council there can only be one primate of a province: see para. 16.5.2. There are a few other instances of provinces being grouped under one primate within the Anglican Communion.

37 When Pope Gregory I sent St Augustine to England in 597, he envisaged that when it had become Christian, the country would be divided into two provinces, the southern with its centre in London and the northern with its centre in York. Each province would have its own archbishop and precedence between them was to depend on their seniority of appointment. The southern province was established in the seventh century, but based in Canterbury. The northern province was established only in the following century. Archbishops of Canterbury considered that, because the see of Canterbury was

established first, it was senior to that of York. In the following centuries there were numerous disputes between the two archbishops as to their respective seniority until, in the fourteenth century, the Pope conferred the title of Primate of All England on the Archbishop of Canterbury and Primate of England on the Archbishop of York. For a full account see Makower's *Constitutional History of the Church of England*, pp 281 *et seq*.

38 See further note 37.

39 But it has had some significance. So the Archbishop of York, it would seem in his capacity as Primate of England, confirms the election of an Archbishop of Canterbury (and the Archbishop of Canterbury confirms the election of the Archbishop of York).

40 Ecclesiastical Licences Act 1533; Canon C.17.7.

41 Except in the case of the Archbishop of York, a primate within the Anglican Communion will usually be invited to the Primates' Meeting: see para. 16.27.

42 The Archbishop of York is currently the representative head of the Church of England to the Churches within the Porvoo Communion.

43 See para. 2.14.2.

chapter 3

1 All bishops, and so all archbishops, continue in priestly and diaconal orders: see First Report, Appendix D, para. A.4.

2 See para. 2.4.2.b.

3 Para. 2.14.2. 'President' is used here to denote the Archbishop's various roles in the Anglican Communion: see para. 3.9.1.

4 Primarily in this context England.

5 See para. 15.20.3.

6 The population figures are based on 1999 mid-year estimates and the figures for stipendiary diocesan clergy are those for 2000. In relation to the Southern Province the figures exclude those for the Diocese of Europe. See *Church Statistics* (GS Misc 641) and *Statistics of Licensed Ministers* (GS Misc 638).

7 For example, the Archbishop of Canterbury is *ex officio* the Chairman of the Board of Governors of the Church Commissioners. If the Archbishop of Canterbury is not present at a meeting, the members of the Board elect a chairman for the meeting: in practice, this is the Archbishop of York if he is present.

8 The Anglican Communion as such does not have a president. The Archbishop of Canterbury is *ex officio* the President of the Anglican Consultative Council (see para. 16.71.1) and we use the expression 'President of the Anglican Communion' to denote all of the formal roles which the Archbishop has within the Anglican Communion (see Expressions and their meanings).

9 See further para. 16.73.3 for an estimate of the time of the Archbishop which is taken up with his work in relation to the Anglican Communion.

10 The British and Irish Anglican Churches and The Nordic and Baltic Lutheran Churches are the churches which comprise the Porvoo Communion. See the Porvoo Declaration which is contained within The Porvoo Common Statement: occasional paper No 3 of The Council of Christian Churches, 1993.

11 We do not suggest that secular models should necessarily apply, but reference to them can be helpful in illustrating the nature of the Church models.

12 Diocesan bishops are also not subject to formal review, but in practice an increasing number of bishops voluntarily make arrangements for peer-group or other appraisal.

13 Although legislation may allocate specific responsibilities: see Appendix E.

14 Informal exceptions are the episcopal 'cell groups', which are self-selected groups of mainly or

exclusively bishops, together with, in most cases, their wives. Both Dr Carey and Dr Hope are members of cell groups. The members of the groups meet to share personal and ministerial experiences and to discuss in total confidence issues of common concern. The groups provide some measure of mutual support.

chapter 4

1 First Report, para. 7.3.

2 For example, diocesan and suffragan bishops; the Commissioners and members of the Archbishops' Council; and numerous members of staff employed within the various National Church Institutions. (As to the National Church Institutions, see Expressions and their meanings.)

3 See First Report, para. 4.9.

4 See paras 4.4.1 *et seq.*

5 See paras 5.4.2 *et seq.*

6 See para. 10.4.2.

7 See paras 7.2 *et seq.*

8 See para. 5.20.1.

9 See paras 6.9.1 *et seq.*

10 Paras 7.4.1 to 7.7.

11 Although in exceptional cases, such as that of the Bishop of London, there are some similarities.

12 In Chapter 3.

13 '... we asked [Dr Carey] to suppose that we had somehow managed to provide him with an eighth day in each week. We asked how he would use that eighth day. [Dr Carey] replied that he would not fill the eighth day with new diary engagements; instead he would use it for study, reading, discussion and prayer in preparation for the rest of the week, since under present arrangements it was these activities for which he badly needed more time.' (The Hurd Report, Chairman's Introduction, para. 4.)

14 See, for example, the Hurd Report, Chapter 6, p. 38.

15 First Report, para. 3.32.

chapter 5

1 Chapter 4.

2 Chapter 8.

3 Chapter 7.

4 Chapter 10.

5 Chapter 14 (Lambeth Palace); Chapter 15 (Old Palace, Canterbury) and Chapter 21 (Bishopthorpe).

6 First Report, paras 10.8.1; 11.4.

7 First Report, para. 11.6.

8 See in particular Chapter 11 (the Archbishop of Canterbury) and Chapter 18 (the Archbishop of York).

9 See further, First Report, para. 10.19.

10 First Report, para. 12.9.

11 First Report, para. 12.15.1.

12 As to the Commissioners' powers to provide funds for resourcing, see First Report, para. 4.11.4.

13 See para. 4.4.9 and Chapter 7.

14 Most of such decisions are in practice taken by the Bishoprics and Cathedrals Committee. At the present time, neither of the Archbishops is a member of that committee.

15 See the discussions in paras 17.39.1 *et seq.*

16 See para. 12.16.2.

17 By the Archbishops' Council.

18 See Expressions and their meanings.

19 The Bishop of Dover is, formally, a suffragan bishop in the Diocese of Canterbury. Apart from two Provincial Episcopal Visitors, who are also, formally, suffragan bishops in the diocese, the Bishop of Maidstone is the other suffragan bishop in the diocese.

20 See para. 15.25.3.b.

21 See para. 15.38.1.

22 See paras 18.17.1 *et seq.*

23 The Vicar-General and the Provincial Registrar are the legal officers of the Province. Broadly, the Vicar-General has a judicial role, acting on behalf of the metropolitan, and presides at the ceremony of confirmation of the election of a bishop. The Provincial Registrar may be described as the metropolitan's legal adviser. The Vicar-General and the Provincial Registrar are lawyers: they may be, but are by no means necessarily, ordained.

24 Either by the Commissioners or the Archbishops' Council.

25 See paras 13.13.1 *et seq.*

26 See para. 13.21.2.

27 First Report, para. 12.23.2.

28 Paras 7.4.1 *et seq.*

29 First Report, paras 15.1 *et seq.*

30 First Report, para. 10.20.

31 See further para. 13.8.

32 First Report, paras 10.30.1 *et seq.*

33 First Report, paras 10.4.1 *et seq.*

34 See, for example, para. 15.29.3.

35 See para. 21.38.1.

36 See further First Report, paras 16.34.1 *et seq.*

37 First Report, para. 16.40.

38 First Report, para. 7.16.2.

chapter 6

1 Chapter 14 (Lambeth Palace); Chapter 15 (Old Palace, Canterbury); and Chapter 21 (Bishopthorpe).

2 First Report, paras 4.38.1 *et seq.* See also Note 18 to the Commissioners' Accounts for 2000.

3 Para. 14.15 (Lambeth Palace); para. 15.24.2 (Old Palace, Canterbury); and para. 21.18 (Bishopthorpe).

4 Para. 6.2.3.

5 Although the same point applies, Lambeth Palace is not a see house: see para. 14.7.1.

6 Paras 14.38.1 *et seq* (Lambeth Palace); paras 15.8.1 *et seq* (Old Palace, Canterbury); and paras 21.36.1 *et seq* (Bishopthorpe).

7 First Report, Chapter 19.

8 First Report, para. 18.32.2.

9 First Report, para. 18.37.3.

10 First Report, para. 18.32.3.

11 First Report, para. 18.37.1.

12 First Report, para. 19.38.

13 The see house of the Bishop of Durham. Broadly similar arrangements are in force in relation to the see house of the Bishop of Bath and Wells.

14 The constitution of the Auckland Castle charitable company provides for the Commissioners in consultation with the Bishop of Durham to apply any surplus for charitable purposes.

15 The Auckland Castle arrangements have been in force since 1994.

16 As to the Commissioners' obligations to provide, and maintain, a see house, see First Report, para. 4.11.3.

17 Both the specific statutory obligations which arise from the fact that the palaces are heritage properties and general fiduciary obligations for the maintenance of the property.

18 First Report, paras 19.7 *et seq.*

chapter 7

1 They are published, annually in advance, in the Commissioners' Annual Report and Accounts.

2 Namely, what the Commissioners bring into account as 'bishops' working costs', although we recommended the discontinuance of the use of that expression: First Report, para. 4.28.

3 House of Bishops' booklet *Bishops' office and working costs for the year ended 31 December 2000*. This publication is the product of the work of a joint Disclosure Working Group of the Commissioners and the House of Bishops which was constituted following a decision of the House of Bishops in January 2000. In our First Report we advocated a bold approach to disclosure: First Report, para. 13.11. The booklet in respect of the year 2000 was the first of what we understand will be annual publications.

4 The main areas of difference are:

a. the Commissioners' disclosure is only of costs met by them: we recommended disclosure also of costs met by DBFs;

b. the Commissioners' disclosure is only of 'working costs': we recommended disclosure also of premises expenses;

c. the Commissioners' disclosure is by reference to each bishop: we recommended disclosure by reference to the bishops of each diocese as a group; and

d. the categories by which expenditure is disclosed are different.

The Commissioners' booklet also gives helpful relevant diocesan statistics and other explanatory information.

5 We are in no way suggesting that the operation of the present system is irresponsible.

6 We use the expression broadly to embrace all those who contribute to the formulation of policy, including the Commissioners, members of the Archbishops' Council and members of General Synod.

7 See Chapter 2.

8 As to 'Presidency' of the Anglican Communion, see para. 3.9.1.

9 Paras 5.11.2, 5.12.2.

10 First Report, paras 12.12 *et seq.*

11 Para. 16.80.3.

12 See further para. 17.39.1.

13 See para. 14.22.

14 For details of these costs at the present time, see para. 16.62.1.

15 We do not suggest that there is a *direct* correlation between the amount of costs attributed to a role and the amount of time spent in performing that role, but it is a guide.

16 See para. 7.1.2.

chapter 8

1 First Report, Chapter 14.

2 An Archbishop *is* a diocesan bishop: see para. 2.28.1. For convenience, in this chapter we use the expression 'diocesan bishops' to mean diocesan bishops who are not also archbishops.

3 For the process of appointing a diocesan bishop, see First Report, paras 14.3 *et seq*, and Appendix E thereto, paras 3.1 *et seq*. The differences between the procedure for the appointment of an archbishop and that which applies in the case of the appointment of a diocesan bishop include the facts that:

  a. on the Crown Appointments Commission, the retiring Archbishop is replaced by a bishop elected by the House of Bishops; and

  b. in the case of the appointment of an Archbishop of Canterbury, the Secretary General of the Anglican Consultative Council (see para. 16.36.1) is in attendance.

  See further *Working with the Spirit: choosing diocesan bishops*, A review of the operation of the Crown Appointments Commission and related matters, CHP 2001.

4 A vacancy in an archiepiscopal see arises when the Archbishop in office announces his intention to retire. The interregnum begins when the Archbishop actually retires.

5 An Archbishop formally takes up his office when his election has been confirmed and when he pays homage to the Sovereign: see First Report, Appendix E, paras 3.3., 3.4. However, enthronement is generally regarded as marking the start of his archiepiscopal ministry.

6 Not only within the Church of England.

7 See First Report, para. 14.4.6.

8 See First Report, para. 14.4.8.

9 As to the need of the Post Office to increase its staff when the appointment of Dr Carey as Archbishop of Canterbury was announced, see Hurd Report, Chapter 10, p.72.

10 See First Report, para. 14.4.1.

11 We use the expression 'Archbishop-designate' to denote a future archbishop from the time when the announcement of his appointment is made to when he is enthroned.

12 In the case of the Archbishop of Canterbury, it will be both Lambeth Palace and the Old Palace at Canterbury.

13 Not all see houses are large.

14 Chapter 10.

15 See First Report, paras 14.11 to 14.16.

16 See para. 8.12.1.

17 See para. 8.13.

18 For a similar recommendation in relation to diocesan bishops, see First Report, para. 14.46.d.

19 First Report, para. 14.22.1.

20 See paras 2.29.1 *et seq*.

21 See paras 15.23.1 *et seq.*

22 See para. 18.13.2.

23 In Chapter 10, p.74, para. (h).

24 See para. 12.16.1.

25 Para. 8.12.1.

26 Para. 8.13.

27 See First Report, paras 14.6.1 *et seq*, and Appendix E thereto, paras 3.3 *et seq.*

28 For the corresponding recommendation in relation to diocesan bishops, see First Report, para. 14.40.1.

29 See First Report, para. 14.51.

30 During the last fifty years, Archbishops of Canterbury have been in office as follows:

a. Archbishop Geoffrey Fisher (1945–61);

b. Archbishop Michael Ramsey (1961–74);

c. Archbishop Donald Coggan (1974–80);

d. Archbishop Robert Runcie (1980–91); and

e. Archbishop George Carey (1991–2002).

During the same period, Archbishops of York have been in office as follows:

a. Archbishop Cyril Garbett (1942–55);

b. Archbishop Michael Ramsey (1955–61);

c. Archbishop Donald Coggan (1961–1974);

d. Archbishop Stuart Blanch (1974–83);

e. Archbishop John Habgood (1983–95); and

f. Archbishop David Hope (1995–).

31 First Report, para. 14.51.

32 First Report, para. 14.50.

33 On giving up office, an Archbishop ceases, by virtue of his office, to be a member of the House of Lords. However, the recent practice has been to confer a life peerage on a retiring Archbishop.

34 This recommendation relates only to resources and not to stipends. It is presumed that a retired Archbishop will be in receipt of a pension.

35 For the suggested equivalent for the Archbishop of Canterbury, see para. 13.14.

36 Paras 5.11.2, 5.12.2.

chapter 9

1 See para. 2.15.1.

2 For a full list of the National Church Institutions, established under the National Church Institutions Measure 1998, see Expression and their meanings. The Measure was passed to implement recommendations contained in *Working as One Body* (The Report of the Archbishops' Commission on the Organization of the Church of England, the Turnbull Report) CHP 1995.

3 In particular, long-serving members of staff working for the Archbishops' Council have different terms and conditions from those working for the Commissioners. The staffs of both Archbishops are generally employed on the same terms as those working for the Commissioners.

4 Para. 12.50.2 (the Archbishop of Canterbury's staff); para. 19.25.3 (the Archbishop of York's staff).

5 We regard press officers as being concerned with all aspects of the media.

6 The current arrangements for the Archbishop of York do not follow this principle, but appear to be satisfactory. See further para. 19.11.6.

7 We understand that the cost of this equipment would be in the region of £20,000.

8 Paras 16.91 *et seq.*

9 Para. 12.39.2 (Lambeth Palace); para. 19.19.2 (Bishopthorpe).

10 Para. 14.42.2 (Lambeth Palace); para. 21.35.5 (Bishopthorpe).

11 Paras 15.8.2 *et seq* (The Old Palace, Canterbury); para. 21.36.2 (Bishopthorpe).

12 Opportunity cost is the amount which could be expected to be received if the rooms set aside for official guests were let or used for some other income-producing purpose.

13 See First Report, para. 18.14.

14 Para. 10.3.

15 Paras 5.9.1, 5.12.2.

16 First Report, paras 15.22.1 *et seq.*

17 See First Report, para. 15.21.1.

18 See paras 12.16.1 *et seq* (at Lambeth Palace) and paras 19.15.1 *et seq*, for the equivalent at Bishopthorpe.

19 Para. 5.20.3 (Bishopthorpe).

20 Para. 5.20.1 (Lambeth Palace).

21 As to 'Presidency' of the Anglican Communion, see para. 3.9.1.

22 In practice, during the archiepiscopate of Dr Carey this has applied particularly to visits to the United States.

23 Detailed arrangements and preparation for these visits are made by the Archbishop's personal staff at Lambeth Palace as part of their other duties.

24 For further reference to these journeys, see the Hurd Report, Chapter 7, p.46.

25 Hurd Report, Chapter 7, p.54., para. (g).

26 Within the twelve months prior to the writing of this report, the Archbishop of Canterbury has been accompanied by:

   a. February 2001: Nigeria: 3 members of staff;

   b. March 2001: Primates' Meeting, USA: 2 members of staff;

   c. July 2001: Jerusalem: 1 member of staff;

   d. September 2001: America: 1 member of staff;

   e. November 2001: the Gulf: 2 members of staff;

   f. January 2002: Inter-Faith Initiative, Egypt: 2 members of staff;

   g. January 2002: World Economic Forum, USA: 2 members of staff.

27 See para. 18.6.3.

28 The Commissioners maintain separate overseas travel accounts in their books. Travelling expenses incurred by the Archbishop of Canterbury and his staff, or by other bishops travelling at the request of the Archbishop, in relation to ecumenical and Anglican Communion business are debited to this account.

29 Described by the Commissioners as working costs: see Expressions and their meanings. By contrast, the cost of some overseas visits made by Lord Habgood when Archbishop of York was charged to the overseas travel account.

30 Para. 4.5.5.

31 Some travel first class, irrespective of the duration of the journey. Examples are ministers of cabinet rank; the most senior ambassadors; and the most senior directors of some major commercial companies. Some, irrespective of grade, travel business class if the duration of the journey exceeds a specified minimum. We have seen examples from major commercial companies (4hrs) and the civil service (2½hrs). Other examples provide for business class travel where the duration exceeds a minimum, but where the minimum is lower as the grade of the individual is higher.

32 Where any person travels on the business of the Anglican Communion and the cost is borne by the Anglican Consultative Council, the Council only provides funds for economy class travel. As to the Anglican Consultative Council, see further paras 16.19 *et seq* and 16.40.1 *et seq*.

33 Accordingly, travel by a 'no frills' low cost airline may not be appropriate.

34 The class of travel used might be covered under this heading.

chapter 10

1 First Report, para. 17.1.

2 First Report, para. 17.4.1.

3 First Report, para. 9.8.

4 See para. 10.14.1.b.

5 First Report, para. 17.6.

6 Para. 8.12.3.

7 Para. 8.13.

8 This is the case with Lambeth Palace and Bishopthorpe. The Old Palace at Canterbury is a much smaller building and has only a modest, albeit attractive, garden.

9 See para. 12.17.1.

10 Para. 8.12.3.

11 Only about a quarter of all see houses are heritage properties.

12 Paras 5.20.1 and 5.20.3.

13 Para. 6.5.3.

14 Para. 14.29.2 (Lambeth Palace); para. 15.4.3 (The Old Palace, Canterbury); para. 21.23.2 (Bishopthorpe).

15 The basic meaning of 'state' in this sense is that the rooms are intended for ceremonial or special occasions: see Expressions and their meanings.

16 During the present and immediately preceding archiepiscopates of Archbishops of Canterbury, long-standing improvements have been made from such endeavours to the main palace building and gardens of Lambeth Palace, mainly with external funds donated for the purpose.

17 Experience at Lambeth Palace indicates that it is likely that this can be obtained *pro bono*.

18 See para. 10.14.3. In some circumstances she may be able to share the services of another secretary.

19 See paras 12.18, 19.10.1 and 19.15.1.

20 Whether setting aside rooms as official guest bedrooms is making the best use of these rooms has to be considered in each case. This is particularly so at Bishopthorpe (see para. 21.36.2) and the Old Palace at Canterbury (see para. 15.10.1). For corresponding considerations in relation to other see houses, see First Report, paras 18.23.1 *et seq*.

21 In accordance with the principle expressed in para. 10.4.2..

22 See para. 9.16.2.

23 See para. 10.3.

24 First Report, paras 17.13.3, 17.13.4.

25 In the case of the wife of an Archbishop of Canterbury, this would usually be the equivalent of the Resources Group for the Archbishop at Lambeth Palace: see para. 5.20.1.

26 In so acting, the wife of an Archbishop would, in effect, be the Archbishop's representative, and it seems that on this basis it would be within the Commissioners' powers to pay for these resources.

27 See paras 16.24 *et seq.*

28 There is an analogy with the principle that the wife of an archbishop, or of any other bishop, should not be precluded from following her own career because of the demands made on her by her husband's ministry: see para. 10.4.3.

29 From 1 April 2002, this has been £2,650.

chapter 11

1 Paras 2.28.1 to 2.30.

2 There is no finally settled classification of these offices. There can be differences of opinion about the category into which a particular act falls. Furthermore, there can be overlap between categories, so that the same act or group of acts can fall into more than one category.

3 As noted previously, in para. 2.14.2, formally, there is no office of President of the Anglican Communion, but there is of President of the Anglican Consultative Council: see para. 16.71.1. We use the expression 'President' of the Anglican Communion to denote all of the offices held by the Archbishop within the Anglican Communion.

4 Para. 16.73.3.

5 See paras 15.8.2, 15.22.1.

6 In addition, issues relating to some other churches overseas over which the Archbishop does not have metropolitical authority are, by virtue of the standing of his office, from time to time referred to him for advice or resolution.

7 In the aftermath of the terrorist attacks in New York and Washington on 11 September 2001, Dr Carey has been heavily engaged on inter-faith issues, as have many other bishops. By re-ordering his priorities Dr Carey has been able to deal with these matters with his existing resources.

8 See First Report, paras 3.16.1 *et seq.*

9 Namely the Lambeth Conference (para. 16.24), the Anglican Consultative Council (para. 16.19) and the Primates' Meeting (para. 16.27). As to Presidency of the Anglican Communion, see note 3, *supra.*

10 A part-time chaplain and a personal secretary: see para. 15.14.1. The Commissioners also employ a steward at the Old Palace.

11 In relation to the vesting in the Commissioners of the episcopal estates, see First Report, paras 4.6, *et seq.*

12 The Commissioners provide the see house for the use of the bishop; pay his agreed operational costs; and pay his stipend and pension contributions.

13 Although not all resourcing requests are agreed. Furthermore, we are aware that Dr Carey has not put forward, or has delayed putting forward, requests which he would otherwise have made had the financial circumstances of the Church of England been less stringent. In considering requests from an Archbishop, the staff of the Bishoprics and Cathedrals Department are hampered by the absence of comparators.

14 Para. 5.8.3.

15 As well as a room at Church House.

16 See further para. 5.14. For an indication of some of the work of the Provincial Registrars, see Appendix E.

17 See para. 14.23.1.

18 Throughtout chapter 12.

19 See para. 15.24.1.

20 Particularly in paragraphs 15.27.1 *et seq*.

21 See P. Hinchcliff, *Frederick Temple, Archbishop of Canterbury: A Life*, OUP, 1996.

22 See Appendix E, para. 8.3.1.

23 See para. 11.15.

chapter 12

1 Para. 15.14.1.

2 Para. 17.19.1.

3 Hurd Report, Chapter 10, p.68.

4 Para. 14.16.1.

5 Para. 14.23.1.

6 The sensitivity would to some extent be reduced if the Archbishop's home were in a separate house in the grounds of the palace: see para. 14.29.4.

7 See, for example, the Hurd Report, Chapter 10, p.65.

8 There are two other points of access, but they are in much less frequent use.

9 Despite attempts, such as providing the Archbishop with a room for his use in Church House.

10 At present there are 12: see paras 17.19.1, 17.19.2.

11 Not all are principals, but they usually attend principals' meetings.

12 Para. 12.9.1.

13 The job descriptions do not specify that role.

14 Hurd Report, Chapter 10, p.73.

15 Hurd Report, Chapter 10, p.73, para. (a).

16 Para. 19.15.1.

17 Paras 14.31.2 *et seq*.

18 Hurd Report, Chapter 10, p.73, para. (c).

19 Hurd Report, Chapter 7, p.53, para. (d).

20 Para. 16.98.3.

21 Para. 8.12.1.

22 Para. 5.20.1.

23 Hurd Report, Chapter 10, p.73, para. (d).

24 Hurd Report, Chapter 10, p.73, para. (d).

25 At the rates applicable for 2001/02, this would give a range between £70,905 and £116,904.

26 Para. 16.36.2.

27 Para. 16.71.1.

28 The Archbishop's present chaplain has expertise in this field and was able to assist materially.

29 Para. 5.9.1.

30 Para. 14.23.1.

31 Para. 14.42.1.

32 Para. 9.16.2.

33 Para. 14.43.

34 Para. 9.2.3.

35 Para. 12.14.2.

36 Para. 12.18.

37 Excluding the Archbishop's Private Secretary, who is treated as a principal.

38 Paras 9.2.1 *et seq.*

39 Para. 12.21.

chapter 13

1 See First Report, Chapter 6.

2 See Expressions and their meanings.

3 The role of this department in relation to the Archbishop's personal staff has previously been described: see paras 9.5.2 *et seq.*

4 The Bursar reports to the Archbishop's Administrative Secretary.

5 For the position in respect of other diocesan bishops, see First Report, Chapter 6.

6 See para. 12.36.1.

7 See para. 12.9.4.

8 It would be open to the Archbishop of York also to charge the cost of his official overseas travel to this amount, but in practice the present Archbishop does not do so.

9 See para. 2.17.1 and Appendix E.

10 See para. 5.14.

11 The fees are prescribed by the Legal Officers (Annual Fees) Orders made under the Ecclesiastical Fees Measure 1986. See further First Report, paras 7.12. and 7.13.

12 See further First Report, Chapter 6.

13 First Report, Chapter 10.

14 Except the Lambeth Palace Library.

15 See paras 12.17.1 *et seq.*

16 Para. 17.25.1.

17 Para. 5.9.1.

18 Paras 14.31.3 *et seq.*

19 Para. 12.34.3.

20 Ibid.

21 The Chairman declares an interest as having been a trustee since 1995.

22 The Lambeth Partnership is a group of nearly 400 individuals who contribute – financially or by offering their skills and efforts, as well as by prayer – to the work of the Archbishop in general or more particularly to some of his specific initiatives.

23 Springboard is a major initiative of the Archbishop to encourage evangelism.

24 First Report, paras 10.20 *et seq.*

25 See para. 5.11.1.

26 It has been the practice for the Bishop at Lambeth to attend these meetings.

27 Para. 12.27.

28 They are registered with the Charity Commission and their accounts are open for public inspection.

29 Para. 15.23.2.

30 It was £13,300 for each of the years 1999, 2000 and 2001. Grants can be made from the discretionary fund for any deserving purpose which the Archbishop thinks fit: it is not confined to purposes connected with the Diocese of Canterbury.

31 About £1,400 at the end of 1998; about £800 at the end of 1999; about £800 at the end of 2000; and about £3,500 at the end of 2001.

32 First Report, para. 13.16.

33 Paras 7.4.1, 7.7.

34 In subsequent editions of the House of Bishops' paper *Bishops' office and working costs for the year ended 31 December 2000*, December 2001.

chapter 14

1 As to which, see para. 2.15.1.

2 At that time, the property was a manor owned by the monks of Rochester Cathedral priory.

3 For further information see *Lambeth Palace, A History of the Archbishops of Canterbury and their Houses*, Tim Tatton-Brown, SPCK, 2000.

4 The Archbishop's flat is officially termed his 'lodging'.

5 The main state rooms are two drawing rooms and the Guard Room. The basic meaning of 'state' in this sense is that the rooms are intended for ceremonial or special occasions: see Expressions and their meanings. The state rooms within Lambeth Palace are frequently used for meetings and the reception of visitors.

6 See para. 17.20.b.

7 Although they are not very suitable for this purpose: see para. 17.21.

8 In 1986 the Commissioners granted to the trustees of the hospital a long lease of the site at a premium. The trustees erected the hostel at their expense.

9 The property was vested in the Commissioners by a scheme made under the Episcopal Endowments and Stipends Measure 1943 and confirmed by an Order in Council made in December 1946.

10 At least one lease was drawn up on this basis.

11 See para. 15.12.

12 There are separate, controlled, accesses to the Lambeth Palace Library and to the Head Gardener's House.

13 As to the effect of this on the atmosphere and ethos of the palace, see para. 12.5.3.

14 Para. 14.38.1.

15 Paras 13.21.2 and 13.22.

16 The figure represented the cost of general improvements (£55,000) and improvements to the crypt and crypt chapel (£107,000). The Commissioners also incurred £151,000 which was the net cost of the replacement of a house for the Archbishop's Anglican Communion Officer. The Commissioners bring that expenditure into account by attributing it to the Archbishop. The house remains in the Commissioners' ownership.

17 As to whom, see para. 12.36.1.

18 These obligations arise principally from the listing of the main palace building and certain other parts of the property: see the Town and Country Planning Act 1971 and the Planning (Listed Buildings and Conservation Areas) Act 1990.

19 One member of the staff is engaged as the maintenance officer and the Archbishop's driver assists when he is not on driving duties. In addition, when necessary outside contractors are employed under a standing arrangement.

20 See para. 13.3.1.

21 To or through The Lambeth Fund: see paras 13.13.1 et seq.

22 See para. 6.3.3.

23 Ibid.

24 We have not made detailed enquiries, but with the reduction in the size of the staff of the Archbishops' Council it seems likely that such space could be made available. If not used in this way, it would no doubt be let to third parties.

25 More accurately, managed by the Archbishops' Council: see para. 9.2.3.

26 See the discussion about the Archbishop's Anglican Communion Officer in paras 16.85 et seq.

27 Paras 11.5.1 et seq.

28 See para. 12.5.5.

29 See para. 12.16.2.

30 Para. 12.9.

31 Even if no infrastructure staff were employed elsewhere, a proportionate part of equivalent costs would be reflected in the rent or service charge.

32 Paras 13.21.2, 13.22.

33 For example, they include Council Tax payments which would need to be paid in respect of the occupation of alternative residential accommodation.

34 See para. 12.12.3.

35 See para. 5.10.2.

36 See note 33, supra.

37 Paras 6.5.2 et seq.

38 Paras 6.12.2 et seq.

39 Para. 14.23.1.

40 This is officially described as his lodging.

41 See para. 14.39.2.

42 Paras 14.45.1 et seq.

43 See para. 14.46.1.

44 Para. 12.36.1.

45 Paras 14.45.1 et seq.

46 At any one time two Sisters of Religion serve duty at Lambeth Palace.

47 For this purpose, up to, say, 2 years.

48 See para. 6.6.1.

49 For the equivalent recommendation in respect of see houses, see First Report, para. 18.45.3. We understand that since our First Report was published the Commissioners are acting on that recommendation.

50 Not necessarily in the main palace building: see para. 14.29.4.

51 See para. 12.39.3.

Notes

52 Paras 14.23.1, 14.31.3.

53 Para. 14.23.1.

54 Para. 17.20.

55 Planning Policy Guidance 15.

56 Para. 14.29.4.

57 Para. 14.30.4.

58 Paras 14.39.1 *et seq.*

chapter 15

1 See para. 16.96.

2 The option was not referred to in the Scheme by which the property was vested in the Commissioners, but whether or not it is binding in law, there is in our view a very clear moral obligation on the part of the Commissioners to give effect to it.

3 Many of Dr Carey's teaching missions in the diocese have been conducted at weekends.

4 No doubt, on specific request, the Archbishop would be glad to permit them to be so used.

5 This is in accordance with the Commissioners' general policy in respect of heritage properties which are not planned for disposal: see para. 6.3.3.

6 See para. 6.3.3.

7 In para. 15.5.2.

8 Para. 15.18.

9 See paras 12.36.1, 14.11.1.

10 Fax and email.

11 Para. 15.27.

12 Para. 15.7.

13 We understand that Archbishop and Mrs (now Lady) Runcie also found these arrangements very unsatisfactory.

14 First Report, para. 13.14.

15 The figures for 2000 and 2001 are included in those given in paras 13.21.2 and 13.22.

16 Bishop Llewellin used the title sparingly.

17 Hurd Report, Chapter 4, p.29, para. (a).

18 Following a decision of the Commissioners' Bishoprics and Cathedrals Committee on 12 May 1999.

19 Ibid.

20 See First Report, para. 15.14.2.

21 Amending Canon 25, promulgated and executed by the General Synod on 8 July 2000.

22 Hurd Report, Chapter 4, pp. 27, 30 para. (d).

23 This would apply, for example, to grants from discretionary funds for purposes related to the diocese: see para. 13.17.

24 See para. 15.15.2.

25 Any bishop's office must be organized so that confidentiality is safeguarded. We recognize that some communications to the Archbishop are ultra-sensitive.

26 Para. 15.21.2.

27 Para. 15.33.1.

28 Para. 15.34.

29 Para. 15.32.1.

30 The Commissioners are under a duty from time to time to review the suitability of the property for this purpose: see First Report, para. 4.11.3.

31 Para. 15.30.1.

32 First Report, Chapter 19.

chapter 16

1 See resolution 21 passed at the meeting of the Anglican Consultative Council at Limuru, Kenya, in 1971.

2 The Church of England includes the Diocese of Europe.

3 See paras 16.31 et seq.

4 See Article 3(a) of the Constitution of the Anglican Consultative Council. Although that article defines the expression in relation to the narrow purpose of determining membership of the Anglican Consultative Council, the word has more general use within the Communion in this sense.

5 Para. 16.31.

6 Although the Church of England is manifestly a member of the Communion, it is not apposite to refer to it as being in communion with the see of Canterbury.

7 The extra-Provincial bodies are so represented.

8 Provided that they are in active episcopal diocesan ministry.

9 This does not apply to extra-Provincial bodies, which do not have Primates. Those bodies are represented at Primates' Meetings by the Archbishop of Canterbury.

10 Notwithstanding that they bear some of the marks of certain controversies of the time.

11 Examples are the Lusitanian Church of Portugal and the Reformed Episcopal Church of Spain. The historical connection with Great Britain of some of the other Churches is tenuous. For example, the connection of the Episcopal Church of the Philippines is indirect, being through the Episcopal Church of the United States of America. There is an analogy with the position of Mozambique in the Commonwealth. Mozambique is a member of the Commonwealth although it has not had an historical constitutional connection with the United Kingdom.

12 As to 'see' generally, see First Report, page xvii.

13 So a minister ordained by a Church other than the Church of England would fall within the Overseas Clergy Measure in relation to officiating in England. Similar legislation is in force in other countries.

14 Para. 16.22.

15 Under the Charitable Trustees Incorporation Act 1872, now Part VII of the Charities Act 1993.

16 Clause 2 of the Council's constitution.

17 See para. 16.36.1.

18 Para. 16.30.

19 As to the definition of 'Primates' see para. 16.7.2.

20 Para. 16.9.1.

21 Para. 16.9.2.

22 The appointed members of the Anglican Consultative Council are:

   (a) Three persons from each of the following, consisting of one bishop, one priest, and one layperson:

   Anglican Church of Australia

   Anglican Church of Canada

Church of England
Church of Nigeria (Anglican Communion)
Church of the Province of Rwanda
Church of the Province of Southern Africa
Church of South India
Church of the Province of Uganda
Episcopal Church (United States of America)

(b) Two persons from each of the following, consisting of one bishop or one priest plus one layperson:
Anglican Church of Aotearoa, New Zealand and Polynesia
Church of the Province of Central Africa
Province of the Anglican Church of Congo
Church of Ireland
Anglican Church of Kenya
Church of North India
Church of Pakistan
Episcopal Church of the Sudan
Anglican Church of Tanzania
Church in Wales
Church in the Province of the West Indies

(c) One person (preferably lay) from each of the following:
Church of Bangladesh
Episcopal Anglican Church of Brazil
Church of the Province of Burundi
Anglican Church of the Central American Region
Hong Kong Sheng Kung Hui
Church of the Province of the Indian Ocean
Nippon Sei Ko Kai (Anglican Communion in Japan)
Episcopal Church in Jerusalem and the Middle East
Anglican Church in Korea
Church of the Province of Melanesia
Anglican Church of Mexico
Church of the Province of Myanmar
Anglican Church of Papua New Guinea
Episcopal Church in the Philippines
Anglican Church of the Southern Cone of America
Scottish Episcopal Church
Church of the Province of Southeast Asia
Church of the Province of West Africa

The extra-Provincial bodies, which do not have appointing rights in relation to the Anglican Consultative Council are:
The Anglican Church of Bermuda
The Anglican Church in Ceylon
The Episcopal Church of Cuba
The Lusitanian Church of Portugal
The Reformed Episcopal Church of Spain
The Anglican Church in Venezuela

The Anglican Church of Puerto Rico

The Church in the Falkland Islands

23 See the *Church of England Year Book*.

24 See John Rees 'The Anglican Communion: Does It Exist?' (1998) 5 Ecclesiastical Law Journal 14.

25 Para. 16.82.1.

26 Para. 16.23.2.

27 Including some, but not all, of the extra-Provincial bodies: see footnote 22, *supra*.

28 See para. 16.54.1.

29 Excluding donations from the Compass Rose Society which were restricted to special projects and not available for general expenditure.

30 Primarily from publications.

31 The target level of General Reserves as returned for Charity Commission purposes is £270,000. Even after this transfer, the actual level of the reserve was only £186,464.

32 Para. 16.40.1.

33 Under Section 501(c)(3) of the United States Internal Revenue Code. Accordingly, donations by US citizens to that corporation are tax deductible.

34 Para. 16.46.

35 The Archbishops' Council receives most of its funds from dioceses under the system of synodical apportionment.

36 Paras 16.61, 16.62.1.

37 Para. 16.47.1.

38 Para. 16.49.1.

39 Para. 16.47.3.

40 First Report, para. 2.5.1.

41 First Report, para. 2.5.3.

42 See, for example, Norman Doe, *The Legal Framework of the Church of England*, Clarendon Press, Oxford, 1996, page 7.

43 See paras 16.19.1 *et seq*.

44 Formally, the Secretary General supports the Archbishop in his capacity as President and a member of the Anglican Consultative Council and in relation to the Lambeth Conference and the Primates' Meetings (clause 6 of the Council's constitution; Resolution 30 passed at the Eighth Meeting of the Council). In practice, the support is more generally in relation to the Communion.

45 See para. 16.1.

46 See para. 16.18.1.

47 See para. 16.95.2.

48 First Report, para. 3.30.3.

49 Namely those available to the Church Commissioners and those available to the Archbishop's Council.

50 Para. 5.9.1.

51 See para. 5.17.1.

52 Para. 7.4.3.

53 Para. 6.6.1.

54 The lease of the Anglican Communion Office will shortly expire, although the Anglican Consultative Council has statutory rights to continue in occupation.

55 See para. 11.5.3.

56 See para. 16.82.1.

57 Para. 16.94.2.

58 See Hurd Report, Chapter 7, p.46.

59 Paras 9.19.1 *et seq.*

60 Paras 9.34.1 *et seq.*

61 The centre will also host many guests, students and pilgrims from all over the Communion.

62 Para. 15.24.1.

63 Hurd Report, Chapter 7, p.53, para. (d).

64 See p.50.

65 See para. 12.18.

chapter 17

1 As to the Archbishop's corporate capacity, see paras 2.15.1 *et seq.*

2 By the Ecclesiastical Commissioners Act 1866.

3 Pursuant to the Church Commissioners Measure 1947.

4 See Section 7 of the Ecclesiastical Commissioners Act 1866.

5 Whether on paper, electronically or audio or visually.

6 In October 2000 a fund derived from a bequest for the Library and until then administered by the Commissioners was transferred to the trustees.

7 See Expressions and their meanings.

8 Para. 17.29.2.

9 See para. 14.4.3.

10 Letter from the Historical Manuscripts Commission dated 22 March 2001.

11 Para. 17.37.1.

12 Letter cited in footnote 10, *supra.*

13 Para. 17.37.1.

14 Both of these bodies are registered charities. Their accounts are filed with the Charity Commission and are open to public inspection.

15 Para. 17.15.2.

16 Para. 17.16.2.

17 See paras 14.33.; 14.37.2.b.

18 The earning potential of the Library Buildings if the Great Hall and the other buildings are available for use as a conference centre is much greater: see paras 14.39.1 *et seq.*

19 First Report, para. 4.28.

20 Para. 17.40.

21 Para. 17.6.5.

22 Para. 17.42.1.

23 At the present time, in practice the Archbishop of York chairs most meetings of the Board of Governors.

24 Para. 17.41.2.

25 For example, the main Public Records Office building is at Kew.

26 The point arose in relation to the possible construction of an underground facility: see para. 17.22.2.

27 Section 7, Ecclesiastical Commissioners Act 1866.

28 Para. 17.27.2.

29 Para. 17.24.1.

30 Para. 5.9.2.

31 In the Commissioners' statutory accounts and, for so long as the Commissioners, notwithstanding our view, treat it as part of bishops' costs, in the disclosure booklet referred to in note 3 to para. 7.1.2.

32 Subject to minor exceptions which occur from time to time when accommodation is provided at Lambeth for individuals working on short-term Church projects who may not be members of the Archbishop's staff.

33 Formally, all the National Church Institutions – see para. 9.2.2. – are the joint employers, and the Archbishop, in his corporate capacity, is the managing employer.

34 Likewise formally, the trustees of The Lambeth Palace Library Trust are the managing employers of the Librarian.

35 See para. 12.10.1.

36 First Report, para. 18.45.3.

37 Para. 14.7.1.

38 Unless express provision was made for it in the lease.

39 The Librarian would therefore be in a position comparable to that which we have recommended (in para. 12.36.1) for the Commissioners' agent, that is, having a managing employer other than the Archbishop, owing duties to the managing employer, but concurrently being a member of the Archbishop's staff.

40 Para. 12.17.1.

chapter 18

1 According to the classification used in this report: see para. 2.29. There is no finally settled classification of these offices. There can be differences of opinion about the category into which a particular act falls. Furthermore, there can be overlap between categories, so that the same act or group of acts can fall into more than one category.

2 House of Lords Precedence Act 1539 s.3. In the Table of Precedence the Archbishop of York is placed next after the Lord Chancellor, and before non-Royal dukes. In practice, Dr Hope has not been a frequent attender.

3 The suffragan sees of Hull, Selby and Whitby.

4 The Bishop of Beverley. See First Report, paras 16.34.1 et seq.

5 In marked contrast to the extensive delegation by the Archbishop of Canterbury of his powers as diocesan bishop of the Diocese of Canterbury: see para. 15.20.3.

6 Para. 2.24.3.

7 Para. 3.9.2 and note 10 to that paragraph.

8 In the last three years, the number of days Dr Hope has spent on official business outside the United Kingdom, including, but not restricted to, the business of the Porvoo Communion, are:

   a. 1999: 25

   b. 2000: 15

   c. 2001: 3

9 For the time commitment of other diocesan bishops, see First Report, para. 3.32.2. As to the time commitment of the Archbishop of Canterbury, see para. 11.4.

10 Para. 11.5.2.

11 Ibid.
12 See para. 18.14.3.
13 Para. 5.8.3.
14 Paras 3.4 to 3.9.3.
15 See further Appendix C, para. 5.4.
16 Para. 8.9.2.
17 Para. 19.5.
18 The DBF has assisted on matters such as employment contracts.
19 See paras 19.8, 19.12.1.
20 See para. 5.14.1.
21 Para. 21.21.
22 See para. 21.23.2.
23 See para. 19.14.
24 Para. 19.14.
25 Para. 14.35.2.
26 Although not the exclusive use of a flat, as at present: see para. 14.35.1.
27 Hurd Report, Chapter 6, p.39.
28 Hurd Report, Chapter 6, p.41.
29 Hurd Report, Chapter 6, p.42, para. (d).
30 Hurd Report, Chapter 7, pp 51, 54, para. (h).
31 Hurd Report, Chapter 6, pp 41, 42, para. (c).
32 See para. 18.7.
33 At the time when this report is written, the Measure has not been considered by Parliament.
34 See Appendix E, para. 8.3.2.
35 Para. 9.11.2.
36 See First Report, Chapter 8.

chapter 19

1 See para. 21.21.
2 Although this does not happen frequently.
3 As to which see 'Expressions and their meanings'.
4 See paras 19.10.1 *et seq.*
5 The range of duties is indicated in the job descriptions.
6 See paras 21.32.1 *et seq.*
7 See First Report, paras 14.33.1 *et seq.*
8 See para. 20.3.3 and, as to local expenses accounts, see First Report, paras 6.4 *et seq.*
9 See para. 21.29.1.
10 See First Report, paras 5.14.3. and 7.17.1.
11 See paras 18.17.1 *et seq.*
12 Para. 5.12.2.
13 Para. 19.1.1.

14 Para. 19.8.

15 As contrasted with the Archbishop himself, who uses IT extensively.

16 Hurd Report, Chapter 6, p.39. See also paras 18.17.1 *et seq.*

17 As to the requirement for, and desirability of, such an agreement, see para. 8.9.2.

18 Para. 21.38.1.

19 Paras 21.34 *et seq.*

20 Paras 12.16.2 *et seq.*

21 Paras 21.25 *et seq.*

22 In respect of our recommendation for the appointment of a Financial Secretary at Lambeth Palace, see paras 12.34.1 *et seq.*

23 See para. 20.8.1.

24 See para. 21.25.

25 See para. 21.29.1.

26 See para. 21.30.2.

27 They are mainly natural woodlands, together with some formal garden.

28 See Expressions and their meanings.

29 See para. 9.9.2.

30 See further para. 9.5.2.

31 See First Report, para. 15.4.

32 First Report, para. 15.13.1.

33 See para. 21.38.1.

34 Strictly, employed by the National Church Institutions and managed by the Archbishop.

chapter 20

1 First Report, Chapter 6.

2 These are described by the Commissioners as 'working' costs: see First Report, paras 4.28 and 10.41.2 *et seq.*

3 The amount for 2001/02 is £13,500 a quarter.

4 See First Report, paras 6.3 *et seq.*

5 The Commissioners' agent for Bishopthorpe is an external professional firm. See also First Report, para. 4.24.1.

6 See para. 21.12.1.

7 For example, in travelling to other Churches within the Porvoo Communion.

8 See para. 13.4.1.

9 By the Legal Officers (Annual Fees) Orders made under the Ecclesiastical Fees Measure 1986. See further, First Report, paras 7.12. and 7.13.

10 Para. 19.10.2.

11 Such as the Ramsey flat (see para. 21.27.1) and work to the Great Hall (see para. 21.12.1).

12 See further para. 21.29.2.

13 See para. 5.12.2 and First Report, paras 10.15 *et seq.*

14 Para. 5.12.3.

15 Para. 5.20.3.

16 First Report, para. 13.16.

17 This recommendation accords with our principles with regard to Transparency and Disclosure: see paras 7.5 and 7.7.

chapter 21

1 Para. 21.15.1.

2 Para. 21.35.2.

3 Para. 6.16.2.

4 By Order in Council dated 23 April 1943, giving effect to a scheme made pursuant to the Episcopal Endowments and Stipends Measure 1943.

5 Paras 21.30.1, 21.31.

6 Para. 20.15.

7 As to these arrangements generally, see First Report, paras 4.24.1. and 6.13.1.

8 Other than cleaners.

9 With effect from 1 January 1999. See First Report, para. 6.14.

10 That report will not be available in time for it to be considered by us.

11 See para. 6.3.3.

12 Ibid.

13 See para. 19.5.

14 Para. 19.14.

15 See First Report, paras 5.10 *et seq* and 17.7 *et seq*.

16 Para. 21.23.3.

17 Para. 21.36.2.

18 The Ramsey flat – see para. 21.27.1 – may also properly be regarded as a resource for the diocese.

19 We record that this finding is the result of our own observation, and not by virtue of any complaint which has been made to us by Dr Hope.

20 See First Report, para. 5.11.

21 Para. 21.35.2.

22 Para. 21.7.1.d.

23 Para. 21.24.1.

24 Para. 21.35.2.

25 Para. 20.14.2.

26 These are the capacities if the rooms are laid out theatre style. The capacities are less if they are laid out boardroom style.

27 Para. 21.33.2.

28 See para. 19.19.2.

29 Para. 21.24.1.

30 According to a report dated October 2001 commissioned by the Palace Manager.

31 Para. 21.35.2.

32 Para. 21.23.3.

33 Para. 21.33.1.

34 Para. 21.15.2.

35 Para. 21.4.2.g.

36 There is one public house with rooms in the village and at least five houses offering bed and breakfast accommodation within a short distance from Bishopthorpe.

37 According to the report referred to in footnote 30, *supra*.

38 See First Report, paras 19.17 *et seq*.

39 At that time the DBF was under pressure to vacate the property which it then occupied.

40 First Report, paras 18.36.1 *et seq* and 19.1 *et seq*.

41 Paras 18.17.1 *et seq*.

42 Para. 6.12.2.

43 The Commissioners are under an obligation to provide accommodation for the Archbishop in his capacity as diocesan bishop of the Diocese of York: see First Report, para. 4.11.3.

appendix A

1 In some instances in the course of plenary meetings and otherwise on separate occasions.

2 In five instances in telephone interviews.

appendix C

1 The Rt Revd and Rt Hon the Lord Habgood was Archbishop of York from 1983–95.

2 The Revd Professor W.O. Chadwick OM, KBE, was Dixie Professor of Ecclesiastical History in the University of Cambridge from 1958–68, and Regius Professor of Modern History from 1968–83.

3 The Most Revd Dr R.D. Williams was Lady Margaret Professor of Divinity in the University of Oxford from 1986–92, Bishop of Monmouth from 1992–99 and Archbishop of Wales from 1999.

4 *Episcopal Ministry* p. 129, para. 283.

5 *To Lead and to Serve* (Report of the Review of the See of Canterbury, CHP, 2001) especially pp. 37–42.

6 First Report pp. 23–24, paras 2.8.2 – 2.8.7.

7 Op cit p. 18, para. 2.4.5 – ' Consequently it is imperative that the bishop is committed to teamwork, and understands his leadership in these terms. The whole theology of the church as the Body of Christ implies that the church's leadership will exemplify and promote this understanding.'

8 *Episcopal Ministry* p. 98, para. 212 – J.H. Newman on 'The Catholicity of the Anglican Church' (Essays Critical and Historical 1890).

9 Op cit p. 130, para. 284 – Lambeth Conference Report 1968.

10 Op cit p. 147, para. 321 – ARCIC (Anglican–Roman Catholic Commission) Final Report.

appendix E

1 *First Report*, para. 2.5.3.

2 See, for example, below with regard to clergy discipline, where the Archbishop's present role as decision-maker upon reference from the diocesan bishops under section 55 of the Ecclesiastical Jurisdiction Meaure 1963 becomes that of appellate tribunal from decisions of the diocesan bishops, under the new Clergy Discipline regime.

3 'There are, we think, two keys to the situation. The first is to distinguish between the pastoral and administrative aspects of the [metropolitical] functions …' (Hurd, p. 32).

4 For example, parishes to which presentation is being made by the Archbishop of Canterbury are routinely included in intercessions.

5 N Doe, *Canon Law in the Anglican Communion* (OUP, 1998), p. 107.

6 *Working with the Spirit: Choosing Diocesan Bishops* (CHP, 2001); the correlative functions performed by the Crown, through the Prime Minister, are attractively described in Palmer, *High and Mitred*, SPCK 1992, and there is some useful material in the report of the working party on *Senior Church Appointments* (CHP, 1992, GS1019).

7 See GS Standing Order 122(a)(iv), which would permit the Archbishop, if unable to attend a meeting of the Crown Appointments Commission, to nominate a member of the House of Bishops from the Southern Province as his deputy, with full voting rights. It is thought that this power has never been used and is unlikely to be used on a regular basis, for the ecclesiological reasons we have identified above.

8 Which permits delegation of certain of these metropolitical functions to the Bishops of London and Winchester; regular delegation of this sort would result in a degree of additional administrative cost through duplication, and would be ecclesiologically questionable, as an abdication of one of the Archbishop's core functions.

9 Canon C17.2.

10 Canon G5.

11 According to the preliminary judgment of the Privy Council in *ex parte Reed* 1888 13PD 221.

12 It is believed the last occasion on which a visitation took place may have been the trial of Bishop King and that the manner in which the Archbishop dealt with the trial on that occasion may have been open to challenge – see Newton, *The Trial of Bishop King (Reed –v- Bishop of Lincoln)* 1999 5 Ecc.L.J. p. 265 *et seq.*

13 Canon C17.3 authorizes such delegation in an appropriate case.

14 Canon C8.2(c).

15 Which permits ministry for up to seven days, in appropriate circumstances, by a person not otherwise licensed to do so.

16 Under the Overseas and Other Clergy (Ministry and Ordination) Measure 1967.

17 For example, recognition of orders, particularly in relation to the orders of those ordained by women bishops in other provinces whose own orders are not interchangeable with the episcopal orders of the Church of England.

18 108 Permissions were granted under the 1967 Measure in the calendar year 2000.

19 18 licences were granted to service chaplains and readers in the calendar year 2000.

20 Canon C4.3A.

21 From the summary revocation of the licences of, respectively, clergy, lay readers and lay workers. There have been no appeals to the Archbishop under these Canons for well over a decade.

22 See clause 38 of the Clergy Discipline Measure 2000.

23 Para. 1.2, n. 2.

24 See clause 30 (2) Clergy Discipline Measure 2000.

25 GS 1217.

26 Ibid, para. 10.3.

27 *Just Cause or Impediment* – GS 1436.

28 Halsbury's *Laws*, volume 14, para. 776.

29 Patronage (Benefice) Measure 1986, S.8(3).

30 See Halsbury's *Laws*, volume 14, para. 826.

31 Which has met only twice during its 40-year life.

Index

Note: Where more than one sequence of notes appear on one page, index references are distinguished by the addition of a or b to the note number. References to tables are indicated in italic

Index